DATE DUE

DEC 0 6 2000			
MAY 1 0 2001			
APR 30 02			

THE FLORIDA

DEMCO 38-297

Flori
Florida
Florida
Florida International University, Miami
Florida State University, Tallahassee
University of Central Florida, Orlando
University of Florida, Gainesville
University of North Florida, Jacksonville
University of South Florida, Tampa
University of West Florida, Pensacola

University Press of Florida

Gainesville · Tallahassee · Tampa · Boca Raton · Pensacola · Orlando · Miami · Jacksonville

THE
EVERGLADES

An Environmental History

David McCally

Foreword by Raymond Arsenault and Gary R. Mormino

04 03 02 01 00 99 C 6 5 4 3 2

05 04 03 02 01 00 P 6 5 4 3 2 1

Library of Congress Cataloging-in-Publication Data

McCally, David, 1949–
The Everglades : an environmental history / David McCally ;
foreword by Raymond Arsenault and Gary R. Mormino.
p. cm. —(Florida history and culture series)
Includes bibliographical references and index.
ISBN 0-8130-1648-7 (alk. paper)—cloth
ISBN 0-8130-1827-7 (alk. paper)—paperback
1. Everglades (Fla.)—Environmental conditions—History.
2. Drainage—Florida—Everglades—History. I. Title. II. Series.
GE155.E84M34   1999
333.91'8'0975939—dc21   99-18766

The University Press of Florida is the scholarly publishing agency for
the State University System of Florida, comprising Florida A & M
University, Florida Atlantic University, Florida International
University, Florida State University, University of Central Florida,
University of Florida, University of North Florida, University of
South Florida, and University of West Florida.

University Press of Florida
15 Northwest 15th Street
Gainesville, FL 32611–2079
http://www.upf.com

To Patrick . . . Lionheart.

The master came because it was time.
He left because he followed the natural flow.
The wood is consumed but the fire burns on,
and we do not know when it will come to an end.

CHAUNG TSU

CONTENTS

TABLES AND FIGURES

FOREWORD

The Everglades: An Environmental History is the eighth volume in a new series devoted to the study of Florida history and culture. During the past half century, the burgeoning population and increasing national and international visibility of Florida have sparked a great deal of popular interest in the state's past, present, and future. As the favorite destination of countless tourists and as the new home for millions of retirees and other migrants, modern Florida has become a demographic, political, and cultural bellwether. Unfortunately, the quantity and quality of the literature on Florida's distinctive heritage and character have not kept pace with the Sunshine State's enhanced status. In an effort to remedy this situation—to provide an accessible and attractive format for the publication of Florida-related books—the University Press of Florida has established the Florida History and Culture Series.

As coeditors of the series, we are committed to the creation of an eclectic but carefully crafted set of books that will provide the field of Florida studies with a new focus and that will encourage Florida researchers and writers to consider the broader implications and context of their work. The series will continue to include standard academic monographs, works of synthesis, memoirs, and anthologies. And, while the series will feature books of historical interest, we encourage authors researching Florida's environment, politics, literature, and popular and material culture to submit their manuscripts for inclusion in the series. We want each book to retain a distinct personality and voice, but at the same time we hope to foster a sense of community and collaboration among Florida scholars.

David McCally's environmental history of the Everglades is a fascinating study that complements two earlier volumes in the Florida History and Culture Series: *Gladesmen: Gator Hunters, Moonshiners, and Skiffers* by Glen Simmons and Laura Ogden and *The Enduring Seminoles: From Alligator Wrestling to Ecotourism* by Patsy West. As we noted in the foreword to *Gladesmen,* "The natural wonder known as the Everglades has been a subject of enduring fascination, for naturalists and ecologists, for frontier buffs, and for countless others who have felt the strange allure of hidden and remote places. Over the centuries this unique ecosystem adapted to innumerable natural and man-made disasters, penetrations and explorations, the construction of roads and canals, the follies of agribusiness, and the siphoning of water and other precious natural resources." In 1947 Marjory Stoneman Douglas captured much of this saga in her classic study *The Everglades: River of Grass,* which a half century after its publication remains a source of insight and inspiration for environmental activists and scholars. However, Douglas, who died in 1998 at the age of 108 years, would have been the first to acknowledge that a great deal has happened during the past five decades, not only in her beloved Glades but also in the exciting new field of environmental history.

Led by William McNeill, Donald Worster, Alfred Crosby, William Cronon, Carolyn Merchant, and Jared Diamond, a new generation of scholars has greatly expanded our understanding of natural history and the biological and environmental context of human history. Drawing upon a wide array of disciplines—including biology, climatology, demography, epidemiology, geography, and geology—environmental historians have taken us well beyond the confines of traditional human-centered political, economic, and social history. We now have access to specialized historical analyses of everything from ergot poisoning, sugar consumption, and cod fishing to snow, fire, and air-conditioning—and, perhaps even more important, to emerging syntheses that recognize the importance of environmental and nonhuman forces.

David McCally's richly nuanced study represents an important addition to the ongoing environmentally based reconsideration of American history. He is the first professional historian to have applied, in a sustained and conscious manner, the perspectives and methods of environmental history to the Everglades, one of the world's most distinctive and fragile ecosystems. The story he tells is a complex tale that defies easy categorization or summation. No slogan, metaphor, or sound bite can do justice to the complexities and subtleties of the region's past and present. To understand the Everglades on its own terms we need to accompany David McCally on his figurative journey through space and time—through the evolving hammocks and forests, grasslands and islands, streams and sloughs of this remarkable place. Once taken, this is a journey no reader will ever forget.

Raymond Arsenault and Gary R. Mormino, Series Editors

PREFACE

In spite of all the man-made changes that have been introduced in Florida, the Everglades remains the state's most distinctive feature. Well known throughout the world, this extensive wetlands system represents, in the minds of many, a living example of nature's disregard for the needs of human beings. The countless pictures of its dense saw grass stands, abundant aquatic birds, and menacing alligators remind moderns that there are places on earth where people are, at best, unwelcome intruders. In spite of the Everglades' notoriety, however, the story of man in the Everglades is little understood by the public at large, and it is these largely anonymous people who have been asked to decide the complex system's fate.

As part of the 1996 election, Floridians were asked to pass judgment on three proposed amendments to the state's constitution. All three proposals dealt directly with environmental problems in the Everglades. Numbered 4, 5, and 6, the first proposed a one-cent-per-pound tax on unprocessed sugar—sugar being the principal crop grown on the reclaimed Everglades. The second amendment provided that those who polluted the Everglades would be responsible for the cost of cleanup, and the final proposal established a trust fund for Everglades cleanup money.

The election results were ambiguous. The measure that would force polluters to pay proved the most popular, with 62 percent of Floridians approving of it, and the trust fund, too, was carried by a rather comfortable margin of 57 percent in favor and 43 percent opposed, but the amendment that would have authorized the sugar tax failed when 52 percent of the state's electorate voted against it.[1] Many observers attributed the failure of the sugar tax to the massive advertising campaign conducted by the sugar industry, but certainly the general lack of knowledge about the history of reclamation contributed to that campaign's success.

Although a broader readership is certainly hoped for, this study is primarily directed toward the voters of Florida, and it is intended that this work will become a part of the Everglades public policy debate. In the process of examining the Everglades' environmental history, this study addresses three questions. First, what sort of environment was the undisturbed Everglades? Second, why were these wetlands drained? And, third, have the economic gains that followed reclamation been worth the environmental costs?

The first and most essential consideration for those who want to understand the environment of south Florida is, what were the environmental components of the predrainage Everglades? This is essential knowledge to people who have been asked to evaluate restoration proposals. The answer to this question has been obscured by the universal prevalence of Marjory Stoneman Douglas's "river of grass" metaphor. Although I in no way intend to criticize Douglas or her fine book, the dominance of this metaphor is unfortunate, because it gives an inaccurate portrait of the undisturbed Everglades and allows halfway restoration measures to masquerade as realistic solutions. The following detailed account of the Everglades' predrainage wetlands will illustrate that this region was decidedly not a river of grass. Rather, it was a river obscured by grass that supported a diverse assemblage of forests and swamps.

The answer to the second question entails assessment of responsibility. Simply, why were the Everglades drained? I maintain that this process represents the conversion of a natural system into a developmental system. From the first, the expressed goal of drainage was the establishment of agriculture in the reclaimed Everglades, and subsequent reengineering of the region's water control works was developed so that agriculture would prosper. As a result of these reclamation efforts, the commercial growers who occupy the land around the south shore of Lake Okeechobee grow their crops on what amounts to a twenty-mile-thick dam, a barricade that separates the former Everglades river from its headwaters, and these farmers have continually opposed any attempt to reestablish anything resembling the pristine environment of the region. I believe study reveals that no real restoration can take place in the Everglades until something like the natural flow of water is reestablished. Although such a restoration does not require the complete abandonment of agriculture, it will require a far-reaching restructuring of current farming practices.

Finally, this study provides useful information for those who want to think about the broader implications of modern development practices and notions of profit.[2] The relatively ephemeral nature of the Everglades, at least when compared to other more ancient and durable landscapes, offers a stark illustration of the destructive potential implicit in so much current economic thinking. The Everglades was an exotic landscape that Americans converted to the familiar. This process of converting the exotic to the familiar dates from the earliest European habitation in the New World, but the magnitude of the change in south Florida's wetlands is among the most dramatic of any in the Americas. Indeed, draining the Everglades created environmental conditions that assured the eventual demise of not only the region's indigenous plants and animals, but also the very soil that supported this flora and fauna. Among all the exotic landscapes of North America, the Everglades, the most strange, will suffer the greatest loss.[3] From an economic standpoint, this vast environmental destruction created an agricultural system in the Everglades that flourished only because government subsidies financed the construction of water-control works, supplied access to inexpensive labor, and guaranteed profits to producers.

This book could be described as a biography of the Everglades. The term is appropriate because the Everglades is a completely organic system, and it will, in all likelihood, have a finite life span. Within its confines, living organisms prepared the way for and sustained future generations of life. The forests and sedges that white Americans encountered when they explored the region grew in organic soils created by earlier generations of plants. Indeed, even the district's bedrock consisted of the bodies of untold generations of aquatic life that accumulated over the aeons. The emergent properties of the wetlands system ceased, however, after Americans drained south Florida. Since that time, much of the indigenous plant life and most of the organic soil has been destroyed, and Floridians must acknowledge that, barring restoration, the death of the Everglades is near at hand.

This biography of the Everglades divides itself into three parts. The first three chapters describe the creation of the Everglades, the life ways of its indigenous people, and the emergence of what I term the derelict system following the demise of those native people. The second section, which occupies the next three chapters, describes the conversion of the Everglades from a derelict to a developmental system—that is, a natural system that has been reengineered to accommodate modern development. Finally, the last chapter examines the agricultural system that came to fruition in the reclaimed Everglades.

The first chapter recounts the natural history of south Florida. After a long interval as a sea bottom, peninsular Florida was repeatedly inundated and raised from the seas, as the polar ice caps alternately expanded and contracted. The land that comprises the modern-day Everglades did not escape the sea for the last time until after the end of the last Ice Age, and environmental conditions did not favor the existence of the modern plant assemblage until about five thousand years ago. It was only after this date, a scant few hundred years before the Egyptians began building pyramids, that the Everglades came into existence.⁴ Over the course of the last five millennia, the marsh plants of the Everglades provided the organic remains that formed the highly organic soils that characterized the region.

The second chapter provides an account of south Florida's native inhabitants. The Indians who inhabited this land lived in the region before it was wetland, and their cultures evolved with the landscape. These natives shunned agriculture. Instead of farming, these native inhabitants relied on the bounteous supplies of saltwater and freshwater fauna for their subsistence. When Spanish explorers encountered the region, they discovered an unpromising, watery land that was inhabited by a warlike people, and the Europeans quickly concluded that south Florida was not worth the trouble of conquest.

The third chapter provides a detailed account of the predrainage Everglades. The firsthand accounts and photographs of the people who explored these wetlands provide adequate evidence that the unaltered Everglades was much more than a river of grass. The first three chapters provide readers with a good understanding of how the Everglades came into existence, how the wetlands were used by its native inhabitants, and how the region appeared to its explorers. Taken together, these chapters tell the story of the predrainage Everglades.

The next three chapters describe the developmental system that Americans created in south Florida. Ambitious Americans fervently believed that, once drained, the Everglades would provide an agricultural cornucopia unequaled anywhere in the world. It was not until the 1880s, however, that anyone seriously attempted the project. During that decade, the young millionaire Hamilton Disston purchased 4 million acres of Florida land and set the dredges to work. Although Disston's company succeeded in connecting Lake Okeechobee to the Gulf of Mexico, via the Caloosahatchee River, the task of draining the Everglades proved too vast for even his great fortune, and reclamation ceased, not to be resumed until the administration of Florida governor Napoleon Bonaparte Broward (1905–1909) applied the largesse of the state to the task. But again the Everglades proved intractable, and it was not until after 1928, when the vast resources of the federal government were applied to the task, that effective drainage became a reality.

After Broward committed the State of Florida to the task of draining the Everglades, the wetlands system entered a new phase of its life. Before drainage, the marshlands had been emergent; that is, organic remains continued to create new soil. But after drainage became effective, this process reversed itself, and the Everglades began the dying process as its finite supply of soil, the legacy of five thousand years of life, began to disappear. The newly dried land experienced dramatic subsidence and smoldering fires that could burn for years. Less dramatic, but even more insidious, was the toll taken by the aerobic bacteria that lived in the organic soils. Once the water was removed, these microbes had ready access to oxygen, and the bacteria literally began to consume the muck. It is widely agreed that, as a consequence of drainage, about 88 percent of these organic soils will have disappeared by the year 2000.[5]

The final chapter examines the agricultural system that came to fruition in the reclaimed Everglades. In the Everglades, the operant assumptions for those who sought to establish commercial agriculture on the reclaimed wetlands was that the domination of nature, no matter how environmentally destructive, was justified if the end result was monetary profit. These were capitalist farmers, who viewed nature as a free good, created for no other reason than to be used by people. Even though these growers relied on various government programs to subsidize the drainage system, to secure a pliant labor force, and to guarantee their profits, they insisted on the unlimited right to the enjoyment of their private property.

The environmental health of south Florida's wetlands ultimately affects the lives of the millions of Americans who have chosen to live along their margins. In south Florida, the close relationship between the interior wetlands and the coastal cities means that the destruction of one will ultimately lead to the destruction of the other. In the words of historian Jack Temple Kirby, "Nature, too, has agency"; such forces as climate and geologic morphology have the power to "forbid, discourage, or invite human settlement."[6] Accordingly, the epilogue consists of recommendations for how the Everglades can be changed from the current developmental system into a sustainable system that will help to assure that south Florida will remain a desirable place to live rather than degenerating into merely a site suitable for human habitation.

Acknowledgments

This book grew from work that I did, first on a master's thesis and, later, on a Ph.D. dissertation. Accordingly, I would like to thank Professors Ray Arsenault, Lawrence Harris, Gary Mormino, Bertram Wyatt-Brown, Charlotte Porter, Robert Zieger, and Vassiliki Smocovitis for all the advice and guidance that they gave me on those projects. Similarly, I would like to thank three members of the University of Florida's library staff, Bruce Chappell, Carl Van Ness, and Lib Alexander, along with Joe Knetsch of the Bureau of Survey and Mapping in Tallahassee, for their help with my research.

My family and friends were no less important than my professional colleagues. A work such as this affects an entire family, but I must single out my wife, Linda, and my mother, Betty, for special thanks; they each played crucial roles in completing this work. Of my friends, Robert Lauriault and Paul Wojtalewicz were the most intimately connected with this work. As for the rest, knowing you cared meant a great deal.

Finally, I would be remiss if I did not thank those who played crucial roles in converting this manuscript into a book. Steve Morello helped to prepare the illustrations, and Meredith Morris-Babb and Jacqueline King-horn Brown, my editors at the University Press of Florida, helped save me from myself.

1

A Changing Landscape

Although the Everglades elicits for many the image of a primordial wilderness, the region is quite young, having been formed within the last five thousand years. Like all ecosystems, the Everglades represents a complex association of interdependencies. Despite all the changes that human beings have introduced in the region, the basic fact of interdependency remains. This is not to say that the same matrix of interdependencies controls the modern Everglades as dominated the region before drainage, because it most manifestly does not. The drained Everglades is a man-made construction. As such, the relations between its component parts follow the direction of human needs and expectations that have transformed its trees into timber (or dross, depending on the evaluation), wild animals into game, and the very earth itself into soil. The task of the environmental historian is to examine this man-made ecosystem, against the backdrop of the predrainage environment, and evaluate its long-term viability. Toward this end, the first chapter of this study will explicate the interrelations that dominated the predrainage ecosystem.

What follows should be characterized as a biography of the Everglades. In contrast with human biography, however, gestation occupies a much larger portion of this story, involving the movement of tectonic plates, the expansion and contraction of continental ice sheets, and the slow accumulation of aquatic remains. Not until the demise of the Wisconsin glacier, and the onset of the modern era, the Holocene, did this gestation give birth to a peninsula in its modern configuration. Only then could the interrelationship between the organic rock of an ancient seafloor and the waters of a modern ocean begin the biotic transformation that became the Everglades. Fire became the third crucial element in the peninsula's evolution from erstwhile ocean bottom to freshwater wetland, and together these three elements—rock, water, and fire—created the mature system in the Everglades.

Rock

First in significance is the evolution of the solid rock bed upon which the Everglades rests. The rock divides into three categories: basement rock at the bottom, then marine sediments, and then Ice Age strata. Each of these categories had a role in the formation of the Everglades. First, there could have been no Everglades if the dynamics of plate tectonics had not attached Florida's basement rock to the North American landmass. Similarly, because Florida's marine sediments, formed during the area's ancient career as a shallow sea, experienced little deformation, the emergent peninsula featured very little relief. Finally, the thin layers of rock that formed in south Florida during the glacial periods had varying porosities, and these differences meant that some areas of the peninsula absorbed water more slowly than others, a characteristic that proved crucial to the future location of south Florida's wetlands[1] (see table 1.1).

Modern peninsular Florida occupies the southeast corner of the Florida Platform, also called the Florida Plateau, a ridge that separates the waters of the Atlantic Ocean from those of the Gulf of Mexico. The platform's basement rock, Osceola granite and high-feldspar volcanic rocks, indicates an African origin for the Florida Platform, and the movement of tectonic plates accounts for this unlikely source.[2]

Geologists believe that the Florida Platform was originally a part of west Africa, near Senegal, and it became attached to the North American plate after Pangaea, the super continent that once encompassed all of earth's landmass, broke up during the Triassic. After Pangaea's split into two continents, Laurasia and Gondwana, the new landmasses drifted apart and an ocean formed between them. By 450 million years ago, Gondwana was

Table 1.1. Chronology of Glacial and Interglacial Periods

Period or Epoch	Age	Years before Present	Sediments and Rock-Forming Events	Terraces and Higher Sea Level Stands
Holocene	(Probably interglacial)	0 to 10,000	Formation and development of Everglades, beginning 5,000 YBP	Rising sea level; coastal marshes advancing inland
Pleistocene "Ice Age"	Wisconsin (glacial)	10,000 to 67,000	Erosion	Low sea level
	Sangamon (interglacial)	67,000 to 128,000	Miami Limestone, Anastasia formation, Key Largo formation	Silver Bluff (18 ft.), Pamlico (25 ft.)
	Illinoisan (glacial)	128,000 to 180,000	Erosion	Low sea level
	Yarmouth (interglacial)	180,000 to 230,000	Fort Thompson formation	Talbot (40 ft.), Penholoway (70 ft.)
	Kansan (glacial)	230,000 to 300,000	Caloosahatchee formation	Wicomico (90 ft.)
	Aftonian (interglacial)	300,000 to 470,000	Caloosahatchee formation	Okefenokee (120 ft.)
	Unnamed in U.S.	470,000 to 2,000,000	(Brooks Unit 1)	
Pliocene		2,000,000 to 5,000,000	Caloosahatchee and Tamiami formations	(140 ft.)

Source: Patrick J. Gleason and Peter Stone, "Age, Origin, and Landscape Evolution of the Everglades Peatland," in *Everglades: The Ecosystem and Its Restoration,* ed. S. Davis and J. Ogden (Delray Beach, Fla.: St. Lucie Press, 1994), 153.

separated from Laurasia by the Iapetus Ocean, but over the next 100 million years these continents converged until they collided. When they again parted, about 225 million years ago, both continents became dismembered—Gondwana splitting into South America, Africa, Antarctica, Australia, and India, while Laurasia divided itself into North America, with the Florida Platform attached, and Eurasia. Even though the Florida Platform was on the leading edge of an area of continental convergence, it somehow escaped any significant deformation, and the basement rock for the modern Florida peninsula remained very flat.[3] Either as a result of this collision, however, or perhaps stemming from subsequent volcanic activity in the vicinity of the Bahamas, the Florida Platform was tilted ever so gently to the west, a factor that proved crucial to the establishment of the general Everglades drainage pattern.[4]

Although the Florida Platform had been sutured to the North American landmass, it would be millions of years before peninsular Florida would become dry land. A long marine interval accounts for some 95 percent of Florida's geologic history, and that span allowed a thick layer of limestone to accumulate on the basement strata. All through the Mesozoic Era—that is, from about 225 to about 65 million years ago—Florida lay beneath the sea. During this time terrestrial life underwent great changes; fauna such as frogs, turtles, lizards, crocodilians, and dinosaurs appeared, as did new flora such as ferns, conifers, and cycads. Beneath the waters life had to be virtually recreated. The largest mass extinction of all time marked the birth of the Mesozoic, when as many as 96 percent of the world's marine species passed from existence. During all of these vast changes, the Florida Plateau remained on the ocean floor, and the new marine genera of the Mesozoic contributed the bodies of untold generations to the Florida Platform's emergent limestone.[5]

Another mass extinction, this time spelling the end of the dinosaurs, marked the demise of the Mesozoic and the rise of the Cenozoic Era. During these millennia the Florida Plateau remained a shallow seabed, and the limestone strata continued their slow accumulation. Not until about 25 million years ago, with the emergence of the Ocala Arch, which forms the spine of the modern northern peninsula, did any portion of peninsular Florida escape the ocean. Even then, the area destined to become Florida's Everglades continued as a shallow sea. Here, plate tectonics played a trick that significantly prolonged the plateau's career as a sea bottom. Just before the end of the Mesozoic, the basement strata of the Florida Plateau began to settle slowly. For the next 70 million years, the rate of basement rock subsidence roughly equaled that of limestone deposition. Although layer upon layer of limestone accumulated, this deposition only allowed the shallow seafloor to maintain a more or less constant position with relation to the water's surface.[6]

Because of this subsidence, the limestone deposits of south Florida range from 13,000 feet near the south shore of Lake Okeechobee to approximately 20,000 feet at the modern peninsula's southern extremity, compared to only 4,000 feet in the vicinity of Ocala (these are, of course, not all the same limestones).[7] This limestone would, in its turn, serve as the substrate upon which the Everglades bedrock would form. But first, Florida had to escape the ocean.

The interaction between an emergent limestone stratum and fluctuations in sea level finally allowed peninsular Florida to become dry land. During latter stages of the Pliocene and for the entire Pleistocene epoch, which began some 2.5 to 3 million years ago, episodic glaciation greatly influenced world sea levels. During this time, the Florida peninsula experienced repeated cycles of inundation, as melting glaciers released water, or expansion, when growing continental ice sheets converted water to ice.[8] (Figure 1.1 provides a view of two of Florida's relic shore lines, while figure

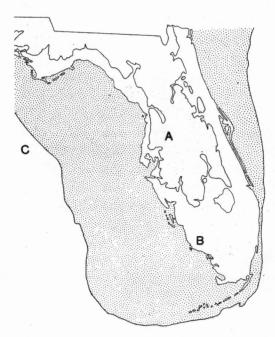

Figure 1.1. Three Florida shorelines: *A*, Wicomico shoreline; *B*, present shoreline; *C*, Wisconsinan glacial shoreline. Source: S. David Webb, "Historical Biogeography," in *Ecosystems of Florida*, Ronald L. Myers and John J. Ewel, eds. (Orlando: University of Central Florida Press, 1990), p. 93. Reprinted with permission.

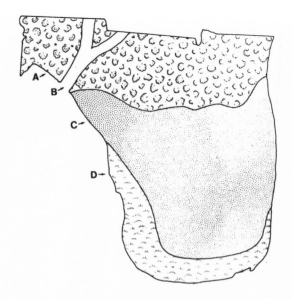

Figure 1.2. Wisconsinan glacial vegetation: *A,* mesopythic forest; *B,* riparian forest; *C,* scrub; *D,* swamp and mangrove. Source: S. David Webb, "Historical Biogeography," in *Ecosystems of Florida,* Ronald L. Myers and John J. Ewel, eds. (Orlando: University of Central Florida Press, 1990), p. 94. Reprinted with permission.

1.2 presents the distribution of plant life on the expanded peninsula.) During periods of inundation, Florida's bedrock experienced deposition, and, during periods of exposure, these strata were eroded (see table 1.1). Because of these oscillations, glacial-period strata, which total less than one hundred feet in thickness, little resembled the thick, even layers of limestone that accumulated during Florida's marine interval. The repeated rise and fall of sea level represented dramatic changes in environmental conditions, changes that found their expression in the remarkably heterogeneous composition of the future Everglades' bedrock.

The emergent peninsula's thick deposits of marine limestone were quite porous and very flat, and these characteristics were crucial to the subsequent development of the Everglades' ice-age bedrock. First, highly permeable limestone could not hold water at the land's surface during periods of low sea level. Because freshwater floats on salt, a declining sea level resulted in a drastically lowered water table in strata as highly permeable as Florida's marine limestone. Consequently, expansive ice sheets produced a south Florida landmass that was not only much larger than that of the modern peninsula, but also much cooler and, in the absence of any significant surface water, more arid.

During periods of extreme glaciation, of which the Wisconsin represented only the latest episode (see table 1.1), the relatively close proximity of a large glacier produced an exaggerated temperature gradient between the ice's surface and the large Florida peninsula. Such temperature differences subjected the Florida peninsula to incessant high winds. When combined with the arid climate, these winds created an environment characterized by large, shifting dunes on the peninsula's interior.[9] As the ice sheets melted, the winds abated, and the dunes became stationary, until the advancing seawaters inundated these sandy formations. During the course of repeated expansion and contraction of continental ice sheets, these sandy strata, the Talbot and Pamlico formations, assumed a position as shown in figure 1.3,

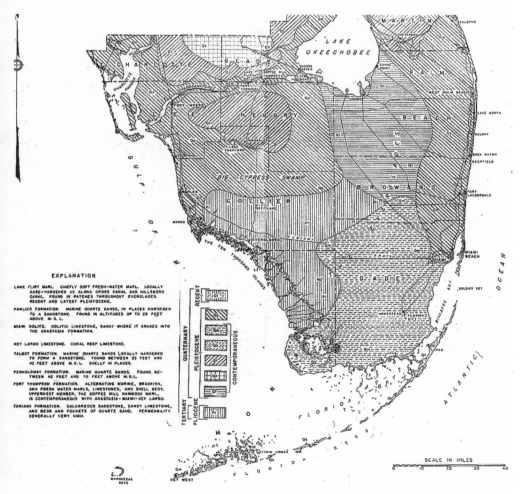

Figure 1.3. South Florida stripped of organic soils. Source: Garald Parker and C. Wythe Cooke, *Late Cenozoic Geology of Southern Florida, with a Discussion of the Ground Water*, State of Florida Department of Conservation, Geological Bulletin No. 27 (Tallahassee: Florida Geological Survey, 1944), plate 14.

and these formations eventually formed the eastern and western boundaries for the developing wetland ecosystem.

The extreme flatness of Florida's marine limestone proved crucial to the survival of the glacial periods' limestone strata. Between the sandy formations, periodic inundation deposited numerous thin layers of calcite sediment, as shown in figure 1.3. Because the Florida Plateau's thick layers of marine limestone offered little relief, these thin strata survived the weathering associated with periods of exposure. The level surface of the Florida Plateau tended to minimize erosional forces, allowing the vulnerable new calcite strata, although damaged, to maintain at least a modicum of integrity. Garald Parker's description of the Fort Thompson formation as consisting of "Alternating marine, brackish, and fresh water marls, limestones, and shell beds" provides an apt illustration of the diverse nature of these strata.[10] Only in a topography of such slight relief could such relatively fragile layers of soluble materials survive.

If the marine limestone had experienced any significant geologic deformation, the resultant increased relief would have spelled the end of the thin ice-age formations of the central peninsula. If weathering had destroyed these strata, the underlying marine limestones would have produced a much more homogeneous environment than the one that eventually took shape atop south Florida's glacial strata. These ice-age strata, with all their variability, provided the basis for the diverse hydroperiods that allowed the development of the Everglades' rich mosaic of wetland environments. In the absence of a variegated bedrock, then, the Everglades ecosystem would not have resembled its modern configuration.

In summary, the rock formations of the Florida Plateau provided three crucial elements to the formation of the modern environment. The basement rock, a one-time piece of Africa, provided the basis for the generally westerly direction of drainage. In the aeons that followed the attachment of this rock mass to North America, continued marine conditions allowed countless generations of sea animals to contribute their bodies to the limestone that was slowly accumulating upon the basement strata. This limestone stratum's high porosity and flat surface proved crucial to the formation of the future Everglades bedrock. Finally, the glacially driven rise and fall of sea level provided both the sandy formations that confined the Everglades to the central portion of the Florida peninsula and the limestone bedrock that accounted for the emergence of a diverse wetlands system.

Water

In 1940 Garald Parker, at the time a hydrologist in the employment of the United States Geological Service (USGS), was dispatched to Miami in the hope that he could discover the cause of a saltwater intrusion into the city's drinking-water wells. Parker had not been in the city long when he discovered that traditional USGS division of authority hindered the pursuit of his goal. Until this time, the USGS had maintained an administrative separation between those investigating surface water and those interested in groundwater. Because of the incredibly high rate of recharge, the rate at which water percolated through overlying strata to the aquifer below, these distinctions were not appropriate in south Florida. Parker had, in effect, discovered a hydrologic system where surface water and groundwater were one.[11]

This intimate relation between surface and groundwater represented not only a key to understanding the city of Miami's drinking-water supply, but also a crucial element in the creation of the lower peninsula's wetlands system. This relation actually involves three elements: rising sea level, solution, and hydroperiod. *Solution* refers to slightly acidic rainwater's propensity to dissolve limestone, and *hydroperiod* refers to the number of days per year any given section of south Florida can expect to be flooded. Both of these elements involve a dynamic relation between rock and water, but this relation did not fully come into play until after sea level rose to its modern level, following the demise of the Wisconsin ice sheet.

The end of the Wisconsin ice age was a precondition to the development of an extensive wetlands system in south Florida. As melting ice caused sea level to rise (a process referred to as the Flandrian Transgression), the Florida peninsula shrank, and the water table rose nearer to the surface, with the porous limestone substrata becoming more saturated. Since freshwater floats on salt water, the rising water table caused a new abundance of springs and sinkholes to appear on a formerly arid landscape. These new sources of freshwater provided habitats for new flora in south Florida (a transformation that scientists have documented with pollen studies). Near the new water sources, wetland flora such as hazelnut, birch, ash, willow, cypress, cattail, water lily, and arrowhead flourished. The new abundance of surface water also provided a source for added evaporation-convection precipitation, and the increased precipitation allowed scrub oak savanna to appear in areas of south Florida that had been until then dominated by sand dune scrub.[12]

Plentiful rainfall also allowed solution to play a greater role on the proto-Everglades landscape. As precipitation percolated through the limestone, it dissolved some of the rock. When coupled with the rising water table, this chemical reaction tended to bring the groundwater into contact with the land's surface, a process that greatly expanded the range suitable for wetlands flora. But solution affected the emerging system from below as well as from above. Underground aquifers dissolved limestone too, and this action proved crucial to the emerging Everglades. The modern Kissimmee River valley drains a 2,500-square-mile basin into Lake Okeechobee, and this valley owes its existence to subterranean solution. In this area, groundwater dissolved enough of the supporting rock so that the land's surface sagged, creating a valley. This sag did not destroy the surface features of the affected area, nor did it create a deep gorge; rather, the sagging valley provided a shallow drainage slough whose low relief provided an ideal basin for a slow-flowing, meandering river.

This river delivered its water and sediments to the trough that would eventually contain Lake Okeechobee and the Everglades. Lake Okeechobee now occupies the lowest portion of this trough, in an area where sediments created a deep accumulation of clays. Differential compaction created a depression in these clays, and freshwater arriving from the north created a lake in the low area. Freshwater calcite mud indicates the existence of a lake in this basin as early as 6,300 years ago, but a lake of modern aspect did not appear until about 4,000 years ago, after organic deposits along Lake Okeechobee's southern rim created a sill of sufficient height to impound its waters in the modern configuration.[13]

Although the surface of interior south Florida appears monotonously flat to the casual eye, it represents a complex of lilliputian valleys and plateaus to water (see fig. 1.4). The hydroperiod of these various diminutive peaks and valleys varied, and these differences proved crucial to emerging plant assemblages. But small elevation differentials alone do not account for all the differences in hydroperiod; rather, the nature of the rock itself also played a role. South Florida's ice-age strata offered a variety of more or less porous surfaces for newly abundant water, and these surfaces played a major role in determining how long water stayed on the surface. Figure 1.3 illustrates the division, north and south, in the limestone that underlies the

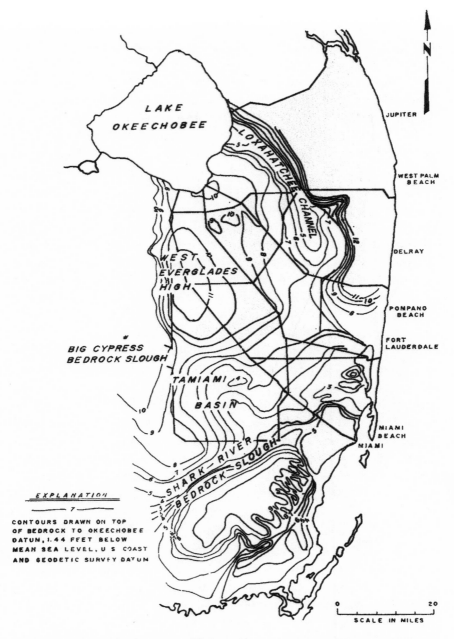

Figure 1.4. Contours of south Florida bedrock. Source: Patrick J. Gleason et al., "The Environmental Significance of Holocene Sediments from the Everglades and Saline Tidal Plain," in Patrick J. Gleason ed., *Environments of South Florida Present and Past II* (Coral Gables: Miami Geological Society, 1984), fig. 3, p. 327. Reprinted with permission.

Everglades. The Fort Thompson formation forms the bedrock of the northern Everglades, while Miami Limestone predominates in the south. The characteristics of both strata bear the imprint of the oscillations in sea level associated with Pleistocene ice sheets, and these characteristics contributed to the hydroperiod of the emerging Everglades.

Both the Miami Limestone and the Fort Thompson formations provide excellent examples of the connection between hydroperiod and Pleistocene sea-level fluctuations. The southern end of the Florida peninsula has experienced marine conditions more recently than have more northerly areas. This marine influence requires one to subdivide the Miami Limestone strata east from west. The surface of the Miami Limestone slopes gently to the west, from a high of some twenty feet on the Atlantic Coastal Ridge to a low of about five feet at its border with the Tamiami formation. The more elevated eastern portion of this formation represents the remains of a mound of sand and shell that formed beneath the sea, and this low ridge was dry land long before the lower elevations to the west.

In the higher east, oolites, the round grains of sand that settled on the former ocean bottom, hardened into oolite limestone when exposed to the air. Behind this erstwhile sandbar—that is, to the west—a shallow sea persisted, and bryozoans, invertebrate colonial marine animals, form the major constituents of this stratum. When peninsular Florida finally attained its modern aspect, bedrock topography directed drainage along the margin of the oolitic limestone (see fig. 1.5). East-west channels in the Atlantic Coastal Ridge, referred to as the Transverse Glades by south Florida's pioneers, allowed some of this water to flow into the Atlantic Ocean, while the highly porous oolitic limestone directed much of the remaining water to the underlying Biscayne Aquifer (see fig. 1.6). These conditions helped insure that the western bryozoan limestone, itself very porous, had a shorter hydroperiod than the eastern oolitic strata.[14]

As one proceeds north, the terrestrial history of the peninsula has an earlier beginning. Because of this fact, one must also subdivide the Fort Thompson formation, but this time the demarcation must be between the north and the south. Since the more northerly reaches of the Fort Thompson formation have a longer terrestrial history than do those in the south, they also have a longer association with freshwater. The sag valley that served as a drainage basin for the proto–Kissimmee River inundated this area with freshwater even before modern Lake Okeechobee took form.

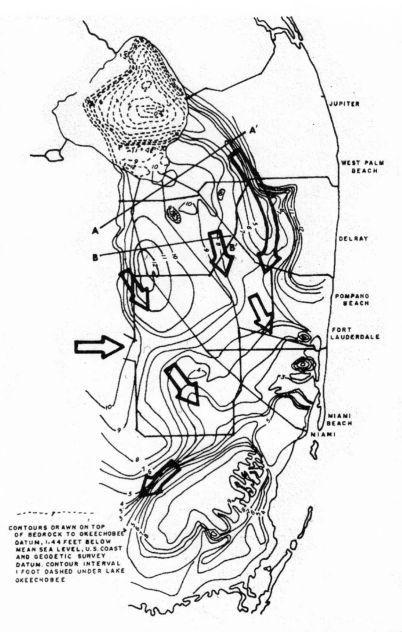

Figure 1.5. Major directions of surface water flow. Source: Patrick J. Gleason et al., "The Environmental Significance of Holocene Sediments from the Everglades and Saline Tidal Plain," in Patrick J. Gleason ed., *Environments of South Florida Present and Past II* (Coral Gables: Miami Geological Society, 1984), fig. 2, p. 327. Reprinted with permission.

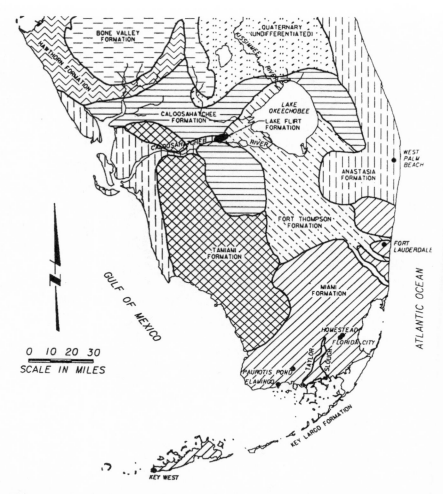

Figure 1.6. South Florida's bedrock formations. Patrick J. Gleason and Peter Stone, "Age, Origin, and Landscape Evolution of the Everglades Peatland," in *Everglades: The Ecosystem and Its Restoration,* S. Davis and J. Ogden eds. (Delray Beach, Fla.: St. Lucie Press, 1994), p. 153. Reprinted with permission.

This situation allowed a thin cap rock of freshwater limestone to form in the north, and this freshwater stratum proved less porous than its saltwater counterparts to the south. Consequently, the hydroperiod increases as one proceeds north along the Fort Thompson formation.[15]

In both the Miami Limestone and Fort Thompson formations, areas that experience longer hydroperiods support vast stands of saw grass, while areas with shorter hydroperiods manage only scattered stands of this sedge and extensive beds of periphyton, a blue-green alga mixed with calcium carbonate crystals. Periphyton grows on poorly drained limestone that experiences inundation interspersed with long dry periods. The presence of such mud indicates an environment too dry for the growth of peat-forming marsh plants.

Calcite muds continue to form in the Everglades, especially on the bryozoan strata of the Miami Limestone. In the northern Everglades, however, calcite mud does not appear on the surface; rather, the mud underlies virtually the entire region, occupying a thin stratum between the bedrock and peat soils. Evidently, accumulations of calcite mud increased the hydroperiod of the strata in the northern Everglades enough so that peat-forming plants could gain a foothold. In this way, periphyton helped prepare the way for plant assemblages capable of forming organic soils.[16]

Peat began widespread formation in the northern and central Everglades about five thousand years ago. But peat formation did not create a homogeneous soil throughout the Everglades; rather, differing hydroperiods support plant assemblages that created their own unique soils (figure 1.7 provides a soil map for the Everglades). There are five major classifications of peat within the Everglades, and two of these, Okeechobee muck and Gandy peat, occupy the highest elevations. Okeelanta peaty-muck occurs in the transitional zone between the higher elevations of the Lake Okeechobee impound sill and the lower Everglades, where Everglades peat predominates. Finally, Loxahatchee peat occupies the marsh's lowest land, areas usually referred to as sloughs.[17]

These varieties of peat owe their characteristics to the plant assemblages from which they were formed, and these, in turn, represent the flora that flourishes in areas of different hydroperiods. In the lowlands, the hydroperiod is longest (if not perpetual), because water flows to these sloughs from surrounding areas. Here, water lilies and other slough-type vegetation predominate and promote the formation of a spongy, light-brown soil called Loxahatchee peat. Occupying some 730,000 acres within the Everglades, this soil never achieved agricultural significance and underlies much of the undeveloped Everglades.

If enough Loxahatchee peat accumulates to form a ridge of sufficient height, tree islands form and begin the creation of Gandy peat. Gandy peat is the rarest soil type within the Everglades. Covering only about 19,000

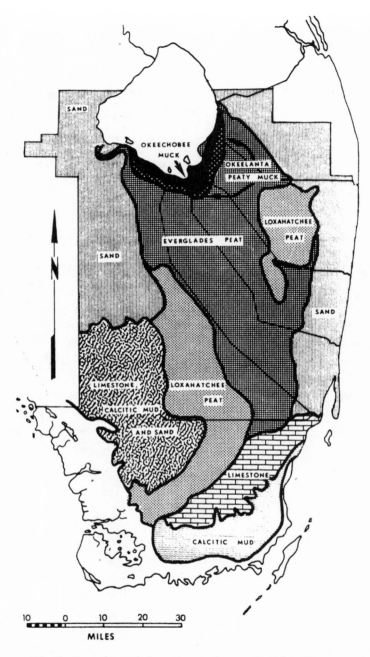

Figure 1.7. Distribution of Everglades soil types. Source: Patrick J. Gleason et al., "The Environmental Significance of Holocene Sediments," fig. 8, p. 332. Reprinted with permission.

acres, it is found mostly in the ridge and slough area of the southwest and northeast Everglades. This peat usually overlies Loxahatchee peat, but it can be found above Everglades peat or interbedded with either of these soils. Gandy peat forms on tree islands in the zone above high water, and, unlike other peats, forms in an aerobic environment.

Everglades peat, for its part, forms wherever saw grass has been the dominant vegetation. This type of peat covers some 1,091,000 acres of the Everglades, and its black color comes from the abundance of charcoal within this soil, the result of recurrent fires. Everglades peat has proven to be the most widespread peat with agricultural utility, and sugar cane has found this soil type a fertile home.

Okeechobee muck refers to a multilayered sediment that covers 32,000 acres around the southern shore of Lake Okeechobee. This type of soil occupies a three-mile-wide strip on the south shore of Lake Okeechobee, and it is considered an allocthonous peat—that is, a peat whose components are formed elsewhere and then deposited in their present location. These components, mostly sand and organic material, entered the lake with the waters of the Kissimmee River and the other streams that drain into Okeechobee from the north, and their deposition created the sill that impounded the lake's waters. Okeechobee muck has the highest percentage of inorganic components among the Everglades soils, and the relatively high elevation of this soil allowed a forest of custard apple to flourish around the lake's southern shore. But because this soil was the first to support successful agriculture, these forests had virtually disappeared by 1930.

Okeelanta peaty-muck occupies about 26,000 acres that occur in a thin band between the Okeechobee muck and the Everglades peat to the south. Widely viewed as a transitional zone between regions of lake and Everglades influence, the Okeelanta peaty-muck supported a plant assemblage of saw grass, willow, and elder. Some modern observers believe the region's willow and elder growth owed its existence to early drainage efforts, and they maintain that saw grass dominated the region in its natural state. But on closer scrutiny this argument does not seem plausible, because Everglades soil types so closely reflect an area's flora. It seems more probable that, as a transitional zone, the Okeelanta peaty-muck belt was especially sensitive to water-level fluctuations. Although drainage could indeed have altered the hydroperiod enough to aid willow and elder dominance, this change surely represented no more than a single man-made episode within a larger natural cycle. Precipitation in the Everglades has varied over time. During dry cycles, the hydroperiod was shorter, favoring a willow and elder assemblage in this location, while wet cycles allowed saw grass to thrive. The distinctive soil that developed in this transitional zone testifies to these fluctuations in hydroperiod, and willow, elder, and saw grass all contributed organic remains to the Okeelanta peaty-muck. Extremely fertile, this soil type, too, was favored by agriculturalists who eventually planted the entire region in crops, relegating arguments about the relative dominance of saw grass or willow and elder to academia's arcane world.[18]

The Everglades soils represent the culmination of a five-thousand-year-old process. The end of the Wisconsin Ice Age, and the subsequent Flandrian Transgression, brought south Florida's water table to a position at or near the land's surface. This wetter environment not only provided a home for different plant assemblages, but also allowed solution to play a larger role in south Florida's environment. Florida's limestone bedrock was liable to alteration by solution, and this chemical reaction expanded the wetter environment. Slight differences in the Everglades Basin's limestone bedrock, combined with slight undulations in the old seafloor, created an environment characterized by different hydroperiods. These hydroperiods controlled the subsequent proliferation of floral communities, and the organic remains from these plant assemblages provided the key ingredients to the Everglades' organic soils. When agriculturalists arrived in the Everglades, the varieties of organic soils proved crucial to the success of their endeavors. Through this chain of events, an element as mundane as water emerges as the second crucial element in Everglades development—both natural and human.

Fire

The third crucial element to the Everglades, fire, is closely associated with hydroperiod and soil formation. In the Everglades, precipitation cycles largely dictate both hydroperiod and fire frequency. Because most naturally occurring fires are the result of lightning strikes, the majority of natural Everglades fires occur during the wet season, and they can be characterized as superficial. These fires cause no long-term damage, and they in fact play a key role in maintaining many plant assemblages. Some fires do, however, ignite during dry periods, and such blazes, although fewer in number, usually cause more damage than wet-season fires. Such deep fires often induce plant succession, by destroying even the fire-resistant plants' root systems, and can even consume the dried-out organic soils. In close association with the region's water, then, fire plays a key role in plant assemblage maintenance and subsequent soil development.

In the hyperorganic environment of the Everglades, only water restricts the activity of fire; conversely, the total absence of water would allow fire to consume the entire tangible environment—plants, animals, soils, and all. Most of the water within the Everglades comes to the region as rain, and Everglades precipitation is highly cyclical. Evidence exists for at least three fire cycles in the Everglades, and these cycles are closely associated with variations in the area's rainfall. The fire cycle of shortest duration is based on the variability of the region's precipitation throughout the year. South Florida's rainfall is highly seasonal, with the wet period occurring from May to October and the dry season from November to April. Most naturally occurring fires result from the lightning generated by summertime thunderstorms, and this season experiences more fires than the winter. These summertime fires can be characterized as superficial, and they allow fire-resistant flora to flourish. But dry-season fires can cause deeper damage, especially in May, when early season thunderstorms encounter the region's driest conditions.

In addition to this yearly cycle, researchers have discovered a mid-range fire cycle based on ten- to fourteen-year climatological variations. Although the entire mechanism of this cycle is not understood, it has been observed that fluctuations in fire frequency coincide with similar variations in other significant environmental variables. Water levels, water flows, and pan evaporation all vary with a similar decadal time span, and these variables contribute to the occurrence of fires. As evidenced in the yearly cycle, fires during this mid-range cycle can be characterized as numerous and superficial during wet periods or scarce but destructive in times of drought.[19]

Although the general climatological trend in the Everglades has been toward moderation throughout the Holocene, scientists have identified a 550-year cycle to south Florida's climate. These cycles of long duration represent alternating cool and warm periods within this larger trend toward modern conditions. In the Everglades, *cool* means dry, and alterations in marl and peat strata reflect these changes in past precipitation patterns— marl accumulating during periods of low rainfall, and peat during wet times. As with the other precipitation cycles, lower rainfall resulted in damaging fires. During the Sub-Boreal period (2730–940 B.C.), layers of charcoal indicate five periods of severe burning associated with the period's prolonged droughts. Since that time, however, Everglades climatological conditions have seemingly moderated, and no evidence exists for a repetition of such widespread deep burns.[20]

In the evolving Everglades system most fires occurred during wet cycles, in close association with thunderstorms, and the high incidence of such superficial fires played a key role in the development of plant communities. The relation between water, fire, and saw grass provides the best illustration of the influence fire frequency has on plant communities and subsequent organic soil development.

For many Americans, saw grass has become emblematic of the Everglades, and dense stands of the sedge have become the living symbol of Florida's wetlands. But, in reality, saw grass represents only one plant community within the larger marsh system of the Everglades. Saw grass thrives in a particular relation between wetness and dryness, the hydroperiod, and that relation can be precarious. No marsh plant is more adapted to the normal Everglades fire cycle than is saw grass. Its leaves provide abundant fuel for flames, supporting fire even in standing water, while its root mass, firmly ensconced in wet muck soil, easily survives the fires above. Indeed, one might argue that the plant's leaves invite flames, since recurrent fire discourages invasion of the sedge's realm by woody plants, and the Everglades' vast monocrop stands of saw grass testify to the efficacy of such a strategy.

If the balance of wetness to dryness changes, however, these stands contract, and they can even disappear in cases of extreme alteration. As the hydroperiod increases, saw grass tends to give way, first to flag marsh and then to water lily, if wet conditions persist. But dryness can present a greater long-term threat to the saw-grass environment, because the deep fires associated with dry conditions so drastically alter the natural setting. Deep-water marshes experience fire, on average, every three to five years, while shallow marshes burn every one to three years.[21] In dry conditions, these burns can kill the roots of saw grass, and a continuation of such arid conditions often allows woody plants to invade the former saw-grass environment. If they become firmly established, the shade created by trees and shrubs prohibits regeneration of saw grass, and a former habitat is forever lost.[22]

In addition to affecting plant succession, deep fires can inhibit, or even reverse, peat formation. Modern estimates maintain that twenty-eight crops of saw grass, with an average life span of eight years, are required to create one foot of saw grass peat. That is, a foot of such peat should form every 225 years.[23] These data indicate that continuous peat development over five thousand years would have accumulated more than twenty-two feet of these organic soils. As measured in 1912, however, nowhere in the Everglades did muck accumulations amount to more than seventeen feet, and nowhere did Everglades peat extend deeper than thirteen feet[24] (see fig. 1.8). The high incidence of fire in saw-grass environments accounts for this lost peat, especially deep fires that either killed the sedge or consumed the soil. Indeed, fires have so frequently swept the saw grass Everglades, the site of Everglades peat formation, that the area's soils owe their deep black coloration to the ash left behind by such conflagrations.[25]

In summary, the fires of the Everglades fall into two broad categories: superficial and deep. Superficial fires occur during wet-weather cycles, and they are primarily the result of thunderstorm lightning strikes. These fires have a major role in the maintenance of plant communities since they inhibit the invasion by woody plants of grassy marshes. Deep fires, although they occur less frequently than superficial fires, cause more environmental damage, because they are associated with dry periods in the Everglades weather cycles. Dry conditions allow these fires to kill even fire-resistant species, and deep fires retard, or even reverse, peat accumulation. This close association between fire and hydroperiod has had a profound effect on the evolution of the mature Everglades ecosystem.

The Mature System

The interactions among fire, rock, and water created an organic environment in the Everglades Trough. Taken together, the plants and animals of this organic environment formed a living system, and this living system developed traits of its own. Many ecologists will, no doubt, take exception to this statement. Within the science of ecology, the view of what constitutes the dominant paradigm of the natural world has undergone profound change since Frederic L. Clements postulated a system of plant succession

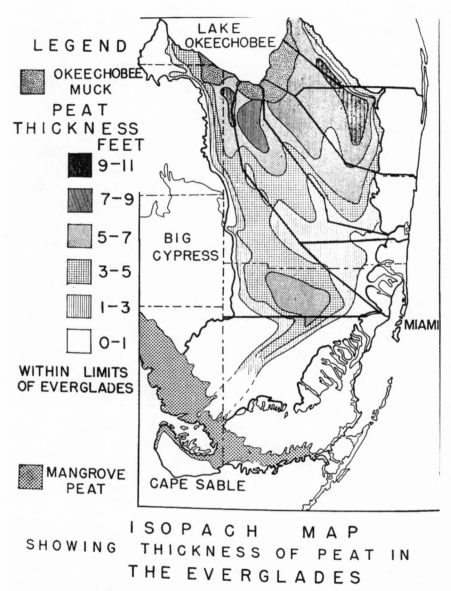

LEGEND

OKEECHOBEE
MUCK

PEAT
THICKNESS
FEET

9–11

7–9

5–7

3–5

1–3

0–1

WITHIN LIMITS
OF EVERGLADES

MANGROVE
PEAT

LAKE
OKEECHOBEE

BIG
CYPRESS

MIAMI

CAPE SABLE

ISOPACH MAP
SHOWING THICKNESS OF PEAT IN
THE EVERGLADES

Figure 1.8. Thickness of Everglades soils. Source: William A. White, *The Geomorphology of the Florida Peninsula*, State of Florida Department of Natural Resources Geological Bulletin No. 51 (Tallahassee: Bureau of Geology, Division of Interior Resources, Florida Department of Natural Resources, 1970), p. 80.

in which the climax ecosystem resembled a superorganism. Modern ecologists have rejected the notion of the natural world as the scene of anything resembling a cooperative steady state in favor of an ecology of chaos, where patch dynamics has supplanted older ideas of the superorganism and the integrated ecosystem. In place of closely integrated environmental systems, ecologists now see a natural world where events are random and succession unpredictable.[26]

But those who think about the environment should take care not to reify what are essentially intellectual tools designed to aid understanding. Whether ecologists view the natural world through the lens of the superorganism, the ecosystem, or the patch, they are not defining reality; rather, they are merely seeking to understand it. Like the Taoist sage Lao Tsu, ecologists should be ever mindful that "the Tao that can be told is not the eternal Tao."[27] Living organisms form systems, and those systems display defining characteristics. That is all.

The three dominant characteristics of the Everglades system are habitat heterogeneity, large spatial extent, and a distinctive hydrologic regime. None of these characteristics stands alone. The hydrologic regime, for instance, has a profound effect on both the extent and diversity of south Florida's wetlands. Similarly, habitat heterogeneity within the Everglades and the large spatial expanse of that system are closely intertwined. The variety of habitats attracts a wide array of flora and fauna to the region, but the full array of plants and animals would not survive in a smaller system, even one that contained the same variety of habitats. For analytic purposes, the wide range of environmental niches will be regarded as the primary contributor to the system's diversity, while its large spatial expanse will be seen as accounting for its resiliency, and the hydrologic regime will be viewed as the agent that maximizes the usefulness of the water.[28]

The Everglades did not emerge as a full-blown wetlands system. Evidence, in the form of calcite mud, points to an intermediate stage between the Everglades as ice-age stratum and that region as a labyrinth of marshes and forests. A thin layer of calcite mud, often hardened into stone, stands between the region's limestone bedrock and the organic soils of the upper Everglades. In the southern portion of the region, calcite mud continues to form, and scientists have concluded that the modern lower Everglades resembles the ancient north. That is, it exhibits the conditions that favor the creation of calcite mud—periods of inundation followed by long dry spells—conditions that once characterized the north. These environmental constraints did not allow the proliferation of peat-forming plants.

As deposits of calcite mud accumulated, they proved less permeable to water than did the ice-age calcite bedrock, and hydroperiods gradually increased throughout the upper Everglades. But micro-topographic features in the bedrock insured that slightly lower elevations, sloughs, had longer hydroperiods than did more elevated sections of the bedrock strata. In areas with the longest hydroperiods, water lily slough vegetation predominated and formed a distinctive soil type, Loxahatchee peat. Since saw grass seeds will not germinate under water, the sedge made its home on slightly elevated sections of the northern Everglades, where hydroperiod was not continuous. Because of its high resistance to fire and cold, saw grass became the dominant plant of this region, often appearing in vast monocrop stands. The sedge's ability to propagate vegetatively—it seldom reproduces by seeds once established—enabled the plant to expand into all but the deepest water environments.[29]

North of the saw grass Everglades, an impound sill began to form on the southern and eastern shores of Lake Okeechobee, composed of the sediments brought into the lake by the Kissimmee River and other smaller streams of the north. Beginning about six thousand years ago the slow accumulation of peat, muck, and inorganic sediments raised the elevation of the lake, as the impounding dike on the southern edge grew. The sill reached its maximum elevation by A.D. 265, and a lake of modern aspect spread out behind it, occupying former wetland habitats. Because of its greater elevation, this sill supported a tropical forest composed of custard apple on the southern shore and cypress along the lake's eastern bank.[30]

At the same time that river-born sediments created the sill around Lake Okeechobee's southern shore, organic peats accumulated in the upper Everglades (see figure 1.9 for a typical cross section of the northern Everglades). At lower topographical elevations, a characteristic ridge and slough landform evolved, which featured numerous tree islands separated by deepwater sloughs. Beginning about twelve hundred years ago, sufficient peat had accumulated so that chunks of the organic soil occasionally broke away from their moorings and formed floating islands. Common in water lily sloughs, these floating islands eventually came into contact with surrounding higher marshland, where they soon became reattached. These newly arrived masses of peat formed slightly higher elevations, and they allowed proliferation of plants unable to survive in lower settings. Through the process of plant succession, these erstwhile floating peat islands often become dominated by red bay trees. Although usually more or less round when they reattach themselves, these islands are transmuted by water currents into a shape resembling spermatozoa—with the tails pointing in the direction of water flow. The low spots created when floating islands break away from their initial positions (often called gator holes), coupled with the high spots created where they reattach, account for much of the rich mosaic of plant assemblages that characterize the ridge and slough provinces of the northeast and southwest Everglades.

Tree islands can form in a number of other ways, however, and these islands also contribute to the heterogeneity of habitat found in ridge and

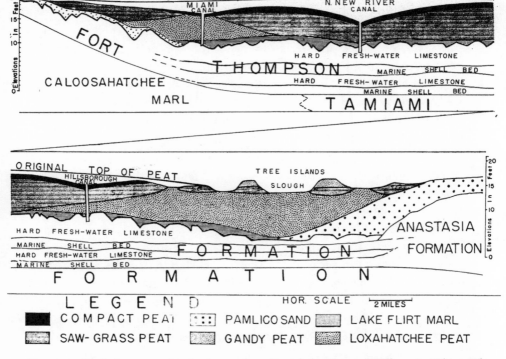

Figure 1.9. Typical cross section in the northern Everglades. Source: William A. White, *The Geomorphology of the Florida Peninsula,* State of Florida Department of Natural Resources Geological Bulletin No. 51 (Tallahassee: Bureau of Geology, Division of Interior Resources, Florida Department of Natural Resources, 1970), p. 81.

slough regions. Limestone or sand mounds, which tower from 0.5 to 1.2 meters above the surrounding water lily sloughs, often provide the basis for tree islands. These elevated mounds often form the heads, areas on tree islands that feature the largest vegetation, with elongated tails stretching out in the direction of water flow.

Dahoon holly tree islands represent another elongated island type, but these do not seem to arise from either floating peat or topographical rises. Dahoon holly islands always have deep deposits of peat, which tell the story of emergence from continually flooded marsh to only occasionally inundated forest. These islands, as their name implies, are dominated by Dahoon holly. These trees grow from slightly elevated root-stump mounds or tussocks, and they usually accommodate an understory of ferns. Regardless of how they formed, the tree islands of the Everglades ridge and slough areas provide congenial homes for a wide variety of plants and the animals they attract.[31]

The Everglades system as encountered by Europeans wholly encompassed the low trough that ran from the southern shore of Lake Okeechobee to the tip of the peninsula. Approximately forty miles wide and one hundred miles long, this system's large size provided environmental resiliency, while its varied vegetation pattern created a vast array of habitats. As so graphically illustrated by modern conditions, this richness of biotic diversity could not flourish in a restricted area. Only on a vast spatial scale is such a system capable of providing an adequate aquatic base for the large vertebrate fauna that complete the ecosystem. Many of these animals have narrow habitat requirements (the snail kite) or require a large feeding range (the Florida panther), and only a vast spatial system can accommodate them. Only in such a large system can viable numbers and subpopulations of such species survive, and only the existence of such a population can insure the long-term survival of these species. Large spatial scale has the additional advantage of minimizing the impact of habitat damage wrought by south Florida's floods, fires, freezes, and hurricanes. Although any of these forces can destroy a localized habitat, the size of the Everglades system insures that suitable specialized habitats will survive somewhere within this large, extremely varied wetlands system.

The third characteristic of the ecosystem, its hydrological regime, allowed the system to maximize its use of the area's highly seasonal rainfall and allowed the wetlands ecosystem to expand to the limits of its range. Stated simply, the major characteristics of this regime, dynamic storage and sheet flow, enabled south Florida's wetlands systems to survive in a climate characterized by a yearly drought cycle. Both organic and inorganic components of the Everglades combined their attributes to, in effect, stretch the area's wet season far into times of drought. But it was the organic components of dynamic storage that insured the Everglades' success, since partially decayed aquatic plants formed the basis for increased water-storage capacity. Because of this characteristic, the water table rose along with emergent peat, and the Everglades continued as a wetlands system far longer than would otherwise be implied by its emergent character.

Peat soils represent one of the key elements in the system of dynamic storage. These soils are capable of absorbing huge amounts of water and are tenacious in their ability to retain moisture. Everglades peats' water contents vary from 80 percent water for saw-grass peat taken from the level of the water table, to 95 percent water for Loxahatchee peat removed from below that level. In addition to the ability to absorb large amounts of water, these soils retain water better than other soil types. As peat soils dry, surface layers assume a granular form, and this transformation reduces the capillarity of the soil. In this condition, the dried surface of the peat serves almost as a sealant, retarding the evaporation of subsurface water. Even plants are prevented from removing much of this deep moisture, since peat can hold water so tightly that roots cannot remove the water from the soil. This dynamic storage capacity of peat soils insures that droughts do not overly dry the region and allows such precipitation as does fall to increase the hydroperiod, since the ground remains in a state of at least semisaturation.[32]

Other characteristics of the Everglades combined with the peat soils to create the huge dynamic storage capacity of the region. Many of these factors have been mentioned previously, but they bear repeating in this context. The area's low relief, dense vegetation, and porous substrata insured that a high percentage of water entering the system would be retained within the region. Much of this water percolated into the ground, where it was retained in superficial aquifers, and this water often reappeared in the streams, lakes, and even surface-water runoff in the southern Everglades. Referred to as "base flow," the contribution of superficial aquifers to south

Florida's surface water is surprisingly high. As an example, scientists estimate that as much as 80 percent of the upper Kissimmee River basin's water owed its existence to base flow.[33]

Firsthand accounts by early explorers and writers confirm the contribution of base flow to the Everglades' surface water. During his canoe trip from the mouth of the Harney River to the headwaters of the Miami River, Hugh Willoughby observed numerous small ponds "like a pretty aquarium"[34] whose water arose from holes in their rock floors. Indeed, the limestone bedrock of the Everglades featured innumerable such openings, called solution holes, created by the corrosive action of rainwater on the calcite rock.[35] The existence of such openings provided ready channels for the confluence of surface water with groundwater and account for much of the base flow enjoyed by south Florida's rivers and lakes. The contribution of base flow to Florida's surface flow was unquestioned by early inhabitants of south Florida, and one popular writer, relying on local knowledge, assured his readers that in the Everglades, "Unnumbered springs fill this vast basin with water."[36] To early observers, it seemed only rational that the vast amount of surface water within the Everglades basin owed its continual existence to something other than rainfall, and modern science has at least partially validated this view.

Modern scientists have employed the term "sheet flow" to describe the slow-motion movement of surface water, and, along with dynamic storage, sheet flow has been characterized as vital to the Everglades wetlands system's hydrologic regime. Sheet flow is viewed as having been driven by the periodic overflow of Lake Okeechobee. As with dynamic storage, the area's low relief, dense vegetation, and porous substrata combine to insure a slow flow-through for the region's surface water. But here, the lack of relief plays a key role, because it insures that the Everglades' surface water experiences only a minimum of channelization, resulting in a pattern of braided drainage.[37] This pattern, in effect, allows the area's surface water to be shared over a much larger area than would occur if relief were greater.

Firsthand accounts, however, force one to question the conventional wisdom that periodic overflow of Lake Okeechobee represented the motive force that drove sheet flow. This idea is based on the assumption that the predrainage lake lacked a southern outlet, and this is not the case. Observers of the undisturbed lake noted at least eight rivers, all of which "run about two or three miles through swamp, and as suddenly as they began, just so suddenly do they cease to exist, the waters spreading out over and forming the swamp."[38] These were no mean streams, as noted by Lieutenant J. C. Ives during the Seminole Wars, ranging from forty to eighty yards in width and "several feet deep."[39] Indeed, one of these streams earned itself a name—the Democrat River—and appeared on Lawrence Will's map of Lake Okeechobee, although in the engineered Everglades it no longer exists.[40]

Periodic overflow of Lake Okeechobee did not provide the water that maintained the Everglades' sheet flow; rather, that water continuously exited the lake through several rivers. These streams disappeared once they passed through the rim that impounded the lake on its southern shore, and here the region's lack of relief allowed them to merge into a stream miles wide and, at times, only inches deep. This slow-moving river allowed the wetland's organic soils to absorb considerable water, and groundwater contributed to its flow downstream toward the southern Everglades. This broad river occupied the entire central portion of the peninsula, and owed its existence to the convergence of the smaller streams that drained Lake Okeechobee's southern shore. The dense vegetation in the northern Everglades obscured this stream from view, and, farther south, the land's lack of relief created a stream so alien to visitors' experience that it was not recognized for what it was—a broad system of braided drainage, not terribly unlike a highly concealed version of the Platte River in Nebraska.

Sheet flow and dynamic storage nurtured the Everglades wetlands system, but these influences owed their existence to the interrelations among rock, water, and fire. The rise of sea level to its current position was an absolute prerequisite to the emergence of a wetlands system on the southern Florida peninsula; a wetlands system began to emerge only *after* the Flandrian Transgression. Similarly, the expanse and heterogeneity of the Everglades' wetlands habitats existed only because of the unique relations between rock and water on the southern Florida peninsula.

The Everglades wetlands system depended on a complex biotic feedback loop to perpetuate itself. Stated simply, the wetlands flora of the Everglades thrived in a biotic habitat composed of its own remains, and those remains contributed to the continuation of a wetlands ecosystem. In keeping with this model, the rivers that drained into Lake Okeechobee from the north contributed their loads of alluvium to the impound sill along the lake's southern and eastern shores. As this sill rose, so did the level of the lake, and its waters formed a key element in both the sheet flow and dynamic storage that nurtured the wetlands environment to the south. These wetlands, for their part, emerged along with the lake, as generation followed generation of marsh plants into the ever-accumulating peat soils of the region. As these soils accumulated, however, they brought entrapped moisture along with them, so that marsh conditions continued even as elevation increased. In the ridge and slough regions, where emergent peat contributed to plant succession, breakaway peat islands left behind depressions that insured the continuation of the extended hydroperiods required for the accumulation of Loxahatchee peat. Even fire contributed to the continuation of a wetlands environment, by destroying dried peat down to the underlying water. Although no one can be sure what the Everglades would have looked like in another five thousand years, it seems clear that its wetland environments used their own biomass to perpetuate conditions favorable to their survival.

The Indians who inhabited south Florida lived in the region before the Everglades began to form, and they continually altered their life ways as the environment of the peninsula changed. But they were more than the passive observers of a changing environment. Like all humans, south Florida's native inhabitants sought to bend the natural world to their ends, and their success was obvious to the Spanish conquistadors who encountered their civilization. The fury with which these Indians defended themselves discouraged Spanish ambitions, and the strangeness of the land insured that Europeans would shun its watery expanse. American agriculturalists, however, lusted after the region's black soils, even if the excess water was an unwelcome intruder. The interrelations among rock, water, and fire seemed to these boosters no more than wasteful excesses of prodigal nature. Those who visualized an agricultural Eden in the Everglades used every means at their disposal to replace the region's interrelations with ones of their own design—the categories of land, labor, and profit. The following chapters will examine the interactions of Indians, Spaniards, and Americans with the wetlands system of the Everglades.

2

Changing Peoples

Indians occupied south Florida before the Everglades came into existence, and their cultures continually evolved to take into account the changing environmental conditions. Stated simply, the particular cultural adaptations of south Florida's indigenous population responded to the creation of a new environment by altering social practices in ways designed to facilitate survival in the emerging conditions. When new food sources became available, they moved to them, and when these sources engendered population explosions, the residents of south Florida created new social relations designed to cope with the changing demographic reality.

The prehistory of the New World's indigenous people is usually divided into three cultural periods: Paleo-Indian, Archaic, and local adaptation. In south Florida, archaeologists have subdivided the Archaic into three time periods, and *Glades* is the name given to the period of local adaptation[1] (see table 2.1). As with any periodization, these categories represent simplifications, and the life ways of south Florida's Indians do not divide into such clearly defined periods. The persistence of such cultural practices as non-agricultural subsistence patterns and a water mortuary cult argues for a certain degree of continuity throughout these periods, and anthropologists, aware of these ongoing practices, regard these three periods as subdivisions within the same cultural tradition.[2]

Table 2.1 Cultural Periods in Prehistoric South Florida

Period	Dates
Paleo-Indian	10,000–7,000 B.C.
Archaic	
Early	7,000–5,000 B.C.
Middle	5,000–3,000 B.C.
Late	3,000–1,500 B.C.
Transitional	1,500–500 B.C.
Glades I	500 B.C.–A.D. 800
Glades II	A.D. 800–1200
Glades III	A.D. 1200–1566
Historic	A.D. 1566–1763

Source: William E. McGoun, *Prehistoric Peoples of South Florida* (Tuscaloosa: University of Alabama Press, 1993), 7.

Paleo and Archaic Indians

Human beings did not evolve in the New World; rather, they migrated to the Americas. Although a number of routes have been proposed for this movement, most scientists view the Ice Age land bridge between Siberia and Alaska as the most probable path for such a migration. The Paleo-Indians who followed herds of big game through this corridor were human beings of fully modern aspect, *Homo sapiens sapiens* in the jargon of the taxonomist.

The exact time of the first Paleo-Indians' arrival in the New World is unknown, but Ice Age conditions presented two periods when such travel would have been possible. A land bridge existed between 50,000 and 40,000 years ago, then submerged for some 12,000 years, only to reemerge about 28,000 years ago. This bridge remained above water until the retreat of the final continental glaciers and the emergence of the Holocene, some 10,000 years before the present. For much of the history of the land bridge, however, the area was unapproachable because of the existence of a thick ice sheet that extended from the polar region to as far south as Long Island in North America. Only near the ends of these cold periods, when the continental glaciers were in retreat, did ice-free north-south corridors exist.

Humans could have arrived in the Americas, then, either about 40,000 or 12,000 years ago, or during both intervals.[3]

Descendants of these early arrivals did not reach Florida until perhaps 15,000 B.C., and what they found was far from inviting.[4] Ice Age Florida was a much larger and more arid place than it is today. Before about 11,500 B.C., especially, peninsular Florida offered conditions only marginally suited to human habitation. As indicated earlier, the arid peninsula was swept by more or less continuous high winds, and the plant assemblage reflected this situation. Pollen profiles from Lake Annie, located about twenty miles west of present-day Okeechobee City, have been obtained for the period between 37,000 and 13,000 years before the present. During this period, south Florida was characterized by shifting dunes whose vegetation was dominated by rosemary scrub. Scattered stands of oak distributed among prairie-like grasses completed the plant assemblage, and the surface water consisted of sinkholes, springs, and spring-fed rivers.[5]

As the continental ice sheet receded, the winds abated, and the sand became stationary. The new environmental conditions allowed dune vegetation to be replaced by greater accumulations of stunted oaks and grasses, with a few pines interspersed among this scrub. The land remained arid, but the less-windy conditions allowed different floral zones to appear. Around sources of water—sinkholes and springs—more mesic conditions prevailed, and these areas became oases on an arid plain. (In the parlance of those who describe landscapes, *xeric, mesic,* and *hydric* are used to describe floral communities in a progression from driest to wettest.) These environmental havens provided Paleo-Indians with locations favorable to settlement, and they especially favored areas where adjacent hills offered a panorama of the water.[6]

The large animals that inhabited the latter Pleistocene and early Holocene Florida offered Paleo-Indians a high-quality food source, and these bands undoubtedly depended on them for a significant portion of their subsistence. Although modern authorities have modified the notion of Paleo-Indians as solely dependent on big game, no one doubts that these attractive sources of food played an important part in these peoples' diet. Indeed, Florida's Paleo-Indians occupied the highlands overlooking scarce water supplies because they knew that their prey must come to these precious pools.

The Paleo-Indian living site at Harney Flats, near Tampa, offered its inhabitants the advantage of access to three distinct ecological zones: the Gulf Coastal lowlands, the Polk Uplands, and the Zephyrhills Gap. Because of the lower sea level, all of these areas lay at greater elevations above mean sea level than at present, and the consequent increased drainage probably made the Polk Uplands unattractive to full-time human settlement. But the Zephyrhills Gap, which contains the modern Hillsborough River valley, provided the water that made this site attractive. Although it is doubtful that a river existed in this valley, the lower elevations within the gap undoubtedly allowed a series of pools to form, and they, in turn, supported a more mesic flora than found in surrounding areas.[7] Although not as wet as the modern Hillsborough River valley, the ancient Zephyrhills Gap offered the sort of environment Florida's Paleo-Indians preferred. Most critically, it was near a reliable source of water. The Harney Flats location allowed its inhabitants either to send hunting parties into the drier inland savanna or to await the arrival of animals in search of water, as the season dictated. Additionally, the area's close proximity to the lower Gulf Coastal Plain allowed its Paleo inhabitants a hedge in the case of prolonged drought, when plant foods may not have been readily available in the Gap.

The Paleo-Indians who lived at this site probably followed life ways similar to those exhibited by modern band-level societies. This implies an egalitarian society, in which authority rested on the desirable personal characteristics each individual demonstrated, and a division of labor based on gender and age. The most skilled hunters exercised the authority required to insure success in the group hunts that the pursuit of wild game required, but that authority evaporated in other situations. These bands undoubtedly had exclusive territories, but they exhibited a good deal of mobility within these home ranges, as the resource base changed with the seasons. Simply stated, Paleo-Indian society consisted of small, unranked kinship groups who lived in an exclusive home range, through which they made cyclic migrations in search of subsistence.

Paleo-Indian reliance on big game, although still considered important, has been modified to include the importance of plant foods and smaller game animals to their diets. Especially in eastern North America, the model of Paleo-Indians as groups of hunters who migrated along with herds of big game has been discarded in favor of a more sedentary model. It now seems apparent that these eastern Paleo-Indians established home bases from which they hunted big game during at least part of the year, then split up into smaller groups during the remainder of the year to pursue plant resources and smaller game. Growing environmental expertise made such a strategy feasible, and the arrival of wetter conditions in south Florida between eight and nine thousand years ago insured its success.[8] These wetter conditions allowed Paleo-Indians to forage farther afield and contributed to a population explosion of sorts.

At about the same time as the wetter climate fully emerged, by 6500 B.C., the Pleistocene megefauna became extinct in south Florida. One must be careful, however, in assigning a cause-and-effect relation between the increased human population and the decline of the large Ice Age mammals. Although human predation undoubtedly played a role in the extinction of Florida's saber cats, mammoths, sloths, and spectacled bears, climatological change cannot be ignored. Although the onset of wetter conditions seemingly boded well for Florida's Pleistocene fauna, the assumption that the emergence of a wetter climate represented an improvement may represent little more than climatological anthropomorphizing. Any number of conditions unfavorable to the survival of desert-adapted animals could arise with the change to a wetter climate. Climatological change has long been associated with other mass extinctions (dinosaurs are the best known example), and the correlation between the disappearance of Florida's megefauna and the arrival of wetter conditions must be more than coincidental.

Similarly, the extinction of these large prey animals had an effect on Paleo-Indian populations, but that effect, too, is more convoluted than can be depicted in neat tables. The demise of the Paleo tradition and the rise of the Archaic does not appear in the archaeological record as some sharp demarcation between two radically different ways of living; rather, the earlier way of living blends into the new tradition. The extinction of the largest game animals did, however, force Paleo-Indians to exercise their powers of cultural creativity to develop social patterns that allowed them to survive in the new environmental setting. If these new adaptations did not leave a dramatic demarcation in the archaeological record, certainly by the end of the Archaic period, Florida's native Americans lived in ways far different from their Paleo ancestors.

The Archaic tradition represents the North-American version of a way of life practiced by people throughout the world. Usually referred to as hunting and gathering, this mode of living has proved highly resilient, lasting into modern times. It is based on hunting small game, collecting wild plants, and catching fish, and the lack of specialization represents the core strength of this tradition. Unlike earlier Paleo-Indians, who relied more or less heavily on big-game hunting, Florida's Archaic Indians were nonspecialists whose cultural hallmark was versatility. In Florida, changing environmental conditions placed a premium on such a pragmatic strategy, as the climate once again became more arid.[9]

The wetter conditions that corresponded with the demise of the Paleo way of life eased the transition to the Archaic, but such favorable environmental conditions did not last. Even though sea level continued to rise, peninsular Florida experienced a prolonged period of drought, beginning during the early Archaic period and lasting throughout the middle. To compound the difficulty, rising sea level was reducing the amount of land surface available from which these people could gain subsistence at the same time that reduced rainfall made the land less productive. This long dry period lasted from about 6000 to 3000 B.C.and severely taxed the adaptive abilities of Florida's indigenous people. The harsh living conditions caused these people not only to exploit more thoroughly traditional food sources, but also to explore new sources of subsistence. An oak mortar, dated at 7000 B.C., was discovered at Little Salt Springs, and it may indicate that a traditional food, perhaps acorns, had gained a new significance in these straitened circumstances. Woven baskets, crucial to the collection of large quantities of plants, further underscore the increased importance of plant foods to these people. Similarly, the nonreturning oak boomerang and bolo helped them to fully exploit small game animals and white-tailed deer. Additionally, freshwater snails and shellfish were widely used for the first time, and oysters may have made their appearance as an important element in the diet of coastal people.[10]

The vast expansion of the Archaic tool kit reflects the diverse subsistence activities of Archaic groups. In addition to stone projectile points, these people fashioned drills, scrapers, knives, and choppers from stone, as well as atlatl hooks and plummets from antler, and awls, fleshers, and pins from bone. Additionally, the poorer overall quality of the workmanship exhibited by Archaic tools indicates a people whose diverse subsistence strategy made them less inclined to lavish careful attention on the creation of their implements.[11]

During this dry period, population declined, as many inhabitants of the peninsula doubtlessly withdrew to the north in search of more favorable environmental conditions. The remaining small population of south Florida, like their Paleo ancestors, chose living sites near water. Again, like their Paleo ancestors, they lived in small, unranked family groups most of the year. These groups surely came together during certain seasons, when the nature of the available food supply allowed it, to form temporary, larger social groups. The distinctions that did exist among individuals centered around age and sex rather than position within any social hierarchy. But this simple social organization apparently worked well. Skeletons of Archaic Floridians indicate that, although some evidence for dietary deficiency exists (especially a lack of iron), these people were at least adequately nourished, and evidence from the Republic Groves site indicates that their height ranged from 5 feet 2 inches to 5 feet 8 inches.[12]

Skulls from the same site, however, provided evidence of widespread occurrence of childhood anemia, probably the result of hookworm infection. Indeed, the evidence of parasitic infections is ubiquitous among the skeletal remains of the Indians who lived in south Florida's wetlands environment. Additionally, there is evidence that these Indians suffered from syphilis, periodontal disease, and arthritis—especially of the elbows, the result of continually paddling canoes. Although none of these ailments took the toll of the epidemic diseases that Europeans introduced, the continual exposure to intestinal parasites sapped vitality. Of sixty-four skeletons examined at Fort Center, on the shore of Lake Okeechobee, ten died between the ages of 18 and 20, forty-four between 21 and 35, and only ten between the ages of 36 and 55. Although no signs of malnutrition were discovered among these remains, their short life spans indicate that these Indians did not live in an ideal environment.[13]

By the late Archaic, however, everything changed in south Florida, and, in the words of one anthropologist, there was a "cultural explosion."[14] Beginning about 3000 B.C., wetter conditions, coupled with the rise of sea level to approximately its modern location, resulted in the emergence of the modern plant assemblage in south Florida, although plant distribution did not assume its modern aspect until about 700 B.C.. The higher position of the water table allowed sedges and aquatic plants to begin the slow accumulation of muck soils in the Everglades basin, and the drainage from this wetter interior provided coastal regions with the nutrient-rich, freshwater runoff that highly productive estuaries require to flourish. These new environmental niches, both interior wetlands and highly productive coastal waters, provided Florida's Indians with living sites that were far more productive than anything previously available in south Florida, and these more productive environmental conditions provided the basis for the emergence of Florida's local adaptation, the Glades tradition.[15]

The most satisfactory taxonomy divides the Glades tradition into three geographic areas: the Glades region, the Caloosahatchee region, and the Okeechobee region[16] (see fig. 2.1). But the people of all these regions knew one another intimately, and their cultures shared many characteristics. In-

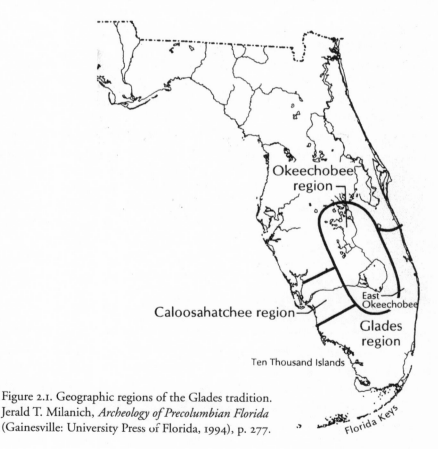

Figure 2.1. Geographic regions of the Glades tradition. Jerald T. Milanich, *Archeology of Precolumbian Florida* (Gainesville: University Press of Florida, 1994), p. 277.

deed, their commonalities enable them all to be grouped within the same cultural tradition.[17] As members of the same cultural tradition (the Glades) all of the people of the various temporal and geographic subdivisions had one thing in common—namely, their ability to adapt culturally to the emerging environmental conditions of south Florida. As the dominant group among south Florida's Indians, the Calusa provide the most graphic illustration of the way of life known as the Glades tradition, and their life ways bear a closer examination.

The Calusa

Recorded history begins in south Florida with the early-sixteenth-century arrival of Spanish explorers. The native inhabitants vigorously repelled these aggressors, but the military prowess of the native people alone did not account for the failure of Spanish attempts to subjugate south Florida. Rather, the area's watery environment discouraged the invaders from launching a concerted effort at conquest. For the Spanish, south Florida offered neither the promise of agricultural productivity nor any potential for commercial development. After initial attempts to subdue the region's indigenous people proved difficult, the Spanish largely ignored this unpromising land.

During the era of European contact, the Indians occupied the same areas that were later settled by Americans; that is, they lived along the southern shore of Lake Okeechobee, on the Miami rocklands, in the Keys, and along the coastal region of the southwest peninsula. Although these groups made seasonal forays into the Everglades proper, the wetlands did not provide an environment that favored permanent human habitation, except on the smallest scale.

The most numerous and powerful of the Indian societies that the Spanish encountered in south Florida were the Calusa (see fig. 2.2). Like the other Indians of the region, the tribe's people did not engage in agriculture; rather, they garnered their subsistence from the abundant freshwater and saltwater resources that flourished in the waters of the southern peninsula. Of all the peninsula's regions, however, the Charlotte Harbor and Pine Island Sound estuary system was the most productive. The estuary received the runoff from three major rivers, the Peace, the Caloosahatchee, and the Mayakka, and these streams created fertile conditions that contrasted sharply with the poorer environment that the drainage from the nutrient-poor Everglades supported. The richer environment, in turn, allowed the southwest Florida coast to support greater concentrations of inhabitants than could any other area of the southern peninsula.

Although Spaniards regarded south Florida as little better than waste-land, to its Indians the region offered a group of highly productive environmental zones in close proximity to one another. But the variability of the south Florida environment also presented challenges. The natural cycles of dry and wet years, episodic storms, and fluctuating game populations created both predictable and capricious times of want and plenty. Although highly productive, the prehistoric environment of south Florida was not an idyllic Eden, and the Indians developed a political organization that helped them cope with the region's variability.

Several Indian groups occupied peninsular Florida at the time of contact (see fig. 2.3), but the Calusa dominated the southern end of the state. Hernando Fontaneda, who was shipwrecked in the Keys in 1549 and lived among Florida's Indians for seventeen years, estimated that the Calusa ruled "fifty towns" stretching from the shores of "Lake Mayaimi" (Lake Okeechobee) in the north to the "Martires" (the Keys) in the south. In addition to these towns were groups that, although nominally independent, paid tribute to the Calusa chief (*cacique,* to the Spanish). The Ais and the Jega, who lived along the southern peninsula's eastern coast, were two subordinated tribes. Fontaneda recounted that although these Indians recovered more than a million dollars in "bars of silver, in gold, and in articles of jewelry" from the wrecks of Spanish ships, they were not allowed to keep their booty because the Calusa cacique "took what pleased him, or the best part."[18] Modern anthropological discoveries bear out Fontaneda's testimony. Although the vast majority of Spanish shipwrecks occurred in the vicinity of the Keys or along Florida's Atlantic coast, nearly all the gold and silver artifacts excavated in south Florida come from either the southwest coast or around Lake Okeechobee.[19]

Calusa dominance rested on demographics—that is, they were able to hold sway over the other Indian groups in south Florida because their greater numbers allowed them to muster more military might than could their less-numerous neighbors. When Pedro Menendez de Aviles landed at the Calusa capital in 1566, he was feted by a party of more than four thousand, and modern archaeologists believe that ten thousand Indians lived

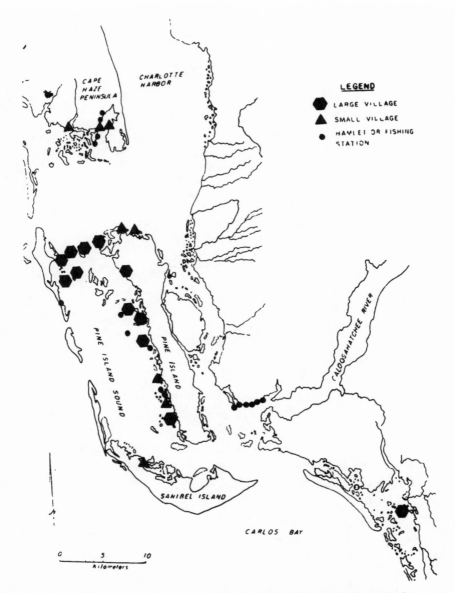

Figure 2.2. Occupation sites in the Pine Island Sound and Charlotte Harbor area. Source: Randolph J. Widmer, *The Evolution of the Calusa: A Nonagricultural Chiefdom on the Southwest Florida Coast* (Tuscaloosa: University of Alabama Press, 1988), fig. 32, p. 258. Reprinted with permission.

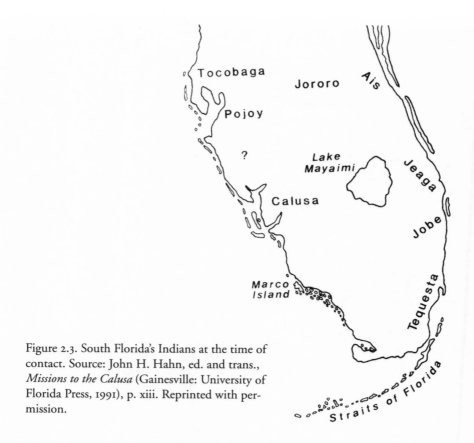

Figure 2.3. South Florida's Indians at the time of contact. Source: John H. Hahn, ed. and trans., *Missions to the Calusa* (Gainesville: University of Florida Press, 1991), p. xiii. Reprinted with permission.

along Florida's southwest coast in early historic times.[20] In contrast, contact-era observations estimated the population along Lake Okeechobee's southern shore at about fifteen hundred, with slightly fewer Indians inhabiting the Dade County rocklands and the Keys.[21]

The Calusa, however, did not have military conquest in mind when they formed their tribal society; rather, they were concerned with the scarcity of foodstuffs engendered by their increasing numbers. The primary function of the precontact Calusa state was the redistribution of scarce commodities within a highly diverse environmental setting.[22] This redistribution became especially important after the growing Calusa population occupied all of the southwest coast's suitable living sites by about A.D. 800. When the anthropologist Frank Cushing visited the area in 1896, he found dramatic evidence of the density of Calusa settlements. In the Charlotte Harbor and

Pine Island Sound estuary alone, Cushing saw seventy-five living sites, of which he described forty as "gigantic," and he estimated that in the Ten Thousand Islands at least one key in five showed signs of human habitation. Additionally, "equally gigantic works" were reputed to lie up the course of the Caloosahatchee River as far as "Lake Okeechobee and the Everglades."[23]

As indicated in the archaeological record, the Calusa heartland was not uniformly productive. Productivity varied at different locations within the region, and also changed at the same location over time. The Charlotte Harbor and Pine Island Sound estuary system contained a number of diverse components, including the mouths of three major rivers, inshore lagoons, salt marshes, mangrove forests, and barrier islands. Each of these components offered a different variety of marine fauna, and fluctuations in sea level insured that any particular site was not always home to the same environmental niche.[24]

Archaeological finds at two sites within the Calusa's estuary system illustrate the link between site location and subsistence. Cash Mound and Buck Key occupy different environmental niches—the first is on a small bay, while the latter is located on Pine Island Sound (see fig. 2.4). Because of environmental differences, the inhabitants of Cash Mound gathered marine fauna that consisted of 58 percent marine bivalves (especially oysters), while the larder of Buck Key residents consisted of 70 percent bony fish. Such differences would not be crucial if bivalves and bony fish were equally available throughout the year, but such is not the case. Oysters can be safely eaten only seasonally—modern Americans have seemingly forgotten the folk wisdom that advised eating them only in months with an *r*—and they are also adversely affected by the increased freshwater runoff that follows Florida's frequent heavy rains. Similarly, most of the species of bony fish upon which these Indians depended for sustenance leave the estuary for the open Gulf during some stage in their life cycles.[25]

The redistribution of estuarine animal resources was especially important to the Calusa because the group apparently placed only slight reliance on plant foods. Florida's southwest coast contained very little arable land, and, with the possible exception of gourds, which the Calusa used for net floats, the tribe did not raise any domestic plants. The Calusa did, however, gather locally available wild plant foods, especially fruits, and they probably made seasonal forays into the interior to take advantage of other opportu-

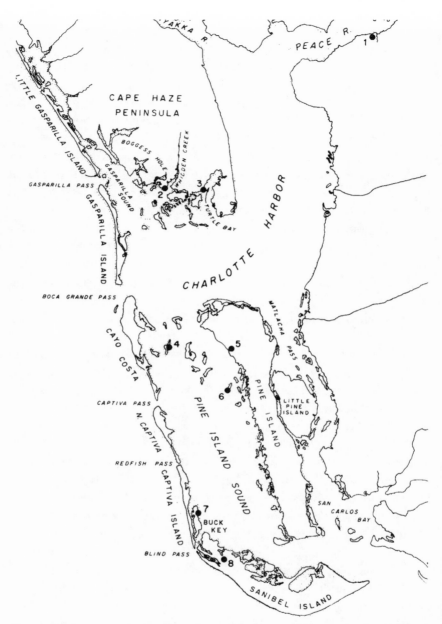

Figure 2.4. Location of Cash Mound *(3)* and Buck Key *(7)*. Source: Karen Jo Walker, "The Zooarcheology of Charlotte Harbor's Prehistoric Maritime Adaption: Spatial and Temporal Perspectives," in *Culture and Environment in the Domain of the Calusa*, William H. Marquardt and Claudine Payne, eds. (Gainesville, Fla.: Institute of Archeological and Paleoenvironmental Studies, 1992), p. 327. Reprinted with permission.

nities, especially during the wet season, when deer become concentrated on the limited areas of high land. Archaeobotanical samples indicate that the Calusa consumed the fruits of a wide variety of plants, including coco-plum, sea grape, prickly pear, cabbage palm, saw palmetto, and others.[26]

It is likely that the Calusa augmented their meager vegetable larder through trade and tribute. Fontaneda recounted that the Indians who lived in the vicinity of Lake Okeechobee placed heavy reliance on root plants, from which they produced a flour that was the main ingredient in a tasty bread. Subjects of the Calusa, the lake Indians included the flour among the items that they sent in tribute to their coastal overlords.[27] But trade also played a role in this relation, and another source from the early historic period recounted that a group of Indians who occupied an island in Lake Okeechobee profited greatly from the exchange in "a flour for bread," and further maintained that "there is no better bread to eat anywhere."[28] Because neither flour nor roots would likely leave a mark in the archaeological record,[29] only circumstantial evidence for this trade exists. Both mortars and pestles, for instance, are common artifacts on Florida's southwest coast.[30] Additionally, the occurrence of such marine products as shells and sharks' teeth along the shore of Lake Okeechobee indicates that the Calusa sent trade goods up the Caloosahatchee River to the interior in exchange for something, and flour or roots would certainly have been desirable to the coastal Indians.

The heavy dependence of the lake district's Indians on root crops makes casual gathering of these tubers highly unlikely. It seems far more probable that these people engaged in what can be viewed as a form of agriculture without full domestication. That is, these Indians employed fire, which encourages the growth of plants that store significant amounts of energy underground, to insure the proliferation of their preferred tubers and then took the simple precaution of lopping the end from each root they un-earthed so that they could rebury it in the already existing hole. In this way, the lake Indians created fields where wild crops could be dependably har-vested, without fully domesticating those plants. That is, unlike maize, which had been altered by human manipulation, the root crops of south Florida remained wild plants, but they were artificially concentrated by human agency.

The seasonality of the resource base was of central concern among the Calusa. The wild fruits that added variety to the Calusa diet each had their time during the course of the year. Seasonal rainfall, concentrated in the summer months in south Florida, often made staple root crops unavailable, and shellfish less than desirable. Similarly, the life cycle of the marine bony fishes dictated that these mainstays of the Calusa diet regularly left coastal waters. Father Juan Rogel, who proselytized among the Calusa in the sixteenth century, provided evidence for this seasonality when he noted that the Lenten season was "the time when the Indians suffer much from hunger," so much so that "other trade goods" did not suffice to bring them to his catechism lessons.[31]

The Calusa conducted a fall fertility ritual that further illustrated their concern with seasonal variations in their subsistence base. Mullet, an important food fish among the Calusa, leave the estuary for their breeding grounds in the open Gulf during autumn. Whether or not these Indians knew the reason for the migration, such an exodus concerned the tribe, and they conducted a ceremony aimed at insuring the return of this important food source. This rite required the beheading of a human victim and the presentation of the severed head to an "idol," which was "required to eat every year the eyes of a man."[32]

As brutal as the practice seems, the Calusa notion of the soul adds further significance to this rite. These Indians believed that a man had three souls, one in "the little pupil of the eye," another in "the shadow that each one casts," and the third in "the image of oneself that each one sees in a mirror or in a calm pool of water." According to Father Rogel, the Calusa believed that when a person died, two of the souls left the body, while the one in the eye remained with the corpse "always." This soul was consulted by the living for advice and counsel, while the other souls entered the body of "some fish or animal," and "when they kill such an animal, it enters into a lesser one so that little by little it reaches the point of being reduced into nothing."[33] In order to insure fertility, then, the Calusa found it necessary to sacrifice the soul that stayed with a body always, but they selected captives, either Spanish or Indian, for this dubious honor.

It is of little surprise, then, that control of seasonal fertility was the basis of the ruling lineage's authority. When confronted with the Christian dogma of the Trinity, the Calusa head cacique Don Felipe replied that "this was one of the secrets that he and his forebears, the kings, held guarded in their breasts and that they did not communicate it to anyone except to their successors."[34] But the Calusa trinity was ranked; the least important god helped in war, while the middling god directed government, and the most important god had dominion over the "most universal and common things," such as "the heavenly movements and the seasons."[35] The Calusa head cacique and other important members of the ruling elite consulted this god in secret rituals "one or two times each year" and performed "certain magic deeds" designed to insure that "the earth brought forth her fruit." Access to this god's ear gave legitimacy to the ruling family's power, and these consultations were the most closely guarded secret of Calusa society. So secret were these proceedings that "if anyone went to see what was done in that place the king had them quickly killed."[36]

In spite of seasonal fluctuations, the environment of the Calusa heartland was extremely productive, and the artifacts recovered at Marco Island (or Key Marco) provide ample evidence that this society flourished. Excavated by Frank Cushing in 1896, Marco Island yielded the most complete assembly of Calusa artifacts ever recovered. Because of the preservation qualities of muck soil, articles such as cordage and wood, which would otherwise have been destroyed, survived, and Cushing's finds amply document both the sacred and mundane aspects of Calusa life.[37]

The Marco Island site, which was continuously occupied from A.D. 750 until contact in the early sixteenth century, was built in the characteristic Calusa style.[38] Wells Sawyer, the artist and photographer who accompanied Frank Cushing to Florida, described the occupied keys of the southwest Florida coast as "shell hammock land" that had been "built up largely or entirely by the shell deposits of the key dwellers." On these hammocks the Indians constructed a "vast network of ridges and lagoons and mounds." In addition to these structures, conch-shell seawalls were constructed to protect vulnerable areas from the surf, and the Indians built jetties so that their settlements would have protected harbors.[39]

At Marco Island, canals led from the protected lagoon to the interior of the key, providing water access to the living sites, where houses were constructed on shell elevations. Cushing's excavations unearthed abundant building materials, and these artifacts provided a comprehensive view of Calusa housing. Descriptions such as "numerous long poles" and "palmetto and marsh grass thatch in considerable mass" indicate housing that was suitable to the climate, if insubstantial by modern standards.[40] But other evidence suggests that the Calusa homes were built with considerable care. Walls were made from "wattled cane matting" and "interlaced or latticed saplings" that "seemed to have been plastered with a clay and ash cement," and the same cement was used to build hearths.[41] Such housing obviously required the investment of considerable effort, and the Calusa willingness to expend so much labor on their homes reflected the sedentary nature of their lives.

Although not the home of the Calusa head cacique—most modern authorities believe that he resided just south of modern Fort Myers on Mound Key in Estero Bay—Marco Island was an important town that not only had a large population of fishermen but also served as a ceremonial center. In addition, Marco Island undoubtedly was the home of a local cacique, whose allegiance was bound to the ruling elite through the exchange of sisters in marriage. This minor chief exercised considerable local power but was required to send tribute to Mound Key, in the form of "food and roots, and skins of deer, and other articles,"[42] as a way of acknowledging the superiority of the Calusa head cacique.

Because of its importance, the artistic artifacts at Marco Island probably displayed a more consistently high level of workmanship than those produced at less-prominent settlements; by the same token, one would expect more grand art from Mound Key. Similarly, year-round occupation probably meant that its residents maintained a larger variety of workaday objects than would members of the peninsula's more transitory groups, such as the Tequesta or Keys Indians, but in spite of these differences, the general design and materials employed at Marco Island represent the typical pattern of material culture for all the southern peninsula's Indians.

The most common materials used at Marco Island were wood, shell, and palm fiber, while bone, antler, pottery, and stone were used to a lesser extent. The Calusa used a wide variety of local wood, especially pine, cypress, and mangrove, and these materials were used to create both artistic and mundane objects. A wide range of shells were used as well, including conch, whelk, scallop, oyster, and Venus clam, among others. Shells, too, had diverse applications, but their most widespread uses were as dippers, bowls, spoons, cutting edges, digging tools, and pendants. Perhaps no single material object had more importance to the residents of Marco Island than did palm fiber, which was used to make cordage for nets, the larger ropes needed by a maritime people, and the mats and thatch used in the Calusas' housing.

Although the Calusa fished with hooks and killed marine animals with harpoons—whales, sharks, manatees, and Caribbean monk seals (now extinct) were among the large marine animals taken in Florida—they were primarily net fishermen. Cushing's excavations revealed numerous nets "of different dimensions," and these nets "were both large and small mesh."[43] Indeed, the most common wooden artifacts recovered at Marco Island, consisting of some 217 whole and 405 fragmentary specimens, were float pegs, and some were still attached to palm-fiber netting. These pegs were tied at short intervals across the top of gill nets so that they floated. In order to enable proper deployment, pierced shell sinkers were attached to the nets' bottoms, and these shells, too, were found in great numbers by Cushing. Like the float pegs, some of these shells were still attached to cordage. Finally, gourds, which served as marker buoys at each end of a deployed net, were recovered, and, like the float pegs and shell sinkers, some of these gourds still had palm-fiber lines attached.[44]

When compared with Indian sites from other areas of North America, the Marco Island site was remarkable for its paucity of stone artifacts and pottery. There are two reasons for these scarcities. First, Florida's southwest coast contained neither abundant supplies of cherts, used to make cutting tools and projectile points, nor of the clays suitable to the manufacture of pottery. Second, the easy availability of materials that readily substituted for these substances made importation unnecessary. The Calusa used abundant, easily worked woods to create the bowls, trays, cups, and other utensils that more northerly Indians made from clay, and they used shells, sharks' teeth, stingray spines, and barracuda jaws as substitutes for stone cutting edges.[45] Significantly, all of the pottery shards that Cushing found had been part of cooking vessels, and many of the stones that were unearthed had been anchors, both uses for which more common local materials made poor substitutes.[46]

The technology of day-to-day living discovered by Frank Cushing at Marco Island was, in all probability, shared by all the Indian groups of south Florida, but the town's artistic creations probably reflected the importance of this settlement. The most sophisticated of these artifacts were certainly not created by fishermen in their spare time; rather, there must have been some full-time artist who lived at Marco Island (see fig. 2.5). Indeed, Sawyer remarked that the levels of skill demonstrated in Calusa art objects were "the superiors in some ways of the ancient Egyptians," especially with regard to their wood carving.[47]

Figure 2.5. Kneeling cat figurine. Source: Barbara A. Purdy, *The Art and Archeology of Florida's Wetlands* (Boca Raton, Fla.: CRC Press, 1991), p.44. Reprinted with permission.

The art of Marco Island falls into three broad categories. First are normally utilitarian utensils that craftsmen's skills have transformed from mundane implements into art objects. Second, Marco Island yielded a fine sampling of Calusa religious art. These objects include the strikingly realistic animal paintings and three-dimensional carvings of animal figureheads, as well as the stylized masks and plaques that the Calusa used in their religious processions and ceremonies. Finally, there are art objects that were created for personal adornment. Many of these items, too, carry religious significance, and, like the more overtly sacred art, reflect the Calusa concern for the soul.

Many of the articles of daily life were so carefully formed or expertly adorned (or both) that they must be regarded as works of art. Artists found the full range of raw materials suitable for such treatment, and they used their talents on wood, shell, bone, and antler. Many wooden trays, bowls, and other vessels demonstrated expert craftsmanship. In addition, such diverse objects as toy canoes, adze handles, and atlatls showed highly developed talent. Similarly, many shell vessels are so carefully formed that, in spite of their functionality, they exhibit considerable artistic skill. The care lavished on such objects as bone pins and bone or antler knife handles exhibits a highly developed aesthetic bent, and the abundance of such artifacts indicates a people whose environment allowed sufficient leisure time to pursue that sensibility.

Sources from the early historic period describe the Calusa as engaging in religious processions that featured "very ugly masks" and "idols," and the Marco Island finds confirm the authenticity of these accounts.[48] Many of the fifteen masks Cushing recovered featured stylized face painting, and some had eyes of inlaid shell. Numerous plaques and tablets were recovered as well, some painted, some carved,[49] and these items may have appeared to be idols to Spanish observers. Although the relics were surprisingly well preserved, many were no more than "pulpy masses," and they could not be removed from the muck. Of the masks that were removed, too many "crumbled to dust or warped out of all resemblance to their original lines" as they dried.[50] It was only through the foresight of Frank Cushing, who thought to hire Sawyer as photographer and artist, that any record of these remarkable artifacts survived.

Cushing found these masks in close proximity with the other genre of Calusa religious art, the realistically carved and painted animal figureheads. Because these artifacts were found together, Cushing examined them for commonalities, and he believed that the painted designs on the masks were actually stylized representations of the lifelike animal carvings. Although the relation between the masks and figureheads is hard to visualize—even Cushing acknowledged that Sawyer's illustrations could not do the relationship justice (see fig. 2.6)—his interpretation fits well with observations from the early historic period. As mentioned previously, the Calusa believed that two of their souls entered animals when they died, and the masks and figureheads that Cushing recovered surely played a role in the ceremonial representation of this relationship.

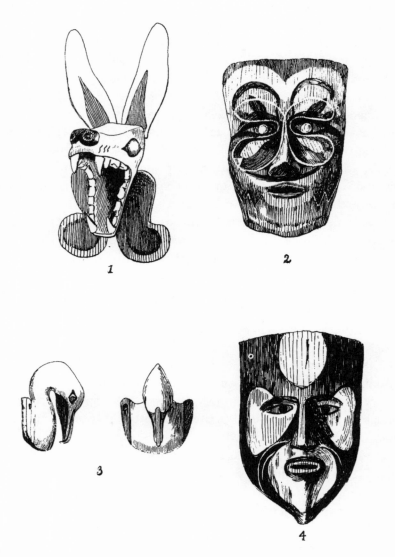

Figure 2.6. *1*, Wolf figurehead; *2*, wolf mask; *3*, pelican figurehead; *4*, pelican mask. Source: Frank Hamilton Cushing, "A Preliminary Report on the Exploration of Ancient Key-Dweller Remains on the Gulf Coast of Florida," *Proceedings of the American Philosophical Society 35* (6 November 1896), p. 96.

These Indians also valued objects of personal adornment, and the artifacts recovered at Marco Island provide a good sampling of their jewelry preferences. Wooden ear spools were common forms of jewelry, and the many with shell inlays so resembled the human eye (Cushing and Sawyer both reached this conclusion separately) that they must have been associated with the soul that lives forever.[51] Numerous other forms of jewelry were also discovered, including painted shells, shell gorgets (gorgets were worn around the neck like a choker), bone gorgets, shell beads, bone beads, and pendants made from the columella of conch and whelk shells.[52] The Calusa readily incorporated gold and silver into their jewelry, once Spanish shipwrecks made these materials available, but Cushing found no such artifacts at Marco Island, indicating that this site was not occupied in the historic period. But Cushing's excavations offered tantalizing clues about the earliest encounters between the Calusa and the Spanish.

Marco Island was hurriedly abandoned. The people who lived at this site left behind beautifully crafted sacred relics, as well as working utensils in good repair, but they took all their canoes with them. A large fire occurred contemporaneously with this exodus that left behind "a mass of charred remains."[53] Among the ruins was a paddle, its blade deeply embedded in the protohistoric lagoon bottom, "while its long handle reached obliquely up nearly to the surface of the muck . . . burned off slantingly on a line that must have corresponded to the original level of the water."[54]

Does this paddle stand as silent testimony of some unrecorded Spanish slaving expedition? While provocative, there is not enough evidence to be sure that it does. What is known is that from the first recorded encounter between Spaniard and Calusa, Juan Ponce de Leon's landing in 1513, there was violence on the part of the Indians, and earlier, unrecorded slaving parties seem the likely cause of such hostilities.[55]

The Spanish

Although Pedro Menendez was not the first Spaniard to lead an expedition to Florida, he was the first to systematically explore the province. On the lookout for good harbors, Menendez sailed along the coast of virtually the entire peninsula, paying particular attention to Tampa Bay, Charlotte Harbor, Estero Bay, the Keys, and the mouth of the Miami River. Menendez had every right to expect a handsome profit if colonization proved successful, and he took careful note of the economic opportunity that Florida's natural setting offered. Although generally sanguine about the future of the colony, he regarded south Florida as "very poor land, subject to inundation."[56]

Menendez was, however, interested in south Florida for another reason; he hoped that one of its bays was the beginning of a water passage across the peninsula. Of course no such route existed, at least for Spanish vessels,[57] and the lack of such a waterway made south Florida the most forsaken area of Spanish Florida, itself a backwater within the context of the larger empire. In spite of a lack of interest, the native peoples of the region endured catastrophic losses from warfare and disease, and their populations declined until a mere handful of survivors abandoned Florida with the Spanish in 1763. After that year, south Florida lay virtually abandoned and derelict, waiting for new arrivals.

The King of Spain, Philip II, valued Florida for its strategic location along a major sea lane between his American colonies and Spain. By the 1560s, regular convoys left Spain bound for Veracruz and Panama, where the merchants exchanged their goods for the gold and silver of the New World's mines. Heavily laden with precious metals, the merchantmen then sailed for Havana, where they again formed convoys for the return trip to Spain. This strategy, although cumbersome, helped to minimize the ravages by the pirates that so disrupted Spain's colonial trade.

The return convoys were scheduled to leave Havana in the spring, when they could depend on favorable winds and currents to provide a rapid crossing of the Atlantic. The weak link in the strategy was in the first leg of the return journey. The route from Havana, through the Bahama Channel (the Florida Strait), was susceptible to unpredictable storms since delays often meant that convoys departed during the hurricane season. Additionally, uncharted reefs made the passage dangerous even in good weather. To compound the peril, the hostile Indians of the Florida coast preyed on shipwrecks, salvaging the cargoes for themselves and either killing or enslaving the survivors. Philip believed that a thriving Spanish colony in Florida would protect this vital colonial trade route and minimize losses following shipwrecks.[58]

Philip II named Menendez *Adelantado* of Florida on 20 March 1565. The *adelantado* system served as the contractual basis for Spanish expansion in the New World. Essentially a regime of conquest by private enterprise, the policy allowed an individual to exploit royal lands in exchange for a pledge to finance the ships and men such a task required. Menendez's agreement granted him extensive lands, slave licenses, and a commercial monopoly in Florida, if he could colonize the region within three years. Stated simply, Menendez had to finance the conquest and settlement of Florida himself, in exchange for the opportunity to become extremely wealthy and powerful.[59]

When Menendez arrived in Florida, the most pressing problem was a recently established French settlement, Fort Caroline, near the mouth of the St. Johns River. Menendez encountered the French fleet at the mouth of the St. Johns on 4 September 1565, and he withdrew his ships to St. Augustine, where the inlet offered a defensible position. Following their initial encounter with Menendez, French ships attempted an attack on the fledgling settlement at St. Augustine, but a storm scattered and wrecked the flotilla. After this, Menendez had little problem defeating the ill-supplied and dispirited French forces, and by 26 November Spain had complete control of Florida.[60]

After Florida was securely in Spanish hands, Menendez could turn his attention to the other aspect of his contract, the profit motive. The Spaniard knew that Florida did not offer the sort of riches discovered in Mexico and Peru, so his plan for Florida's development rested on agriculture and trade. Menendez believed that the *encomienda* system would provide the basis for agricultural prosperity.[61] Using Indian labor, Menendez envisioned that the colony's settlers could produce sugar, hides, timber, and hemp, all of which would bring a handsome profit in the world market.[62]

Menendez visited Florida's west coast for the first time in February 1566. Among the first people the *adelantado* encountered was Hernando Fontaneda, who had been shipwrecked on the Florida coast seventeen years before. Widely traveled in south Florida, Fontaneda knew more about the peninsula's interior than any other living Spaniard, and his description of that land offered little encouragement to Menendez's agricultural ambitions. According to Fontaneda, inland south Florida was "a very rocky and very marshy country," with "no product of mines," where the roots that contributed so much to the Indians' diets were not always available, "because of the lake, which rises in some seasons so high that the roots cannot be reached on account of the water."[63]

But Menendez did not allow these bad tidings to divert him from exploration. While on the west coast, he examined its two large inlets, Tampa Bay and Charlotte Harbor, and secured pledges of fealty from the head caciques of the Tocobaga and the Calusa, the tribes that lived around these bays. During the course of his month-long exploration of Florida's west coast, an intriguing thought occurred to the *adelantado*. He had seen the broad St. Johns River emptying into the Atlantic Ocean on Florida's east coast, and now he knew that another large river, the Caloosahatchee, emptied into the Gulf of Mexico on the west. If these rivers originated from a common source, a reasonable assumption given the dimensions of the Florida peninsula, there was an inland passage through the province.

Florida's midway position between Spain and New Spain provided the basis for Menendez's commercial hopes, and good harbors were a crucial element in this plan.[64] But the possibility of a water passage across the peninsula excited the Spaniard more than any discovery of safe anchorage could. Menendez knew well the dangers of the return convoy—his own son had been lost on such a voyage; moreover, he understood the potential importance of bypassing the hazardous passage. If goods could be transported back to Spain by a safer route, many ships would be saved, and the proprietor of such a route would become extremely rich. But neither Menendez nor any other Spaniard ever found such a passage.

The Spanish experience in south Florida resembled a bad horror movie, in which the climax comes in the first fifteen minutes, and the remainder of the film is little more than a long denouement. In south Florida the climax came between 1566 and 1570, when Spanish colonial authorities realized that the region contained neither a water passage across the state nor agricultural potential in its soil.[65] In contrast, the denouement lasted until 1763, during which time European diseases and imperial ambitions, especially the slave raiding carried out by English South Carolinians and their Indian allies during Queen Anne's War (1702–1713), reduced the region's Indian population to the eighty families who left Florida with the departing Spanish.[66]

The Indians were quickly forgotten, but Spanish ideas were not. Like their Spanish predecessors, Americans regarded south Florida as a wasteland, but these modern boosters believed that it was within their power to reconstruct the region. In the minds of Americans, technology could construct Menendez's phantom waterway, and engineers could create rich agricultural lands from inundated wetlands. If south Florida was unsuited to habitation, Americans saw no reason why human ingenuity could not make it so.

The Indians prospered in south Florida because they understood the environmental setting and lived within its parameters. In Spanish eyes, however, the southern peninsula was little more than a wasteland, and this view persisted in spite of the existence of numerous, obviously prosperous settlements like the one found at Marco Island. Spanish environmental expectations dictated that south Florida was unsuited to habitation, and these expectations transformed the region from an aquatic cornucopia to the backwater of a backwater. This perceptual change became physical reality after Florida's indigenous Indians disappeared, and it became the guiding principle to subsequent American thinking about south Florida.

3

The Derelict Land

The naturalist John Kunkel Small, who visited south Florida each winter from 1902 until the mid 1930s, provided the best description of the region before massive drainage altered the ecology. In his view, the best way to understand this system was to "imagine the keys on a large scale." The lower keys, the islands that stretch in a graceful arc from Florida's southeast coast to the Dry Tortugas, flourished amid a sea of salt water, while the upper keys, actually detached portions of the Miami rocklands that were referred to as Everglades Keys in Small's time, were surrounded by a sea of saw grass. Amid these northern islands and saw grass were numerous "winding river channels" that created a labyrinth of braided drainage within the Everglades Trough. On the main Miami rocklands—itself no more than the largest of the Everglades Keys—another sea, consisting of pine trees, surrounded hammock islands of tropical hardwoods. These hammocks thrived in areas where water protected them from the fires that played the significant role in maintaining the pine forest that dominated the rest of the rocklands. Finally, mangroves lined the shore of this pre-drainage peninsula, making the transition from ocean to dry land an indistinct blur rather than a sharp line.[1]

Americans encountered the wetlands of south Florida soon after the territory passed from the sovereignty of Spain to that of the United States in 1821, but the peninsula's interior was not explored until the decades following the end of the Civil War. By that time, south Florida had been virtually devoid of any meaningful human population for 150 years, and the environment of the region can best be depicted as derelict rather than pristine. That is, following the disappearance of the district's indigenous inhabitants, the environmental configuration of the region represented associations of plants and animals that knew no human management, a situation that, if not unique, was certainly unusual, even in the annals of the exploration of the New World.

These plant associations presented much more diversity than the image transmitted by the popular "river of grass" metaphor. In addition to the heterogeneous marsh system that occupied the Everglades Trough, this derelict system contained the custard apple (also pond apple) swamp of Lake Okeechobee's southern shore, the Miami rocklands, and the mangrove coast. Taken together, the Everglades Trough, the pond apple swamp, the Miami rocklands, and the mangrove coast must be considered integral parts of the greater Everglades.

The Making of a Derelict Land, 1513–1714

The dislocations of the contact era largely depopulated south Florida, and the region remained virtually devoid of people until near the end of the nineteenth century. Indeed, the interior of the peninsula was so empty that its animals did not fear man. John Fritchey, a south Florida pioneer, recalled that the earliest American plume hunters on Lake Okeechobee approached nesting birds closely enough to kill them with "a stick about three feet long,"[2] and alligators so little feared men that they often "impudently" poked their noses into occupied boats.[3] Once the home of numerous Indians, south Florida lay virtually empty for most of two centuries.

Although the Calusa repulsed the Spanish in the sixteenth century, they fared poorly with the Europeans' pathogens, and their numbers declined precipitously after contact. The Calusa death rate from exposure to European diseases was tragically awesome. Although the information on such contacts is scanty, a good example is that of the 280 Calusa who went to Cuba in 1704, of whom 200 died, before the surviving Indians returned to Florida sometime between 1716 and 1718.[4] A more important, if less dramatic, source of disease came from the continual contact between Cuban traders and the Calusa. Even during long periods of isolation, the tribe apparently traded in amber[5] and ambergris, a whale secretion used in the manufacture of perfume,[6] and at least some of these contacts must have introduced infectious diseases to Florida. By the time of a 1697 missionary effort, the Calusa population had shrunk from the estimated ten thousand of Menendez's time to a mere two thousand.[7] This demographic catastrophe contributed to the Calusas' inability to defend themselves from forces of marauding English Carolinians and their Indian allies, who invaded Florida during Queen Anne's War (1702–1713). During this conflict, thousands of Florida's aboriginal Indians were captured and sold into slavery at Charleston, South Carolina, while most of those who escaped sought refuge in the Keys or Cuba.

Although some of south Florida's aboriginal Indians survived this assault, the war severely altered the way they lived. By 1743, even the mighty Calusa had become nomads, and their home waters were fished by Spaniards. A Spanish missionary sent to Florida in that year found the remnants of three tribes—the Cayos (from the Keys), the Boca Raton (who formerly occupied the Miami Beach area), and the Calusa—living at the mouth of the Miami River in a village without huts. No longer sedentary, the Indians did not occupy this site year-round; rather, they migrated to take advantage of seasonal opportunities. The Miami River site was occupied from May until the end of September, when Spanish fishermen arrived to transport the Indians back to the vicinity of Mound Key, their erstwhile homes. Here the Indians exchanged their labor for rum, and they fished with the Spaniards until the season ended, sometime after the first of the year. On their way back to Cuba, the fishermen disembarked their employees at Cow Key, adjacent to Key West, where the Indians stayed until they returned to the Miami River area about the first of May.[8]

After Spain abandoned Florida in 1763, taking with them virtually all of the remaining indigenous Indians, the territory became a colony of Great Britain, but the British interlude in Florida proved brief. In 1783, the Treaty of Paris not only ended the American revolution, but also transferred sovereignty of Florida back to Spain. During this second period of rule, Spanish authority was never firmly established, and the loosely governed territory proved an attractive haven to Indians and escaped slaves, both of whom sought asylum from the authority of the new United States of America.

During the early decades of the nineteenth century, the American republic pursued its own version of what today is called ethnic cleansing, as Indians were removed from desirable lands in the east for resettlement across the Mississippi River. Among the Creeks, one response to this policy was escape across the international border into Spanish Florida, and the influx of Indians was especially heavy in the years following Andrew Jackson's defeat of the tribe at the battle of Horseshoe Bend in 1814. Joining the Seminoles in Florida were a number of American slaves, who either were captured by the Indians in the United States or escaped on their own to Florida. Violence frequently erupted along the Florida border in these years, as plunderers from both sides of the line preyed on the cattle and slaves of those who resided on the other.

These activities became especially ominous, at least from the American perspective, in the years immediately following the War of 1812. During that conflict, British forces had established a fort at Prospect Bluff, about fifteen miles from the mouth of the Apalachicola River, and attracted a following among local Indians and blacks. At the conclusion of hostilities, the British turned this fort, and its weapons, over to the locals, and white slaveholding Americans reacted with predictable anger. Jackson sent an American force into Spanish Florida in the spring of 1816, which destroyed the installation, and he himself led a punitive expedition into the territory in 1818. Known as the First Seminole War, this latter conflict created an international furor, but it did not prevent Spain from ceding Florida to the United States in 1821.

The United States subsequently fought two more wars with the Seminoles, the Second (1835–1842) and Third (1854–1858) Seminole Wars, until all but an estimated one hundred of the Indians were relocated to Oklahoma. Long, costly, and tragic, these conflicts forced the Seminoles who remained in Florida to abandon their traditional woodland homes for living sites in the Everglades, and accounts of war in the wetlands for the first time brought south Florida to the attention of the American public. This initial flurry of interest in the Everglades culminated when the United States Senate instructed Buckingham Smith to form an expedition to explore the region in 1848.[9]

In the wake of secession and the Civil War, interest in the Everglades waned, until the region was rediscovered by northern sportsmen following the peace.[10] But not until 1881, when Hamilton Disston purchased 4 million acres of Florida land (some of it in the Everglades) for $1 million, did the Everglades again capture the American imagination. The region became more accessible after Disston companies improved navigation on the Kissimmee River and dug a canal that connected the Caloosahatchee River with Lake Okeechobee. During the 1880s and 1890s, a number of expeditions explored south Florida, and knowledge of the region, both scientific and anecdotal, increased greatly. These accounts provide modern Americans with a description of the predrainage Everglades that should be used to gauge the effect of decades of drainage and measure the efficacy of more recent rehabilitation projects.

The Custard Apple Swamp

The predrainage environment that Americans encountered in south Florida was not pristine; rather, it was a derelict system. Rising sea level created an environment in interior peninsular Florida that attracted Indians to the area before the region became wetlands. As the sea level continued to rise, however, the wetter environment posed problems for human habitation, and the inhabitants of the region used their ingenuity to maintain their living sites. The south shore of Lake Okeechobee offers a good example of the forms these responses took, as well as the changes that occurred after more than one hundred years as abandoned land.

The impound rim around the south shore of Lake Okeechobee represented highlands within the exceedingly flat landscape of the Everglades Trough, and this area early attracted Indian habitation. As indicated by the archaeological finds at Fort Center and Belle Glade, the Indians of the lakeshore used ditches and mounds to create dry areas, and the inhabitants of other settlements on the impound rim surely used the same technologies to combat rising water. The "many towns"[11] that Fontaneda encountered when he visited the area in the sixteenth century indicated that whatever strategy the Indians of the southern shore employed—and the extreme alterations the region has been subjected to in modern times has obliterated the archaeological record—they were successful.

When Americans explored this region in the nineteenth century, the derelict southern shore of Lake Okeechobee was uninhabitable. A tangled pond apple swamp occupied the area, and eight dead-end rivers provided deep-water passages through the seasonally inundated rim (see fig. 3.1).

Figure 3.1. Along the banks of Anderson's Creek, one of the eight blind rivers flowing south from Lake Okeechobee—water hyacinth in the foreground, custard apple trees in the background. Source: John Kunkel Small Collection, Florida State Archives, Tallahassee. Reprinted with permission.

Perhaps the remains of earlier residents' attempts to channel excess water, these rivers flowed for only two or three miles before they blended with the marsh to the south. Although wading birds and alligators found this derelict setting ideal, the dense forest and underlying swampy mire made human occupation impossible, and a once-vibrant center of settlement had become a trackless wilderness.

This wilderness was remembered as an area of rare beauty. An early pioneer in the region likened the leafy twilight of the custard apple forest occupying Lake Okeechobee's southern shore to a cathedral and recalled an understory consisting of gourd vines, giant ferns, and beautiful epiphytes bedecked with orange and red blossoms. These trees also provided a congenial home for huge spiders and the garish painted bunting, as well as providing a rookery for huge numbers of aquatic birds. Moonvine covered the trees on the outer edges of this forest, and its white flowers, which opened morning and evening, contributed to the beauty. Under the canopy, the ground consisted of a tangle of roots, when it was not flooded, and the buttressed custard apple trunks contributed to the air of other-worldly charm. A scattering of pop ash, buttonwood, rubber trees, and an occasional large cypress completed the plant assemblage of this unusual scene.[12]

Botany professor John Harshberger visited the south shore of Lake Okeechobee and published his botanical observations in 1914. The scientist stayed at a hotel near the entrance of the South New River Canal and viewed the forest from its cupola. He wrote that "the custard apple forest extends east and west, as far as the eye could reach, and in a southward direction from the border of the lake, a distance of 4.8 kilometers (3 miles)." The individual trees of this forest were substantial, consisting of "a close stand of trees nine meters (30 feet) tall, forming a dense shade, so that twilight pervades the solitudes."[13]

Scientists granted the existence of such a plant assemblage, but some questioned its antiquity. Alfred P. Dachnowski-Stokes's 1930 soil survey suggested that the lack of fibrous woody peat within the Okeechobee muck indicated a comparatively recent origin for the lake's custard apple belt.[14] But Dachnowski-Stokes's assessment of the organic components of the Okeechobee muck, the name given to the two-layered soil profile found along the lake's southern and eastern rim, makes three crucial errors.

First, the soil scientists assume a fixed location for the custard apple belt, but this assumption is suspect. The extensive deposits of peaty soils that underlie much of the southern expanse of Lake Okeechobee indicate a dynamic lakeshore, whose position has fluctuated widely during the some five thousand years of peat formation. That is, as the lakeshore moved, so did the custard apple belt. Stated another way, the custard apple belt represents a biotic association rather than a particular location, and the location of that association has presumably always been along the southern shore of Lake Okeechobee.

The second error involves the nature of the custard apple tree itself. Lawrence Will, who provided the most lucid description of the custard apple forest, regarded the tree as "insubstantial." He remembered the wood as "light in weight with spongy roots as light as cork."[15] Indeed, modern fishermen often used custard apple roots to buoy their seine nets when corks became unavailable.[16] Such trees could not be expected to leave a lasting organic record, except under ideal peat-forming conditions.

Finally, Dachnowski-Stokes did not consider the influence of earlier human habitation. The prehistoric inhabitants of the lake's southern shore created a domesticated environment that doubtless little resembled the wilderness Americans encountered at the end of the nineteenth century, but a custard apple forest would surely have been part of the scene. Fishermen themselves, the area's prehistoric Indians no doubt valued custard apple wood for its buoyancy, and they surely encouraged the growth of such a valuable tree. Evidence exists for extensive forest management among the Indians of the Amazon basin, and human agency surely played a role in the creation of the custard apple forest of Lake Okeechobee's impound rim.[17] Although transient, and at times domesticated, the custard apple swamp was a biotic community as old as south Florida's wetlands.

The Everglades Trough

Soldiers who served in the Second Seminole War were the first Americans whose views of the Everglades received any widespread attention. Colonel William Harney led a raiding expedition that crossed the Everglades in December 1840, and one member of that party recalled that "no country that I have ever seen bears any resemblance to it; it seems like a vast sea filled with grass and green trees."[18] Another soldier likened the region to a "vast lake." But this was no ordinary lake because it was "almost entirely over-grown with saw grass about seven feet high" and "studded with numerous little wooded islands," such that the region "presented to the view in every direction an interminable series of beautiful glades."[19]

Although military accounts offered the earliest recollections of the Everglades, the expedition sponsored by the *New Orleans Times-Democrat* presented the most complete account of the environmental setting in the undisturbed wetlands. Interest in the Everglades ran high in Louisiana; many citizens of that state had already settled along the Caloosahatchee River, and sugar growers were particularly keen to hear about the district's prospects. In 1883, accordingly, the newspaper's party traveled from the southern extremity of Lake Okeechobee to the head of the Shark River, which empties into Whitewater Bay on Florida's extreme southwest coast. Major Archie P. Williams was the correspondent who commanded the expedition, and his subsequent newspaper articles provide the only comprehensive account of a north-south journey through the predrainage Everglades.

Williams found that the southern edge of Lake Okeechobee consisted of "grassy waters, which extend for about a hundred yards into the lake around its whole margin," while thin strips of sandy beaches and a "forest of quite large trees" formed the shoreline. Eight rivers "from a hundred to two hundred yards in width" drained the lake into a "dense swamp of custard apple," but these streams flowed for only "two or three miles through the swamp," and "as suddenly as they begin, just so suddenly do they cease to exist." After these rivers dissipated, the party was forced to chop through the remaining custard apple thicket with axes and machetes, but a few hours' work brought them to a marsh dominated by "yma grass, wampu or warmpea, mixed with scrub willow."[20] A transitional zone between custard apple swamp and grassy marsh, this region was only a few miles wide, and its southern margin marked the beginning of an impressive stand of saw grass.

Below the custard apple and transitional zones, saw grass presented such an impenetrable barrier that, even after burning a path through the sedges, Williams considered one and a half miles a good day's travel—in all, the party traveled approximately seventy miles in twenty-seven days. Such stands of saw grass occurred at other locations in the Everglades—one of the largest stands ran along the border of the Everglades Trough and the Miami rocklands—and they presented daunting challenges to travelers. Hugh Willoughby, who canoed from the head of the Harney River to the mouth of the Miami River in 1897, recalled saw grass "of about four feet" in areas where "the rock is near the surface, with little soil." In locations where the soil was deeper, like the area south of Lake Okeechobee, the sedge had "very little water around its roots" and "reaches a height of ten feet."[21]

The *Times-Democrat* party spent eight days, traveling a distance of some twelve miles, in the dense saw grass stand below Lake Okeechobee before the nature of the land changed. Here, Williams wrote, the party encountered "a little stream about ten feet wide and fifteen feet deep," which flowed into "a beautiful little basin, twenty or thirty yards wide, the water clear as crystal, fifteen feet deep, with hundreds of trout swimming in it." This basin had "a dozen little rivulets" flowing from it, but the explorers found that the one they followed, like the rivers that drained Lake Okeechobee, "ends as suddenly as it began."[22]

The explorers traveled through such country for five days, laboriously pushing and dragging their boats from one watercourse to another, before they encountered an island "about three acres in extent" covered with a growth of "wild fig and custard apples," but with an area of dry ground only about "twenty five feet square." The weary men slept on this island, and, when they awoke the next morning, found themselves on the northernmost of the Everglades islands, and "to the east, west, and south, as far as the eye can reach, we see hundreds of little islands," all separated by serpentine flows of "grassy water" and "saw-grass marsh."[23]

After the *Times-Democrat* expedition entered the Everglades islands, near the halfway point in the journey, the traveling became easier. Previously, the footing had consisted of mud that ranged from waist deep to areas where probes with a twelve-foot pole "failed to find bottom,"[24] but now the bottom was rocky and firm. Additionally, the water was generally deeper and "for the first time in many days," the men were able to propel their boats with oars. The streams in this district, however, proved as capricious as had those farther north, ending as quickly as they began, but the nature of the country had undergone another change. In this region waterways were more abundant, and the men had only to drag their boats through a few yards of saw grass to get from the end of one stream to the beginning of another. Indeed, Williams maintained that "the whole face of the country" consisted of "a perfect network of such courses."[25]

As they continued south, Williams noted that "the islands get thicker and timber on them larger," and "rocks begin to crop out above the surface of the water." Only three days from their destination, Williams noted that "all the different water courses seem to have come together" (the Shark River slough), and the saw grass had "disappeared to a great extent," leaving the party on a course that "lies between innumerable islands as far as the eye can see." Before they reached the headwaters of the Shark River, however, there remained one more obstacle, and the men were called on "to lift the boats over ledges of rock" that they encountered "every ten to fifteen yards"[26] (see fig. 3.2).

At the end of the trip, Williams advised all his readers who were interested in the agricultural possibilities of the Everglades to put such ideas aside. Williams believed that "drainage is utterly impracticable." But with regard to human health within the district, he was more sanguine. In more than a month in the district, much of it spent in arduous labor, Williams reported not "a single case of sickness" among his crew. Other explorers agreed with this assessment. Hugh Willoughby, who crossed the Everglades during the next decade, related that the Everglades was a region of "pure water," where "the air is wholesome, pure, and free from disease germs."[27]

When land developers advertised their land for sale, they picked up this theme, and their brochures touted the healthfulness of the region. The Everglades, the promoters gushed, was a region where "extreme heat, as

Figure 3.2. Limestone with scattered saw grass, southwest of Royal Palm Hammock, May 1918. This scene is typical of much of the southern Everglades. Source: John Kunkel Small Collection, Florida State Archives, Tallahassee. Reprinted with permission.

well as frost, is practically unknown," where the water is "not alone healthy but actually wholesome," and its "nature" created an environment where "malaria and its kindred ills cannot exist." Although Floridians recognized this for the boosterism that it was, especially the reference to the heat, the Everglades was never associated with a pestilent environment, and there is no evidence that concern for disease affected either the drive for drainage or the sale of land.[28]

As the *Times-Democrat* party traveled south, they encountered a general pattern of steadily deepening water. Numerous springs contributed the bulk of this water—water that was "pure and clear and drinkable,"[29] moving in a southerly direction at about a mile and a half an hour. Willoughby gave a good account of these springs, noting that he saw pools "eight or ten feet wide and five feet deep," many with holes in the center, from which water poured "with quite a little head."[30] These springs were crucial to the Everglades because they supplied the water the wetlands required during the otherwise dry winter. Without spring-fed water, sheet flow, so crucial to the entire Everglades ecosystem, would not have been so continual, even in the predrainage system.

Throughout their journey the travelers encountered a rich mosaic of dense saw grass stands, deeper water occupied by other marsh plants, and tree islands, but very few animals. The most desolate of all were areas where saw grass dominated. Indeed, Williams contrasted the shores of Lake Okeechobee, with its "10,000 alligators more or less," to the saw grass marshes, where "a deathlike oppressive stillness prevailed." Not only were the regions of dense saw grass "utterly devoid of game of any kind," but "there were no fish in the water, no birds in the air." By contrast, the vicinity of the Shark River was a vast rookery, with "thousands of birds." Here, members of the party shot among them, "killing hundreds, but they continued to return"—an omen of things to come.[31]

The Miami Rocklands

Pine forest occupied approximately 90 percent of the predrainage Miami rocklands, and hardwood hammocks and prairies, which early inhabitants referred to as the Transverse Glades, accounted for the remaining 10 percent of the surface area. This largely forested zone stretched from just north of the Miami River to slightly south of Homestead, where the rocklands turn to the west at the head of Taylor Slough. This slough provided drainage from the Everglades into Florida Bay and separated Long Pine Key and the complex of smaller Everglades Keys to its west from the main north-south rockland formation. Small estimated the size of the region as fifty-five miles long and from two to six miles wide. Although not technically correct, he judged this rockland formation to be a remnant of the ancient Antilles, but certainly the area's flora much resembled that of Cuba and the Bahamas.[32] Other early observers, too, considered the Miami rocklands to be one of the truly unique zones of Florida's vegetation, even though the dominant pine trees themselves sparked little interest among naturalists—except where they grew out of solid limestone (see fig. 3.3). John H. Davis, Jr., for instance, considered the pinelands' chief botanical feature to be "the presence of many sub-tropical and tropical shrubs and bushes."[33]

The solid rock surface that characterized much of this region presented a false impression to people unfamiliar with south Florida. The high porosity of the Biscayne limestone insured that water did not lie on the surface, except in the wettest of seasons, and lack of water, in turn, allowed the surface rock to harden. But those who were familiar with the rocklands

Figure 3.3. Pineland on the Miami rock- lands. These trees are growing in solid rock. Source: John Kunkel Small Collection, Florida State Archives, Tallahassee. Reprinted with permission.

knew that the water table was never far away, and this groundwater insured that the limestone was "soft and crumbling below the surface."[34] Indeed, the water table was close enough to the surface that the rocklands "may steam for several days" after heavy rains, and the solid rock surface represented little more than a thin veneer that covered the water beneath.[35]

The Transverse Glades, actually the remains of old channels that once drained the Everglades, were areas of marshy lowlands that cut through the Miami rocklands. Low and wet, these erstwhile sloughs contained shallow muck soils and were usually bordered by cypress trees and large pines. Banana holes, actually small sinks in the porous limestone surface rock, further pockmarked the surface of the rocklands, and these depressions usually contained more soil than the surrounding rocklands. The moisture and soil of the banana holes allowed broad-leaved trees, ferns, and other shade-loving species to gain a foothold among the rockland pines (see fig. 3.4). Early naturalists believed that these banana holes represented incipient hammocks, but the dewatering of south Florida makes their arguments moot.[36]

Recent usage has imparted a significance to the term *Dade County pine* that would puzzle those who logged that forest. In 1914 Dade County pine was not regarded as first-class lumber because its hardness caused it to crack and split easily.[37] Although lumbermen did log these trees, developers often simply piled and burned Dade County pine after clearing land (see figs. 3.5 and 3.6). Those who used the lumber did so because of its lower price, and they employed it only where its inferior qualities could not cause harm.[38]

In this region, pine trees reached a maximum height of 115 feet and could achieve a maximum circumference of 5 feet, but thin, sandy soils inhibited growth, with some trees taking 90 years to reach 12-inch diameters.[39] Roland Harper regarded rockland pines as little different from those of more northerly climes except that the Dade County pine was "a little smaller and more crooked."[40] Small believed that the density of pine trees per acre increased on the southern portion of the main rockland formation, which he called the "Biscayne pineland," but he distinguished these trees

Figure 3.4. Banana hole, with cabbage palm, Miami rocklands, November 1916. Source: John Kunkel Small Collection, Florida State Archives, Tallahassee. Reprinted with permission.

Figure 3.5. Shields Hammock in the background, with stumps of lumbered pine in the foreground, Dade County, January 1916. Source: John Kunkel Small Collection, Florida State Archives, Tallahassee. Reprinted with permission.

Figure 3.6. Dade County pine piled for burning. Source: John Kunkel Small Collection, Florida State Archives, Tallahassee. Reprinted with permission.

from those that grew on the Everglades Keys. Small viewed the Everglades Keys' trees as "decidedly stunted," achieving only "less than half" the size of their counterparts on the Biscayne rockland.[41]

Early timber records support Small's view of the pine trees on the Biscayne rockland. On 15 September 1911, James T. Hutto secured timber rights to portions of four sections of rockland just to the northwest of Miami. During the time he held the lease, he paid stumpage on nearly seventy thousand board feet of pine timber that he removed. Meanwhile, in December of the same year, D. Frank McCrimmon was granted similar rights to the timber of three sections of land farther south, just west of the small town of Perrine. Eventually, McCrimmon removed nearly 1.5 million board feet of pine timber. These numbers translate into an average of 175,000 board feet per section in the northern grant (273 board feet per acre) and some 500,000 board feet per section farther south (781 board feet per acre).[42] Neither of these figures would astound a lumberman. A 1929 Florida lumber company brochure, for example, boasted of taking an average of six thousand board feet per acre from the prime cypress and pine forests of Dixie and Taylor counties, in Florida's Big Bend district. But McCrimmon's figures do give credence to figures given by Davis, who cited one thousand board feet per acre as the maximum expected yield from rockland pine.[43]

If the rockland pines attracted little attention, the same cannot be said for the hammocks that shared the uplands with the conifers. Early naturalists delighted in the abundance of tropical species present in rockland hammocks, and they noted the progressive dominance of these species as they moved south. Early on, these botanical explorers realized the role played by water in the creation of hammocks. Pine dominated the majority of the rocklands because of its resistance to fire, but in areas surrounded by natural moats of water, other species could gain a foothold.

Rockland hammocks assumed one of two forms: appearing either as islands among the pines or as elongated strands. The elongated hammocks, which followed streams or formed on the borders of lowlands (either the Transverse Glades or the larger Everglades), were generally dominated by cypress, some of which could be quite large. In the island hammocks, tropical hardwood species flourished, and these species dominated the plant assemblage of these formations.

Figure 3.7. Ingraham Highway through Royal Palm Hammock, January 1916. Source: John Kunkel Small Collection, Florida State Archives, Tallahassee. Reprinted with permission.

Royal Palm Hammock, or Paradise Key, is probably the best known of the rockland island hammocks (see fig. 3.7). This hammock once occupied a small Everglades key situated at the headwaters of Taylor Slough (Small called it a river) between the end of the main rockland formation, the Biscayne rocklands, and Long Key, the largest of the Everglades keys. Because the Taylor Slough region offered dependable, long-term protection from exogenous fire, Royal Palm Hammock developed into one of the most spectacular island hammocks of south Florida. An early explorer remembered that the hammock had five hundred royal palms and a large colony of yellow butterflies. When seen among the "vine hung hammock," filled with "waxen magnolias, flaming vines, and brilliant orchids," these butterflies created a "maze of green and yellow."[44]

But Royal Palm Hammock did not represent a typical type. Indeed, as Small noted, the flora of each hammock on the Everglades keys exhibited "individual characteristics," and the vegetation was, to some extent, "distinctive."[45] The main rocklands featured "hundreds of hammock islands" bearing a number of broad-leaved trees. Coco-plum, swamp bay, bustic, wax myrtle, myrsine, gumbo-limbo, buttonwood, and wild tamarind were among the most common trees in these hammocks, but none of these trees attracted as much attention as did the strangler fig. This "tree" begins as an epiphyte that attaches itself to the upper branches of free-standing trees. Once firmly established, the air plant sends down thin tendrils that become roots after they make contact with the ground. At this point in the strangler fig's life, the plant resembles a vine, but, eventually, this "vine" completely surrounds its hapless host, finally killing it. Following the death of its host, the strangler fig begins its own career as a free-standing tree.[46]

The borders of the Miami rocklands—the boundaries with the Everglades Trough on the west, the mangrove fringe to the east, and along the edges of the Transverse Glades—provided congenial habitats for the alligators, crocodiles, and wading birds that also inhabited other areas of south Florida. But the rocklands also provided a home to animals that did not thrive in the lowlands. The Seminoles relied on the rocklands for not only much of their coontie, the roots of which made a tasty flour, but also its game animals, and local residents still referred to the rocklands as the "hunting grounds" in the 1860s.

In 1866, under the auspices of the Freedmen's Bureau, William H. Gleason and George F. Thompson toured the Miami rocklands as part of an inspection of south Florida.[47] Local residents reported an abundance of bear, deer, and panthers in the region, and they traded in the skins of these animals. Additionally, the local waters provided abundant supplies of fish, turtle, and sponges that found a ready market in Key West. Many nongame animals occupied the rocklands as well, including little sparrow hawks, red-shouldered hawks, kingfishers, palm warblers, red-cockaded woodpeckers, opossums, raccoons, otters, cotton-rats, shrews, and marsh-hares.

Like the rest of predrainage south Florida, the Miami rocklands abounded with springs. Small noted that the Everglades keys offered ideal camping because the "delicious cool water" of springs "is always within easy reach."[48] Springs were abundant on the main rockland formation as well, and the largest was located just below the falls (actually rapids) of the Miami River.[49] In addition to all the springs on the surface of the rocklands, Willoughby noted that "all along the shore there are places where the fresh water comes up through the rock . . . with quite a head."[50] Indeed, so many springs discharged beneath Biscayne Bay that a small pumping platform was constructed out in the bay so that boaters could draw freshwater from the bottom of that body of water without the necessity of coming ashore.[51]

The Mangrove Fringe

Mangroves prosper at the confluence of fresh and salt water, especially in areas of limited wave action. Coastal Florida, with its many lagoons and inlets, offered a haven for mangrove, and the trees dominated the shoreline of south Florida on both the Gulf of Mexico and the Atlantic Ocean. Everglades runoff, both surface and subterranean, created especially luxuriant growths of these trees on Biscayne Bay and along the lower southwest coast, stretching from Whitewater Bay north through the Ten Thousand Islands (although the northern reaches of this region owed their existence to drainage from the Big Cypress Swamp). Sandy beaches occurred only on Cape Sable, and on the ocean side of some barrier islands.[52] Elsewhere, in their undisturbed state, these trees created, "perhaps, the most wonderful growth of red mangrove in existence."[53]

The red mangrove, with its extensive prop-root system, is the most salt tolerant of the mangrove species, and this tree created shorelines that resembled a watery Mars to those accustomed to the forests of more temperate climes (see fig. 3.8). The three species of mangrove—red, black, and white—could occur in either strictly segregated zones or mixed together, "all with different shades of green" (see fig. 3.9). In many locations buttonwood *(Conocarpus)* was intermixed with mangrove, and "an entanglement of the stout woody coin-vine *(Dalbergia)* climbed to the tops of the tallest trees."[54]

The mangrove forests also supported understory growth. Numerous epiphytes, including orchids and bromeliads, lived on the mangroves themselves. Tree cacti—with their "erect, reclining, or climbing hawser-like stems and branches, and large white flowers"—were numerous as well, living mainly on rotting logs or the trunks of living trees. In the Cape Sable region, numerous lakes were scattered among the mangrove, and these bodies of water supported aquatic grasses that formed a "Brussels-carpet-like growth" that came within six inches of the surface, forming a mat so dense that it could support a walking man.[55]

Figure 3.8. A mangrove shoreline in south Florida. Source: John Kunkel Small Collection, Florida State Archives, Tallahassee. Reprinted with permission.

Figure 3.9. Grove of black mangrove at Cape Sable. Source: John Kunkel Small Collection, Florida State Archives, Tallahassee. Reprinted with permission.

The remains of ancient Indian middens were frequent among the mangroves, and these elevations provided a home for plants such as palm, live oak, sumac, and myrtle, which could not thrive in the watery world of the mangrove forest.[56] On other naturally occurring areas of high land, mahogany trees thrived. The densest concentration of these trees was at Madeira Bay—an inlet of Florida Bay, on Florida's extreme southern shore—where the "Madeira-redwood" were "exceedingly common."[57]

Mangrove shorelines were forbidding, and few explorers or naturalists even attempted to penetrate the thickets. The labyrinth of roots and trunks, coupled with the hordes of mosquitoes and flies, discouraged any but the most intrepid, and the mangrove belt's lack of commercial appeal, except to the plume hunter, discouraged those who might have otherwise braved the difficult terrain. While traveling up the Caloosahatchee River in 1883, Angelo Heilprin noted that mangroves dominated the banks of the "lower reaches" of the stream, their "dense line of aerial roots forming an impenetrable palisade for miles on the riverfront."[58]

Even plume hunters found the red mangrove daunting. One hunter described the banks of the Shark River as consisting of "mangroves on either bank growing sixty feet high," and these trees were "very thick so the wind did not get us, only a little puff now and then."[59] Coastal mangroves, like their riverine counterparts, presented obstacles to exploration. The red mangroves that grew far out into shallow Florida Bay made travel by boat difficult, and they offered such insubstantial footing that "the weight of a man's body is enough to impart a swaying motion to three or four acres of the floating forest."[60] Mangrove forests rivaled dense stands of saw grass in the obstacles they presented to human travel.

The men who explored south Florida found the mangrove forests uninviting, but to the region's fauna these thickets offered rich possibilities. Mangrove forests provided an ideal nursery for young marine animals because their tangle of roots gave some protection from predators. At the same time, however, the trees offered ideal nesting sites for the wading birds that fed on the animals living in the shallows. And these birds attracted predators, especially snakes, alligators, and an occasional crocodile, which, in their turn, fed on eggs, fledglings, and adult animals. Amid the cacophony of bird noises, the mangrove forests provided a home for a rich diversity of animal life.

In 1907 the ornithologist Frank M. Chapman visited the "Great Mangrove Swamp" on the southern tip of Florida, intent on finding Cuthbert Rookery, famed as a nesting place for a prodigious number of wading birds. Discovered some twenty years earlier by a plume hunter named Cuthbert, the rookery must have contained a truly staggering number of birds. New York buyers paid $28 per ounce for heron feathers, and one authority maintained that Cuthbert sold $1,800 worth of plumes following his discovery of the rookery. Plume hunters usually scalped dead birds, because these were the most salable feathers, and it would have taken 64.3 ounces, slightly more than 4 pounds, of heron plumes for Cuthbert to earn his money—representing a truly enormous number of birds. This site had been "shot over" many times since Cuthbert's visit, but its inaccessibility allowed its birds to make at least partial recoveries.[61]

Cuthbert Rookery lay inland among the labyrinth of channels and lakes that formed the coastline along Florida Bay. Very shallow, the bay's water was only "two or three feet deep," but "for the greater part of the way it measured less than a foot." The bottom consisted of a white marl mud, but, in the absence of storms, the water was unusually clear. Dense growths of "brown, broad-bladed turtle grass" provided footing for the men when they were forced to push their boats through shoal water. This shallow, grass-filled bay provided a home for a wide variety of wildlife. Redfish and drum lived here in large numbers, and these fish attracted the ospreys, brown pelicans, and herons that fed on them. Somewhat surprisingly, Chapman saw "two keen fins of great saw-fish or the single fin of a shark" in the knee-deep water. Most spectacular, however, was the sight of two porpoises "acting in concert, round up a school of mullet and catch them in the air as they leaped from the water"—this in water "scarce deep enough to float them."[62]

To reach the rookery, the travelers were forced to follow a tortuous path, "often so narrow that there was barely room for passage of the boats," through mangroves, "their limbs being burdened with orchids, wild pines, and other parasitic epiphytes." In the distance could be viewed "triangular stalked cactuses, giant ferns, and a small palm" not seen by the author anywhere else in Florida. The winding path took the birders through six lakes, "varying in size from a quarter of a mile to between two and three miles in length," finally ending in a seventh. Here, Cuthbert Rookery occupied an island about one and a half miles long.[63]

Like the bay, this inland area teemed with animal life. Throughout their journey, the explorers encountered "numerous fish," so plentiful that two, "a bass and a small tarpon," leaped into their boats. The number of birds at the rookery, though depleted, remained impressive, and Chapman estimated that the flock numbered thirty to forty roseate spoonbills, "a dozen or more" snowy egrets, "three or four hundred" American egrets, "at least two thousand" Louisiana herons (these birds had little commercial value), "possibly fifty" little blue herons, "several hundred" white ibises, and "a few" cormorants and water turkeys. At least some of them were nesting, and their eggs attracted fish crows and Florida crows that feasted on the bounty.[64]

The inland edge of the mangrove swamps also provided a habitat favorable to animal life. The adventurer Hugh L. Willoughby, who crossed the southern Everglades from the head of Harney River to Miami, saw "very plentiful game at the edge of the Glades." Willoughby counted numerous birds along the border of swamp and marsh, and added that there "must be thousands of otter" in the region because "their trails crossed in every direction," along with plentiful "fresh slides from the night before."[65]

The mangrove that lined the riverfronts and protected shorelines of pre-drainage south Florida occupied a sort of no-man's-land between the water and dry land. In addition to providing homes for a rich diversity of animal life, the growth of mangrove encouraged land formation. In Florida Bay, an especially large area of shallow water, such "incipient islands"—growths of red mangrove that had not yet developed any emergent soil—made the shoreline indistinct and gave early naturalists the impression that the very land itself grew.[66]

The Derelict System

Very few people lived in the south Florida that Americans encountered in the nineteenth century, and it had been largely uninhabited since the early years of the eighteenth century. Three conditions characterized the environmental setting of this derelict land. First, the south Florida of the nineteenth century was much wetter than that district is today, and much of that abundant water came from springs. Second, the interior of the peninsula, the Everglades Trough, contained very little wildlife, and this region was much wetter in the south than in the north. Finally, derelict south

Florida was an extremely heterogeneous environment. Even the Everglades Trough, the area of south Florida that most resembled a river of grass, changed dramatically from north to south.

Like their Indian predecessors, Americans molded the environment of south Florida to suit their needs, but technology allowed this most recent round of alterations to virtually destroy the region's wetlands. The modern dewatering of south Florida so altered the environment that exotic plants

Figure 3.10. Crocodile Hole, a small bay in the mangroves along Indian Creek, opposite Miami. *(Top)* before and *(bottom)* after development. Source: John Kunkel Small, *From Eden to Sahara: Florida's Tragedy* (Lancaster, Pa.: Science Press Printing Company, 1929), plates 5, 6.

Figure 3.11. Custard apple forest below Lake Okeechobee. *(Top)* before and *(bottom)* after drainage. Source: John Kunkel Small, *From Eden to Sahara: Florida's Tragedy* (Lancaster, Pa.: Science Press Printing Company, 1929), plates 13, 14.

flourish while indigenous ones perish. Driving through metropolitan Miami, one can see numerous Australian pines, Norfolk Island pines (neither of which are pines), and melaleuca growing amid lawns of St. Augustine grass, but precious few native pines, even less native grasses, and nothing of the hammocks that inhabited the area before drainage. On the south shore of Lake Okeechobee, cane fields and open-pit sod-mining operations have replaced stands of custard apple trees, willows, and saw grass. Despite its seeming similarity to the sedge saw grass, sugar cane is a grass, and, as such, is as exotic to the Everglades as Norfolk Island pine is to the Miami rocklands. Along the coast, humans have either removed or manicured mangroves so that sandy beaches may flourish. John Kunkel Small's before and after pictures of two locations in Florida, the first set near Miami and the second below Lake Okeechobee, offer startling confirmation of the extent of the environmental change the American search for the good life has caused in south Florida (see figs. 3.10 and 3.11).

The process of converting the Everglades from an exotic to a familiar landscape involved such far-reaching change that few of south Florida's modern residents have an adequate understanding of the district's predrainage condition. Unfortunately, the dominance of the "river of grass" metaphor compounds this ignorance because it provides an inaccurate description of the system. Even in the Everglades Trough, the heart of south Florida's wetlands, the predrainage environment more resembled a river obscured by grass than a river of grass. In addition, this description wrongly suggests homogeneity, little hinting at the diversity of flora and fauna that once existed. Significantly, areas that did play host to dense stands of saw grass supported very little wildlife. If meaningful restoration of the district is to occur, the state's citizens must discard this false metaphor in favor of a more accurate description of the rich and varied predrainage environment.

4

Drainage

What drainage accomplished in the Everglades was the conversion of a derelict system to a developmental one. A developmental system results when the natural world is converted into the basic infrastructure for intensive human development. Ironically, the modern American version of development is actually rooted in extensive destruction. But since that destruction does not lay waste human achievements, it is often ignored, and the close relationship between human development and the destruction of the natural world is overlooked. For Americans of an earlier time, the Everglades was nothing more than a site for development, and the legacy of their vision is the modern environmental reality of south Florida.

The people who developed south Florida were guided by what can best be described as the pursuit of the American dream. The American dream has assumed many different forms, but the variant that occupied the minds of those who wanted to develop the Everglades was the vision of prosperous truck farms, built by the hard work and perseverance of their owner-operators. Truck farming meant to the turn-of-the-century farmer what a consulting career means to the displaced executive of the 1990s—a way to adapt existing skills to a changing economy.

In the years between the end of the Civil War and the turn of the century, the American agricultural frontier was the Great Plains. Here, the combination of a seemingly endless expanse of virtually flat, treeless grassland with the emerging technology of the mechanized farm combined to produce something new, the bonanza farm. Vast holdings of land that were cultivated with state-of-the-art machines, these bonanza farms, as their names implied, returned huge profits to their owners. This extensive cultivation offered advantages in economics of scale that had repercussions throughout the American agricultural economy. The success of these huge Plains farms caused a round of consolidation in the west, and this consolidation, in turn, made it impossible for smaller eastern farms to profit from growing such traditional grain crops as wheat and corn. Some eastern growers, especially those in the Midwest, converted their farms to feeder lots, where they used their grain to finish western grass-fed cattle for the stockyards of Chicago. Others turned their attention to the rapidly growing American cities and decided to cater to their residents' needs for fresh fruits, vegetables, and dairy products.

The truck farms of New Jersey were conspicuous examples of the prosperity that such operations could provide. Beginning in the 1870s and gathering strength as the century progressed, forward-looking New Jersey farmers began converting their holdings to the intensive cultivation of fruits and vegetables for sale in the surrounding cities. This change to intensive agriculture allowed the relatively small farms of the state to make a profit. In 1892, for example, an acre of wheat was worth $9.91, an acre of corn $10.48, while an acre planted in truck crops averaged $163.00.[1] Such increases in income drew the interest of other eastern farmers, and soon most of the growers of the northeast were directing their efforts toward truck and dairy farms.

Ever since Florida came under American control in 1821, the climate of the southern peninsula encouraged the Americans who settled the region to believe that it could support tropical agriculture, and the organic soils of the Everglades convinced early observers that the peninsula's interior would support luxuriant growths of such crops. But the water that inundated, at least seasonally, virtually all of the southern peninsula made even modest-scale agricultural production impossible. Undaunted by the impediment, American Floridians from the first advocated draining all of south Florida so that the region could fulfill what they viewed as its agricultural destiny. Indeed, the first assembly of the Florida state legislature memorialized Congress for the reclamation of the Everglades.[2]

By the end of the nineteenth century, American agricultural trends, Florida's natural features, and the nation's technological advances combined to create a new American dream, that of the prosperous truck farm on the reclaimed muck soils of the Everglades. The success of northern truck farmers illustrated the demand for fresh fruits and vegetables, while Florida's mild winters and rich muck soils convinced developers that the state's growers could produce these crops when northern fields lay idle. Finally, refrigerated railroad cars made the shipment of these commodities possible, and steam dredges made reclamation of the Everglades's muck soils viable.

State-financed drainage of the Everglades was begun by Florida's Progressive politicians. Three inducements, one philosophical and two practical, combined to make the idea of drainage irresistible to these leaders. Although Democrats, Florida's Progressives closely followed the ideological path of Republicans such as Theodore Roosevelt and Gifford Pinchot. Like these brother Progressives, Florida's Democratic leaders viewed the natural world as endangered by the excess of laissez-faire capitalism, but they had little patience with thinkers, epitomized by John Muir, who would preserve the wilderness untouched. That is, Florida's Progressives subscribed to the wisdom of men like Pinchot, who advocated viewing America's wild places in the light of "wise use" and "the greatest good to the greatest number." Under the direction of these dicta, Florida's Progressive politicians viewed the conversion of worthless marshland into productive farmland as no less than a moral imperative.[3]

If this philosophical justification had not been enough to motivate these political leaders to action, the practical effects of drainage proved impossible to resist. Florida's politicians and land speculators both agreed that the farmland created in the drained Everglades would be the richest in the world. In this view, the luxuriant fertility of the reclaimed land would enable families to earn livings on small plots, as little as ten acres, and the notion of creating such a resource "for the people" was particularly appealing to Progressives of all stripes. In addition, the peopling of the Everglades with numerous independent farmers would insure that these state-controlled public lands would stay out of the hands of the railroads. Ever alert to the excesses of railroad tycoons, Florida's Progressive Democrats were convinced that reclamation was the proper course in the Everglades.

The story of reclamation naturally falls into three phases: drainage (1904–1928), flood control (1928–1948), and comprehensive water management (1948 to the present). Although drainage was regarded as a simple engineering problem by early boosters, the marsh system nonetheless proved intractable, and the more drainage succeeded, the more problems it created. As the muck dried, subsidence and soil-consuming fires lowered the surface of the land. In 1926, and again in 1928, hurricanes brought devastating floods to the Everglades, and even the most ardent drainage advocate had to acknowledge the need for flood control. During the 1930s, the largesse of the federal government did much to alleviate flooding around Lake Okeechobee, but, in 1947, another hurricane brought new floods, farther south, where runoff from the northern Everglades inundated the formerly dry land of the Miami rocklands. This new round of flooding graphically illustrated the need for more comprehensive water management, and the Corps of Engineers responded by offering a final solution to south Florida's water problems.

The general trend in this progression of ideas has been toward ever more complex and costly strategies. In 1847, Buckingham Smith, who made the first drainage reconnaissance of the Everglades, believed that the region could be reclaimed at a cost of $300,000 to $500,000, and Florida's first Senator, Democrat J. D. Westcott, believed that the entire region would drain so quickly that the health hazard stemming from "the immense quantity of dead fish and vegetable substances thereby exposed" would present the biggest challenge to the newly reclaimed district's first immigrants.[4] By contrast, the United States Army Corps of Engineers plan of 1948 to enhance the region's water-control structures carried an estimated price tag of $208,135,000 and the admonition that it was only "the basic framework for a practical and permanent solution of the problems of flood protection and water control in central and southern Florida."[5]

Even as reclamation became more complex and expensive, new environmental ills continued to surface, and the solution to one environmental problem often created others. Throughout the process, however, the goal of reclamation, the conversion of a vast marsh system to an agricultural cornucopia, was never abandoned. In spite of tremendous environmental damage, this goal remained paramount, and changes in reclamation strategies doggedly sought to make the dream a reality.

Nineteenth-Century Prelude

In 1847, Buckingham Smith, a Harvard-educated attorney who resided at St. Augustine, conducted the first scientific reconnaissance of the Everglades. The report of his findings and conclusions, which he delivered to the United States Senate the following year, provided the basic intellectual framework for reclamation of the Everglades. This report provided three ideas that guided all subsequent drainage projects. First, Smith believed that the elevation of the region assured the ultimate success of reclamation. The second idea followed naturally from the first, that reclamation could be accomplished at an economically feasible cost. Finally, Smith assured his readers that the drained marshland had the potential to support a thriving agricultural economy.[6]

Senator Westcott made sure that Smith's report received wide circulation, and he forwarded a copy to the offices of the *Commercial Review of the South and West*. This influential magazine embraced Smith's conclusions and urged Congress to deed the Everglades to the State of Florida so that reclamation could begin.[7] The opportunity for such a transfer came in 1850, when Congress passed the Act of Congress to Enable States to Reclaim Swamp Lands, usually referred to as simply the Swamp Lands Act. This law provided that the federal government could give "the whole of those swamp and overflowed lands, made unfit for cultivation" to the several states, provided the proceeds from the sale of this land be applied "to the purpose of reclaiming such lands." Under the auspices of this law, the federal government eventually gave the State of Florida title to more than 20 million of the state's 35 million acres, although title to 2,862,080 acres in the Everglades was not granted until 29 April 1903.[8]

The Internal Improvement Fund (IIF) was the state agency that administered these millions of acres. Created in 1855, the IIF was controlled by a board of trustees that included the governor and his cabinet. In theory, these trustees exercised authority over the sale of all state lands, and they directed all reclamation work. During the years between the IIF's creation and the Civil War, however, state legislatures largely usurped the IIF's powers by granting friendly deals to railroads and, to a much lesser extent, canal companies. In exchange for the construction of transportation facilities, these companies received huge grants of land as well as state backing for their bonds.

The economic dislocations associated with the Civil War forced the railroads into receivership, and their debts, in turn, bankrupted the IIF. With the return of peace, however, both railroad promoters and the trustees of the IIF were anxious to resume business as usual, and the bankrupt lines, along with their debts, were sold at auction for a fraction of their real value. At this juncture, Francis Vose brought suit against the IIF, charging that such sales violated the contract that he, and other prewar investors, had with the State of Florida. In December 1871, the federal district judge at Pensacola agreed and ruled that the IIF could sell public land for cash only, and the money from such sales had to be applied to the outstanding debt. This ruling ended the practice of exchanging various types of script and warrants, all more or less worthless, for public lands.[9]

The court ruling effectively ended the transfer of large blocks of public land until 1881, when Governor William D. Bloxham arranged to sell Hamilton Disston 4 million acres of Florida land for $1 million. In addition to the land he bought outright, the IIF trustees granted Disston a contract that allowed him to claim one half of all the wetland that his corporation, the Atlantic and Gulf Coast Canal and Land Sales Company, reclaimed. In order to take advantage of this agreement, Disston financed an active drainage effort that began soon after his purchase was final and lasted until the Panic of 1893 forced him to suspend all dredging operations.

Disston concentrated his drainage efforts among the lakes that form the headwaters of the Kissimmee River, but his dredges also operated further south, opening a series of canals that connected Lake Okeechobee to the Caloosahatchee River in 1883. Additionally, Disston's chief drainage engineer, James M. Kreamer, developed plans to dig a canal from the Rita River—one of the streams that drained the southern shore of Lake Okeechobee—to Bowlegs Landing, about midway between Lake Okeechobee and the tip of the peninsula. Kreamer believed that this canal would reclaim valuable agricultural land along the lake's southern shore by draining the area's surface water into the Shark River Slough. Although only ten and one-half miles of this canal were actually dug, the idea stirred ambitions around the state, and draining the Everglades seemed more feasible than ever.

As for the trustees, they used the money garnered from the Disston sale to settle all outstanding debt, freeing the IIF from its decade-long receivership. Again master of its public land, the State of Florida resumed the old practice of making generous land grants to the railroads. In 1893, for instance, the legislature granted Henry M. Flagler eight thousand acres, plus rights of way, for every mile of track his Florida East Coast Railroad laid south of Daytona Beach.[10]

The Progressive Drainage Effort, 1903–1913

The decade from 1903, when the state gained title to the Everglades, to 1913, when the first drainage contract was completed, marked the active period of the Progressive effort to reclaim the Everglades. Following Governor Broward's 1905 address to the state legislature, the state launched an ambitious drainage program, but, by 1912, hearings before the Committee on Agricultural Expenditures, the Moss Committee, left the state's drainage effort in a state of national disrepute. The results of these hearings forced a reevaluation of the state's plan, and subsequent studies revealed that simple ditches connecting Lake Okeechobee with the Atlantic Ocean were an inadequate means of draining the Everglades. After 1913, the complexity of the vast reclamation project became more evident, and terms such as *flood control* and *water management* entered the lexicon of south Florida's drainage engineers.

Three principal groups of actors dominated the Progressive drainage effort: Florida's Progressive politicians, United States Department of Agriculture (USDA) engineers, and large holders of Everglades land. Governors William Jennings and Napoleon Bonaparte Broward, along with U.S. Senator Duncan U. Fletcher, played crucial roles in the drainage effort. Like their counterparts throughout the United States, Florida's Progressive politicians believed that the railroads had too much power, and they sought to protect the people from abuse by these largest of American corporations. In Florida, this meant, at least ostensibly, keeping the Everglades out of corporate hands, so that the people could share in the prosperity projected to follow the conversion of these wetlands from worthless marsh to productive farmland. In reality these Progressive politicians were untroubled at the prospect of selling large blocks of the people's land to speculators at bargain prices so that funding would be available to complete the drainage program.

In 1904, before the project began, Charles G. Elliott, the chief drainage engineer in USDA's newly created Bureau of Irrigation and Drainage Investigations, began the painstaking process of gathering accurate information about conditions in the Everglades. By 1909 these investigations became embroiled in conflict between the cautions of Elliott and the boosterism of his employee, James O. Wright—the engineer assigned to write the bureau's report on the Everglades. Wright's finished report contained an enthusiastic endorsement of drainage, but, to Wright's dismay, Elliott believed that the document contained numerous engineering errors that required correction.

In spite of these objections, an excerpt from the yet unfinished Wright report received wide public circulation and contributed to booming Everglades land sales. Lively sales convinced the railroads to acquiesce to the drainage tax that they had lately opposed, and the ensuing settlement seemingly assured the success of the entire drainage project. But the sale of land that proved to be still unreclaimed outraged buyers from throughout the United States. This furor led to a congressional investigation that revealed sufficient chicanery among Florida's Progressive politicians, the USDA, and the Everglades land companies to totally discredit the drainage effort.

Before any of these events could transpire, however, the federal government had to transfer title to the Everglades to the state. The State of Florida received title to the Everglades during the term of the Progressive Governor William Jennings (1901–1905). In 1901, two years before the transfer, Jennings announced a radical change in IIF policy. In the future, the trustees intended to comply strictly with the terms of the Swamp Lands Act by reclaiming all future federal grants of wetlands. Florida's railroad interests reacted with hostility to this change because they expected the state to deed future grants to them—to honor old legislative commitments. Indeed, the transfer of all the Everglades lands would not have fulfilled the state's pledges. By 1904, the State of Florida had received 20,133,837.42 acres of public land from the federal government, including the Everglades, and had already transferred some 17,056,932.74 acres into private hands. But the state was still obligated to supply another 5,359,592 acres to the railroads, which left the government more than 2 million acres in arrears.[11]

The following year, in response to the new land policy, the railroads and their associated land companies sued in an attempt to gain title to all of the state's lands, including all future acquisitions. Led by the Louisville and Nashville Railroad, the corporations argued that the State of Florida forfeited its rights to the Everglades lands because it had not lived up to the mandates of the 1850 Swamp Lands Act; that is, the state had violated this law's provisions by not actively pursuing reclamation of the inundated lands. This lawsuit, in effect, sought to transfer the entire Everglades into private hands as soon as the federal government deeded the land to the state.[12]

During the term of his successor, Napoleon Bonaparte Broward (1905–1909), Jennings served as general counsel to the IIF (Florida governors could not serve consecutive terms at this time), and he led the state's legal response to the corporate challenge. But a pending lawsuit did not deter a man of Broward's mettle. The new governor's career as a boat captain had been every bit as flamboyant as his name—among his exploits was a stint as a gunrunner for Cuban revolutionaries—and Broward approached Everglades drainage with the same abandon that he had displayed during his days on the bridge. In his message to the 1905 state legislature, Broward proposed the creation of an Everglades drainage district with the trustees of the IIF as directors. This district would have the power to levy an acreage tax on property owners within the district, with the money to be used to finance drainage work.[13]

The state legislature readily passed Broward's drainage law, but the Everglades Drainage District soon came under attack. The railroads, potentially the district's largest taxpayers, challenged the constitutionality of the district, and, on 6 April 1907, federal judge James W. Locke ruled that its taxing authority was indeed an unconstitutional delegation of the legislature's power.[14] In response, the 1907 legislature passed a new drainage law designed to overcome this difficulty, but the railroads still refused to pay the tax.

But, again, Broward decided not to wait for the courts, and he elected to spend the IIF's cash on hand, which amounted to $443,995 on 1 January 1905, on drainage. During 1906, construction began on the dredge *Everglades* at Fort Lauderdale, and, after only a hurried survey of the three proposed routes, the vessel began digging in the New River on 4 July 1906.[15] With little thought of possible problems, the State of Florida launched the massive project.

Broward's actions offended the political sensibilities of Florida's more traditional politicians, and they publicly opposed his drainage program. John S. Beard, a state senator from Pensacola, raised the most reasoned objection. Beard considered the feasibility of drainage outside his realm of expertise, but he opposed the venture because ownership of the land targeted for reclamation was uncertain. Beard argued that ongoing litigation stemming from the 1902 lawsuit meant that the state government ran the risk of investing considerable sums of public money in draining the Everglades only to see the courts hand over the improved land to the railroads. This situation, Beard maintained, could be avoided if only Governor Broward would wait for the courts to decide who owned the land.[16]

The ownership question, at least, did not require a long wait for the beginning of a resolution. By November 1907, William Jennings concluded that the IIF's position regarding ownership of Everglades lands was not on strong legal footing, and he informed the trustees that they should attempt to negotiate a compromise with the various litigants. Two settlements, those with the Louisville and Nashville Railroad and with the Wisner Land Company, came within weeks and resulted in the trustees' deeding the railroad 374,831 of the 1,477,000 acres it claimed and granting title to 60,000 of the 860,000 acres claimed by the land company. By the end of 1907, only two large claims remained unresolved, those with the United Land Company for 347,900 acres and with Flagler's Florida East Coast Railroad for 2,674,692 acres. These were settled by granting 68,834 acres to the land company in September 1908, and 210,000 acres to the railroad, the last firm to settle, in 1912. In total, the trustees granted 713,665 acres of land against the litigants' claims to 5,359,592 acres—proving the wisdom of Jennings's advice.[17]

Settlement of ownership questions, however, did not resolve the ongoing dispute over collection of the drainage tax, and the state's reclamation program proved expensive. The money that the IIF had on hand at the beginning of the Broward administration had shrunk to $103,986 by the time his successor, Albert W. Gilchrist (1909–1913) assumed office, and only fifteen miles of the proposed canal system had been dug.[18] The financial strain forced the state to rely on land sales to pay for drainage.

Of all the land sales, none proved more fateful than the deal consummated between the trustees and Richard J. Bolles on 23 December 1908, during the last week of the Broward administration. Bolles, an experienced land developer from Colorado Springs, contracted to pay $1 million for 500,000 acres of Everglades land (see fig. 4.1). Of the $2.00 per acre purchase price, however, the trustees pledged to spend $1.50 on the excavation of five canals—the North New River, South New River, Miami, Hillsboro,

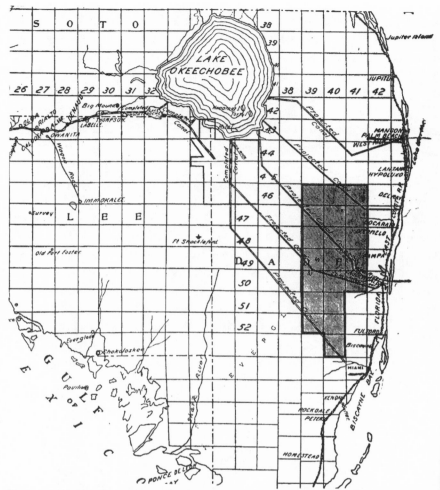

Figure 4.1. Richard J. Bolles's Florida Fruit Lands Company holdings. *Florida Fruit Lands Review* (Kansas City, Mo.: Florida Fruit Lands Company, n.d.). P. K. Yonge Library of Florida History at the University of Florida, Gainesville.

and Caloosahatchee canals—and, if funds remained, they agreed to add two smaller canals on the lowlands between the Miami rocklands and the Atlantic Ocean.[19] This sale irrevocably committed the State of Florida to a specific drainage project even before the first engineering study regarding its feasibility appeared (see fig. 4.2).

The anxiously awaited Bureau of Irrigation and Drainage Investigations engineering report (usually referred to as the "Wright report" for its author,

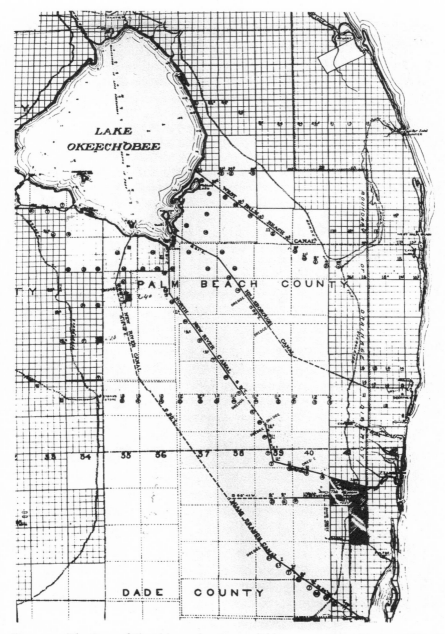

Figure 4.2. The State of Florida's canal system: *solid lines,* as completed in 1913; *dotted lines,* proposed. Source: Nelson M. Blake, *Land into Water—Water into Land: A History of Water Management in Florida* (Tallahassee: University Presses of Florida, 1980), p. 110. Reprinted with permission.

James O. Wright) would not be completed until May 1909. In the meantime, the bureau supplied abstracts of the unfinished report to the trustees of the IIF.[20] Although the bureau cautioned that these abstracts contained information that could be amended—indeed, the conflict between Elliott and Wright over the accuracy of the paper's engineering data eventually delayed publication of the report for more than two years—Governor Gilchrist, in March 1909, obtained permission from Secretary of Agriculture James Wilson to release the document. The abstract of Wright's report assured its readers that digging eight canals from Lake Okeechobee through the Everglades would reclaim some 1,850,000 acres at a cost of about one dollar per acre[21] (see fig. 4.3).

The Florida legislature enthusiastically endorsed the abstract, and land sales companies found it so favorable that they featured it in their advertising, even though the document was, by this time, being extensively revised.[22] Indeed, the advertising campaign generated so much interest that the bureau was forced to print a circular letter that warned its recipients of the speculative nature of any investment in the Everglades and reminded them that farming had not yet been attempted in the area.[23] Banned by Secretary of Agriculture James Wilson within weeks, this form letter had little effect on booming land sales. Indeed, one brochure proclaimed that "Secretary Wilson, of the United States Agriculture Department, says the doubting Thomases who are waiting for the Everglades to develop before buying will regret it all their lives," all of which was sheer invention on the part of the copywriter.[24]

Suppression of the circular letter did not appease the Everglades land merchants, and they chafed at the continued inaction on publication of Wright's report. By January 1910, there were three versions of this document: the original report as Wright submitted it in May 1909, a version that was edited for literary content and resubmitted to the Division of Publications in July of the same year, and a third version, with new engineering data, that was sent to the printers in January 1910. The final version created such disagreement among Florida's congressional delegation, especially between Congressman Frank Clark and Senator Duncan Fletcher, that Joseph A. Arnold, the editor in chief of the Division of Publications, advised that the document should not be published. Secretary Wilson concurred, and he ordered the Division of Publication to discontinue work on the Wright report in June 1910.[25]

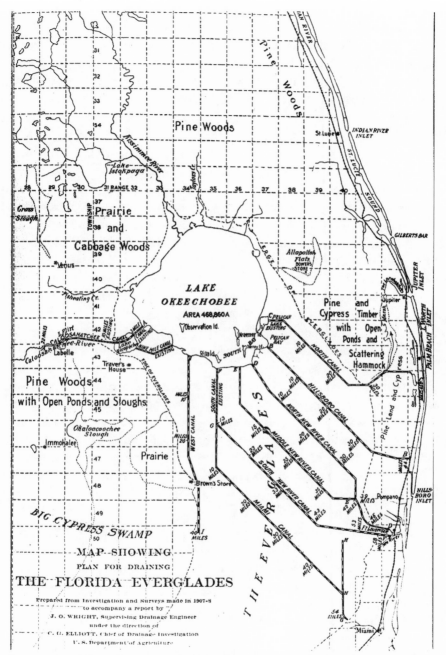

Figure 4.3. J. O. Wright's proposed canal system. Source: U.S. Congress, Senate, *Everglades of Florida: Acts, Reports, and Other Papers, State and National, Relating to the Everglades of the State of Florida and their Reclamation*, S. Doc. 89, 62nd Cong., 1st sess., 1912, p. 168.

Meanwhile, booming land sales caused the region's railroads to reexamine their position on paying the long-neglected drainage tax, and by 3 January 1910, the parties reached a tentative agreement on the question. For their part, the railroads agreed to pay a drainage tax of five cents per acre for the period from 1907 to 1910. In return, the state promised to appoint a competent drainage engineer and turn reclamation over to private contractors.[26] Honoring this agreement, the state hired Wright as drainage engineer in February, and in July contracted with the Furst-Clarke Construction Company of Baltimore to dig the 184 remaining miles in the state's proposed canal system by 1 July 1913.[27]

This settlement, coupled with the glowingly optimistic excerpt from the Wright report, seemingly insured the success of the reclamation program, and the land boom continued throughout 1910 and 1911.[28] Three land companies—the Everglades Land Company, the Everglades Plantation Company, and the Everglades Land Sales Company—combined for sales of 4,000 10-acre farm sites at prices that ranged from $20 to $100 per acre.[29] Of all the land sales companies, however, none prospered more than Bolles's Florida Fruit Lands Company. The largest holders of Everglades land, the Florida Fruit Lands Company employed a lottery scheme to help sell land. The company's sales brochures advertised farms for $240, payable in installments of $10 per month. The sizes of the farms, however, were variable— 8,000 of these farmsteads were of 10 acres, but 3,620 were 20 acres, 250 were 40 acres, 100 were 80 acres, 20 were 160 acres, 8 were 320 acres, and 2 were 640 acres—the size and exact location of any individual parcel to be decided by a drawing after all the land was sold. In addition, all buyers received a lot in the proposed town of Progresso. In the end, the lottery was so successful that the company sold more than 10,000 10-acre farm plots to buyers throughout the country, mostly sight unseen.[30]

It was the dream of the prosperous truck farm that drove these sales. At the same time that farms were consolidating throughout the country, the Florida Fruit Lands Company's advertising campaign assured potential buyers that they could prosper on small plots in the Everglades. An advertisement in a Pittsburgh newspaper, for instance, advised, "Ten acres of Everglades is as good as 100 acres in the north."[31] Similarly, the Everglades Land Sales Company informed prospective buyers in Chicago that on its land along the south shore of Lake Okeechobee, "the soil, deep uniform and black, is absolutely richer than the valley of the Nile."[32] On such land,

Figure 4.4. Holdings of the Everglades Land Sales Company. Source: "The Florida Everglades Land Co.," 1910(?), brochure, P. K. Yonge Library of Florida History, University of Florida, Gainesville.

the company insisted, diligent farmers could prosper on 10 acres. But reality proved the undoing of such claims (see fig. 4.4).

The Florida Fruit Lands Company scheduled its lottery for March 1911, and the company provided discounted train fares for their buyers to travel to Fort Lauderdale. Optimistic buyers flocked to Florida, only to have the reality of the situation dash their dreams. Unlike the agricultural Eden described in the brochures, the investors found an undrained marsh, and the lack of a survey made it impossible even to locate their flooded farms. Outraged by what they found, many investors demanded their money back, and some insisted that the land companies were guilty of criminal fraud.[33]

To make matters worse for the state, by August 1911 Florida Senator Duncan Fletcher found a way to have the original Wright report published. Fletcher, who was to admit during testimony before the Moss Committee that he was widely viewed as associated with "the progressive element that wanted to carry out the drainage project," introduced a resolution in the Senate that called for the publication of a series of documents pertaining to the Everglades.[34] During a congressional recess, Fletcher met with former governor Jennings and engineer Wright in Jacksonville, Florida, where the three men compiled what they believed to be the relevant documents. Included among these was the original Wright report containing the uncorrected engineering data.[35] Once published, this document, the misinformation included, received wide circulation. Indeed, the State of Florida ordered ten thousand copies for distribution to the general public—in essence, adding the government's prestige to the optimistic appraisal of the Everglades' agricultural future.[36] In the eyes of people who paid good money for unreclaimed land, it appeared that land developers had fraudulently used the good offices of the Department of Agriculture to market their real estate.

Denouement

By February 1912, the House Committee on Expenditures in the Department of Agriculture began hearings to examine the land transactions in the Everglades. The committee sat in intermittent session until August, and they uncovered a tangle of deceit and half-truths that totally discredited the land companies and besmirched the reputation of the USDA. The trail of evidence included the flawed Wright report, the circular letter from the Bureau of Irrigation and Drainage Investigations, and Secretary of Agriculture Wilson's decision to suppress both of these documents.

Convened at the insistence of Florida Congressman Frank Clark, whose district included much of the Everglades, these hearings opened amid charges and countercharges from the state's various land developers. On the one hand, pro-drainage people insisted that delays in publishing the Wright report, the USDA's circular letter, and the congressional investigation itself represented little more than an attempt by Flagler's Florida East Coast Railroad to discredit drainage. Florida Governor Albert Gilchrist was among the proponents of this view, and he informed the press that the railroad interests wanted to stop the drainage works so that their real estate on the Miami rocklands would not face competition from the reclaimed Everglades.[37] On the other hand, Elliott and the USDA maintained that the Wright report was withheld from publication because of its flaws, and the department's circular sought only to disassociate the reputation of the USDA from the speculative Everglades venture. USDA officials argued that Everglades land sales companies engineered the suppression of the USDA's circular letter and advocated publication of Wright's unedited report to boost land sales in the unreclaimed wetlands.[38]

On 16 February 1912, Arthur C. Morgan, special drainage engineer for the USDA's Bureau of Irrigation and Drainage Investigations, testified before the investigating committee. Morgan analyzed a laundry list of faults contained in Wright's work that left no doubt about Elliott's motives in refusing to publish the report without corrections. Wright's most critical error involved the interactions among rainfall, evaporation, and runoff. Wright estimated the rate of evaporation within the region at nine inches a month, even though there were only two months of the year during which, on average, more than nine inches of rain fell. This meant, in essence, that the rate of evaporation was greater than the rate of rainfall, and this conclusion meant that, "there would be no run-off whatever." Indeed, taken to their logical conclusion, Wright's evaporation figures meant that Lake Okeechobee "would finally dry up," since the drainage basin could not be expected to maintain its water level.[39]

Similarly, the engineer's canal computations were faulty. Wright's ditches could accommodate only 55 percent of their projected water capacity, and he grossly underestimated their costs. Morgan testified that Wright's estimated excavation costs, four cents per yard for earth and eight cents per yard for rock, caught his attention because they "showed rock to be excavated at a lower cost than I ever knew of rock being excavated anywhere on earth." Indeed, at the time that Wright wrote his report, Florida officials could give him "no logical or clear statement of what the work was costing," and the actual costs of removal were subsequently calculated at eight cents for earth and twenty cents for rock.[40] Additionally, even though he relied strictly on gravity for water flow, Wright proposed using the same ditches for both irrigation and drainage. Finally, Wright understated the necessity for the additional drainage works—the cross canals, laterals, and farm ditches—required for truly effective drainage, and he ignored concerns about subsidence.[41] These numerous and glaring flaws forced Morgan to state bluntly, "I regard Mr. Wright as absolutely and completely incompetent for any engineering work."[42]

After the incompetence of the Wright report became obvious, it was clear that publication of the document had been withheld because of its flaws, rather than as a result of a conspiracy on the part of railroad interests.[43] This conclusion made the other charges of the pro-drainage faction suspect, and subsequent testimony proved these suspicions well grounded. W. R. Hardee, a Florida farmer, testified that he went with Congressman Clark to meet Secretary Wilson in February 1910, after the USDA's circular letter had been suppressed. He recalled that Clark asked Wilson "if he did not think that the statements in the circular letter were correct," to which the Secretary replied that "he supposed they were, but he had suppressed it at the instigation of people who were interested in Everglades lands."[44]

The committee's findings, published on 12 August 1912, agreed with the disgruntled investors. The findings of the majority concluded that Wright "favorably recommended to the public" the Everglades drainage project after "only cursory examination in the field" and that, with his help, land sales companies used these recommendations in their sales promotions before "critical review" by his superiors at the Division of Drainage. The circular letter, the committee found, "gave prominence to certain cautionary statements with respect to the agricultural value of the Everglade lands" and "for this reason was objectionable to certain persons who were offering these lands for sale." As for the Secretary of Agriculture, he issued "an order to suppress the distribution of the circular," and the evidence indicated that "the entire treatment of the project was most unfortunate and subjected the Department of Agriculture to much suspicion and criticism."[45]

After these findings became public, Wright had little choice but to resign his post as Florida's chief drainage engineer, which he did in September 1912. The engineer, however, soon found employment with the Furst-Clarke Construction Company, the same firm that was, by this time, digging the Everglades canals. If he once had expected bigger prizes for his part in the land boom—and circumstantial evidence suggests that he had—the ambitious engineer had to content himself with this lesser prize. In light of the facts uncovered by the Moss Committee, Wright was fortunate that he was not arrested for fraud.

In addition to learning about the flaws in the work Wright did for Florida, the Moss Committee discovered information about his previous activities in North Carolina that brought his integrity into question. While engaged in the Mattamuskeet Lake reclamation project in that state, Wright entered into a number of lucrative deals with land companies interested in the undertaking. Wright secured stock deals valued at $5,000 and $7,500 from two such firms, and he earned a $5,000 finder's fee and $2,200 in additional fees from the same companies. Additionally, while an employee of the federal government, Wright lobbied the North Carolina legislature for a law favorable to the interests of the same land companies.[46]

Circumstantial evidence supports the idea that Wright hoped his Everglades report, with all its inflated estimates, would lead to similar opportunities in Florida. At the Jacksonville meeting with Jennings and Fletcher, Wright actively participated in the attempt to have his original Everglades report printed even though he knew his ditch-flow calculations were grossly in error. Wright could not deny his knowledge of these defects because, while still with the Bureau of Drainage, he and an assistant revised these same figures—on Elliott's orders—at some point between November 1909 and January 1910.[47]

Rather than disavow his original report, Wright did everything in his power to insure its acceptance. In January 1912, while in Washington, he informed the head of the Division of Accounts and Disbursements in the Department of Agriculture of certain minor financial irregularities on Elliott's part during 1909.[48] During the Moss Committee investigation, Wright testified that he had known about the irregularities in 1909. That Wright chose to reveal them on the eve of the Moss investigation can only be viewed as an attempt to discredit one professional critic while cowing the others. Already head of the State of Florida's drainage effort, Wright fought to the end to insure that a report he knew to be professionally flawed escaped public censure.

Even if Florida's politicians did not engage in criminal fraud—and Jennings's and Fletcher's actions raise doubts on that question—they were guilty of critical oversights. As indicated by the inclusion of Kreamer's drainage report in his 1905 message to the legislature, Broward (and, by extension, Jennings too) certainly had at his disposal enough information to alert him to the potential for environmental and financial complications. Written while Kreamer was Hamilton Disston's chief drainage engineer, the report noted that the canals connecting Lake Okeechobee to the Caloosahatchee River overtaxed the river's ability to handle the increased flow from the lake, resulting in the flooding of agricultural sites downstream of Fort Thompson. Before dredging, the area had been dependably dry. Further, Kreamer reported that the existence of the "sand and lime-rock rim" between the Everglades and the Atlantic Ocean made the "cutting of a drainage canal on any of the lines named east of Lake Okeechobee very costly."[49]

Broward had received environmental warnings from other sources as well. By 15 August 1907, a little more than a year after dredging began on the New River, the Bureau of Drainage issued a preliminary report that warned of complications. The bureau's engineers cautioned that, once completed, the state's drainage program would create flood conditions at the southern end of its canals. Additionally, the preliminary report warned that the state's proposed canal routes passed through land where the muck was only three to six feet deep, and the excavation of large quantities of rock would add considerable costs to the project. Finally, the report cautioned that although the canals could reasonably be expected to reclaim land along the lakeshore, further south, where shallow muck predominated, the depth of the state's ditches insured that these works would draw much of their water from the underlying strata of limestone, rather than from the surface of the muck, a prediction that raised considerable doubt about the efficacy of the state's drainage plan.[50]

If Florida's Progressive politicians were not as upright as they might have been, neither were the land developers as sordid. Although their salesmen no doubt exaggerated the favorable aspects of the new lands, the line between salesmanship and fraud remains blurred, and energetic salesmen have little to fear under most state laws. Besides, to support their claims made to prospective customers, the salesmen relied on the good faith of state officials, who promised complete reclamation of the Everglades, and on the scientific conclusions of no less an authority than the USDA, which issued reports promising a rich agricultural future for the region. Finally, like their customers, most of the Everglades sales force had never seen the agricultural Eden they so earnestly promoted, and they could not be charged with knowingly making false claims about the land.

Regardless of their degrees of culpability, no figure connected with the first Everglades land boom spent a moment in jail, although in modern times indictments would have undoubtedly arisen. As for the thousands of unfortunate purchasers of ten-acre farms, they had only one way to voice their displeasure: they stopped making payments. Their withdrawal of financial support proved crippling to a drainage scheme that appeared more and more like just another pyramid scheme. The people's money had seemingly disappeared down the rabbit hole, and, when the Furst-Clarke Construction Company completed its contract on 1 July 1913, the Everglades was still too wet for cultivation. Started with such promise, the Progressive effort to drain the Everglades ended in national disrepute. It would be years before the district escaped from the perception that the region represented little more than land by the gallon.

5

Drainage Reconsidered and Pioneer Settlement, 1912–1924

The conversion of the Everglades from a derelict to a developmental system proved itself a much more difficult task than the one envisioned by Progressive boosters. Indeed, the intractable wilderness of the Everglades Trough had already discredited their efforts by 1912. In the aftermath of scandals that plagued the Progressive drainage effort, however, neither the state nor the land developers abandoned the dream of converting the Everglades from wetlands to productive farmland. Indeed, both the State of Florida and the larger land developers commissioned studies designed to develop a more successful strategy for draining the Everglades. While these studies did develop new plans, implementation of the new strategies proved slow.

The lives of the district's pioneers provide graphic illustrations of the failure to tame the exotic Everglades. Indeed, the earliest arrivals, like their Indian predecessors, depended on their hunting and fishing skills for their livelihoods. Even when reclamation made farming possible, the uncertainty of drainage and the general lack of knowledge about the environmental realities of their new homes insured that many pioneer growers failed. But the arrival of railroads provided Everglades farmers with access to the nation's markets, and the resources of the larger nation set in motion the process of converting the exotic Everglades into the familiar, the Everglades Agricultural Area.[1]

On 2 March 1912, only two days after Arthur C. Morgan concluded his damaging testimony, the Miami Board of Trade sent a telegram to the Moss Committee. Inserted into the hearing's proceedings, the message extended the board's invitation to "your committee or a subcommittee of your body and all critics who have not seen the Everglades" to come "visit this district with a view of ascertaining the actual facts before you submit your report to Congress." The members of the Board of Trade believed that a visit would convince skeptics that the region's soil "is especially adapted to all branches of agriculture" and "that the State has ample funds in view to complete the work." These civic leaders knew full well, however, that funds for drainage would not be forthcoming if drainage taxes were not collected, and they hoped that the proposed junket would help revitalize the faith required to keep the money flowing.[2]

Like the members of the Board of Trade, the trustees of the Internal Improvement Fund (IIF) knew that the ultimate success of Everglades drainage rested on faith; that is, potential investors must somehow be convinced to buy land in a partially reclaimed region so that their drainage taxes would make total reclamation a reality. Hoping to counter "certain reports derogatory to the practicability of the plans which are being followed for the drainage and reclamation of the Everglades," the trustees appropriated $1,000 to pay for a tour of the district by a group representing the national press.[3] The promise of an all-expenses-paid trip attracted a party of twenty-five reporters to Chicago, where they boarded the "Hurry-Up Limited" bound for Jacksonville, Florida. Arriving on 21 April 1912, the newsmen were joined by Governor Albert Gilchrist and other state officials for a tour of the Everglades. From Jacksonville, the party traveled by rail to Fort Myers, where they boarded a steamboat for a trip up the Caloosahatchee River to Lake Okeechobee. After touring the lake's southern shore, the party proceeded down the newly completed North New River Canal to Fort Lauderdale.[4]

Throughout their travels, the reporters were treated in the same manner as were the unwitting buyers who had already purchased Everglades land. Significantly, the tour was planned for April, at the end of the dry winter, when the district's water was at its lowest. Like prospective buyers, the reporters saw "gardens being cultivated along the borders of the ditch"—

the canal banks were always the driest spots in the Everglades—and they were not told these plots prospered only after "the necessary elements of fertility" were "secretly added to the soil."[5] Like so many sales prospects, the newsmen stayed at the Bolles Hotel, specially constructed by the land developer to accommodate promising prospective buyers on the shore of Lake Okeechobee, and they heard enthusiastic reports from Governor Gilchrist—the surrogate salesman on the special junket.[6] Like the numerous investors who preceded them, the reporters came away impressed. One participant gushed, "In the Everglades you simply tickle the soil and bounteous crops respond to feed hungry humanity," while another enthused, "Florida must have been the first part of the world made, early Monday morning when everyone was feeling good without a care or worry."[7]

These attempts at damage control floundered, however, as ruinous facts continued to emerge from the Moss Committee hearings, and indictments against Everglades land agents mounted.[8] As interest in Everglades land declined, holders of large sections of the district's real estate found themselves in a financial bind. The profits of the speculators depended on their ability to sell as rapidly as possible the partially reclaimed land. The absence of sales not only interrupted vital cash flow, but also made the land companies liable for payment of their unsold land's drainage tax—as much as $25,000 per year for Richard J. Bolles, the largest property holder in the Everglades. To deepen the financial morass, lapsed sales contracts meant that the drainage tax on these properties, too, fell back to the land sales companies, and these firms were soon in arrears to the state. Indeed, as one Everglades land salesman admitted in May 1912, "In the past three years, thousands of acres of these lands have been sold here and in the vicinity of this district," but "Now even a ten-acre sale is as rare as a day in June."[9]

In September 1912, the month following the conclusion of the Moss Committee hearings, the representatives of major land firms along with Florida Governor Gilchrist attended a meeting in New York City, where the financial crisis dominated the agenda. Both parties, the state and the private firms, had money woes. By the terms of the Bolles sale, the state bound itself to completion of its proposed canal system, but the work could not continue without money from the drainage tax. As for the landowners, they insisted that they could not afford to pay the tax in the absence of cash flow from the sale of real estate. In addition, the promoters argued, the state's plan was inadequate to the task of effectively draining the marsh system, and they believed it unfair for the state to demand payment for the construction of poorly conceived works.[10]

Drainage Reconsidered, 1912–1913

The land companies based much of their argument on the as yet unpublished Mead, Hazen, and Metcalf report, the first of two documents that reassessed the drainage program. Hired by the Everglades Land Sales Company to study the Everglades problem on 23 July 1912, Mead, Hazen, and Metcalf formed a distinguished board of engineers, and their study reflected their professional standing. Both Leonard Metcalf, of Boston, and Allen Hazen, of Chicago, had national reputations as consulting engineers on water and sewage-disposal questions, while Daniel W. Mead was a professor of hydraulics and sanitary engineering at the University of Wisconsin.[11] In the course of their extensive investigation, the engineers traveled the lengths of the Caloosahatchee and North New River Canals, and they examined the Miami branch of the South New River Canal as far as it was completed. In addition, the group gathered all available data from the trustees of the Internal Improvement Fund, the Corps of Engineers, and the United States Weather Service.[12]

On 12 November 1912, under the auspices of the Board of Consulting Engineers, Mead, Hazen, and Metcalf presented their report to the land companies' executives. Although the engineers reaffirmed the feasibility of drainage, they had little regard for the state's efforts, stating bluntly that, "the present system of canals as outlined by the state of Florida is not sufficient to take care of the runoff from the Upper Everglades as a whole."[13] The inadequacies of the canal system, but especially the deficits in the Miami Canal's ability to drain the Everglades Land Sales Company's lands that lay along its southern course, caused the Board of Consulting Engineers to recommend diking the company's holdings into either two or four parcels. Within this impounded land, the construction of outlet canals would be required for effective drainage, and pumps would have to be employed to insure reclamation of the western areas.[14] A prescient assessment, this approach—that of creating what were, in effect, islands of true water control in a sea of partially reclaimed land—was the strategy that eventually allowed for the success of large-scale agricultural development in the Everglades.

As for the rest of the Everglades, the engineers offered three suggestions. First, they advised that drainage should be a "progressive development," with efforts concentrated on "lands adjacent to centers of population and to transportation facilities, and which are close to natural or artificial outlets."[15] Second, the consultants argued that the trustees would encourage future development if they abandoned their practice of selling Everglades land in alternating sections, a device employed to maximize the state's potential profits. Finally, the report called on the state legislature to pass a "sound drainage act" that would "simplify the obtaining of consent to proceed with effective private drainage."[16]

Although the Mead, Hazen, and Metcalf report was a private report, not meant for widespread public circulation, the document did exert considerable influence among insiders with an interest in the state's drainage program. Among these insiders was Park Trammell, who occupied the governor's chair during the rocky years following the Moss Committee hearings (1913–1917). Trammell worked his way up through Florida's political system, serving in both houses of the legislature, acting as president of the senate, and, in the years before his election as governor, occupying the office of attorney general. As a cabinet officer, Trammell acted as both a trustee of the IIF and a board member of the Everglades Drainage District (EDD), and these positions insured that the new governor was intimately aware of the problems that bedeviled the reclamation of the Everglades.[17]

During the 1913 term of the Florida legislature, Trammell proposed the drainage act advocated in the Mead, Hazen, and Metcalf report.[18] Concentrating largely on financial questions, the measure, signed into law on 6 June 1913, sought to reassure investors and insure their continued support for reclamation. The new law allowed drainage commissioners to borrow money for up to one year, and they could, in addition, sell up to $6 million in bonds. These debts were secured by the receipts from a new progressive drainage tax, which varied from five to twenty-five cents per acre, based on the calculated benefit derived by various parcels of land from drainage. In addition, even the IIF lands were liable for the tax. This provision seemingly insured that taxes would be paid on all of the land within the EDD all of the time—since real estate with delinquent taxes would revert to the IIF, and this body would presumably pay the overdue assessment. Combined with the more flexible borrowing policy, the graduated tax apparently placed reclamation on a sound financial footing and provided the basis for renewed investor confidence.

But the drainage act did not stop there; to further facilitate reclamation, the state's new drainage law allowed for the creation of subdrainage districts with taxing and borrowing powers of their own. To start such a district, all a majority of landowners, or the owners of the majority of the acreage in any particular area, need do was petition either the county commission or the state circuit judge who had jurisdiction in their county or counties.[19] A powerful tool, such subdrainage districts allowed for the corporate separation of drainage works from land holdings. This situation made possible the complete bankruptcy of the district responsible for paying for drainage works, while the land that these works drained remained free to turn a profit—even though both entities, in reality, could belong to the same people.

The new drainage law alone, however, would not solve the crisis of confidence that threatened to halt Everglades development. Before financial institutions could be persuaded to make loans, or investors could be expected to risk their funds, the state needed to insure these sources of capital that its drainage plans were technically as well as economically feasible. These ends could be most effectively accomplished if a highly reputable engineering firm studied the Everglades situation and concluded that effective drainage could be accomplished at an acceptable price. On 30 April 1913, during the same legislative session that passed the new drainage law, the service of such a firm was secured when the State of Florida contracted with the J. G. White Engineering Corporation of New York City. By the terms of the agreement, J. G. White appointed an engineering commission and charged that body with gathering such existing information and conducting such new surveys as necessary to determine what additional works would be required to complete drainage of the Everglades and what those projects would cost.[20]

The members of the Everglades Engineering Commission, Isham Randolph, Marshall O. Leighton, and Edmund T. Perkins, represented some of the most prestigious engineers in the United States. Leighton came to the commission after having served as the chief hydrographer of the United States Geological Survey, and he had also served as a consultant on the U.S. Inland Waterway Commission and, in the same capacity, with several New

Jersey flood commissions. Perkins, too, had considerable experience. A civil engineer, he had worked for the U.S. Geological Survey from 1885 to 1902, and with the U.S. Reclamation Service from 1902 until 1910. Perkins left government service so that he could serve as president of the National Drainage Congress, the post he held when he was selected to sit on the Everglades Engineering Commission.[21] But it was Randolph, the chairman, who was the most distinguished member of this distinguished commission. Trained as a civil engineer, Randolph served as chief engineer of the Chicago Sanitary District, where he supervised the digging of the Chicago Drainage Canal. In 1905, Theodore Roosevelt appointed Randolph to the Panama Canal Commission, a high honor for a civil engineer, and Randolph served as William Howard Taft's personal technical advisor during a 1908 tour of the project. So great was his reputation that one observer noted, "The name of Isham Randolph attached to any enterprise was a guarantee of honesty, integrity, and technical efficiency."[22]

The Engineering Commission established its headquarters at Miami on 3 May 1913 and presented its finished report on 25 October. This document surely pleased state officials. Where the Mead, Hazen, and Metcalf report characterized the state's canal system as totally inadequate, the Randolph report simply asserted, "Until completed as planned this system of main canals will not wholly accomplish the purpose of reclamation."[23] On the feasibility of drainage, however, both studies agreed, and the Randolph report assured its readers, "Our conclusion, based on our study of ascertained facts, is that the drainage of the Florida Everglades is entirely practicable," and, further, the drainage made economic sense because it "can be accomplished at a cost which the value of the reclaimed land will justify."[24]

The Randolph report proposed a three-point program designed to improve the state's system of main canals. The most important innovation was the St. Lucie Canal, which would discharge water from the eastern shore of Lake Okeechobee to the St. Lucie River, and, from there, to the Atlantic Ocean. Proposed as a control canal, the new structure would eliminate the flood surges that entered the lake from the north, via such streams as the Kissimmee River, Taylor Creek, and Fisheating Creek, following heavy rains. Channeling these waters to the ocean meant that Okeechobee would no longer overflow its southern rim, and the main canal system need only drain the rainwater that fell within the Everglades, a task the Engineering Commission believed could be accommodated once the second innova-

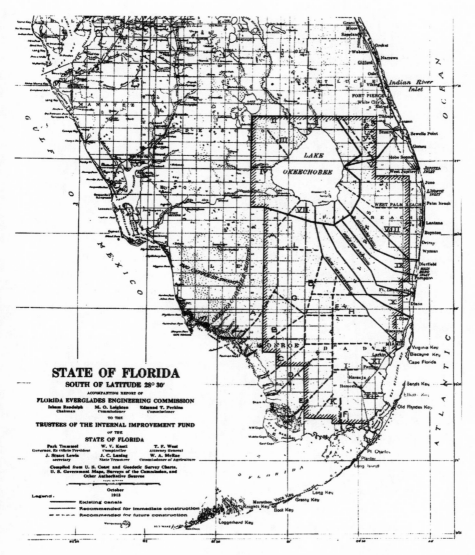

Figure 5.1. The Engineering Commission's proposed canal system. Source: U.S. Congress, Senate, *Florida Everglades: Report of the Everglades Engineering Commission to the Commissioners of the Everglades Drainage District and the Trustees of the Internal Improvement Fund State of Florida*, S. Doc. 379, 63rd Cong., 2nd sess., 1914, p. 15.

tion, "a grand total of 390 miles of canal," were either dug or enlarged[25] (see fig. 5.1). Finally, the Engineering Commission recommended the construction of a hydroelectric power plant on the St. Lucie Canal that would generate "5,000 horsepower," and the sale of this electricity "will return to the drainage district an income that will contribute largely toward the future maintenance of the drainage systems."[26]

The Randolph report offered the state a hopeful vision of an effective drainage system that generated a considerable portion of the costs attendant on its maintenance, and this rosy scenario continued when the Engineering Commission estimated the cost of their proposals. According to their figures, the St. Lucie Canal and its hydroelectric plant could be built for $2.5 million, and the improvements to the system of main canals could be made with an expenditure of $4,281,000. All this work seemed possible because the total was only $781,000 more than the $6-million bond issue that the legislature had authorized earlier in the year.[27] Indeed, the Randolph report offered such a reassuring assessment of the practicality of draining the Everglades that the indefatigable Duncan U. Fletcher made sure that this report, too, was issued as a federal document, and the IIF trustees responded by buying five thousand copies of the newly published document in 1914.[28]

For a second time state politicians demonstrated more boosterism than reasoned judgment, and the Randolph report became the master plan for all drainage work, even though the Mead, Hazen, and Metcalf report more accurately presaged many of the environmental problems caused by drainage. Mead, Hazen, and Metcalf, for example, predicted a subsidence rate of 30–50 percent for all organic soils above the water table—30–36 inches below the surface was considered ideal at the time—while the Randolph report predicted that subsidence would not exceed 7.8 inches, or 1.2 inches less than the Mead, Hazen, and Metcalf minimum.[29]

Most importantly, however, the Mead, Hazen, and Metcalf report demonstrated an understanding of the environmental changes that accompanied drainage. Mead, Hazen, and Metcalf understood that drainage from the upper Everglades meant the possibility of increased flooding in the more heavily populated areas near the canals' mouths. The engineers also realized that draining marshland caused plant succession, and they pointed out that reclaimed saw grass areas became dense jungle if farmers did not follow quickly in the wake of the dredge. Additionally, this report warned that overdrainage allowed fires to consume potentially fertile muck soils. Overly rapid development of the Everglades represented a danger, and this document viewed "slow, substantial, progressive development" as "ultimately the best for all concerned."[30]

But the state's politicians were not the only ones to have their reason overcome by the siren song of Everglades drainage. An article that Randolph wrote in 1917 reveals that he too became an avid booster of the huge reclamation project. Randolph had never been to Florida before 1913, and he knew little about the state before he chaired the Engineering Commission—he readily admitted that "the land of flowers was terra incognita to me."[31] After working on the engineering project, however, Randolph became convinced that "the value of these Everglades lands when drained is great beyond question." In his view, the reclaimed marsh would produce agricultural land so rich that "If this vast area was devoted to raising oranges, grape-fruit, and such fruits as the soil is suited to, the yield would far surpass any human demand for it." The glutted market would force the district's farmers to devote much acreage to "staples such as corn, broom corn, alfalfa, etc." But the district's productivity did not end there. Randolph believed that the drained Everglades had the potential for pasturage so extensive that "the meat supply can be greatly augmented by the cattle which may be raised in tremendous number in this land where there is no winter."[32]

The enthusiasms of Isham Randolph and the state's policy makers were not peculiar to them. The Everglades drainage project offered the promise of such rich possibilities that even the revelation of political chicanery, fraudulent engineering data, and financial fast dealing could not kill the enterprise. Although the faith so critical to the ultimate success of the project wavered during the mid 1910s, the reaffirmation of the financial and technical feasibility of drainage breathed new life into the undertaking. The project survived what could have been its death blow, and if reclamation faltered, the fact that it was even alive testified to its resilience. In the coming years, the project would cast the same sort of spell over thousands of Americans as it had over Isham Randolph.

If some engineers became boosters and placed undue emphasis on the positive aspects of a reclaimed Everglades, the people who actually settled there did not have the same luxury. Rather, these pioneers had to face the reality of life in an unfamiliar and largely untried environment. If they had known of it, and most presumably did not, these early settlers would surely have found more agreement with Arthur C. Morgan's testimony before the Moss Committee than with the enthusiasms of those who, like Isham Randolph, became swept up in the excitement of the reclamation project.

Morgan's congressional testimony revealed that he had more actual experience with the reclamation of muck lands than any of the engineers who wrote the various studies of the region. The engineer told the Moss Committee that he had been closely involved in reclamation projects in "20 drainage districts in Minnesota where the problem of the drainage of muck lands was prominent." In addition, the engineer assured the congressmen that he "read the literature on the subject and traveled in Wisconsin, Indiana, Illinois, and Minnesota making myself familiar with the drainage of muck soils in those states." During his travels, Morgan told the committee, he had encountered a number of farmers from "Germany, Holland, Denmark, and Sweden," all of whom were familiar with the special techniques that farming such soils required, and the engineer recalled that he "made it a point to inquire of them concerning the practice in these older countries in regard to drainage and the handling of muck lands for agriculture." Relying on this extensive experience, Morgan testified, "The drainage of muck lands, in the majority of cases, is the simplest part of their handling." The really difficult task, the drainage engineer assured his congressional audience, "lies in making them useful for agriculture after they are drained."[33]

When Isham Randolph submitted the Engineering Commission's report to the IIF trustees, however, the Everglades was still a wilderness and agriculture consisted of no more than a scattering of kitchen gardens. In 1913, the naturalist W. S. Blatchley traveled from Fort Myers, up the Caloosahatchee River, and around Lake Okeechobee. On the entire lake, Blatchley encountered only "three houses on the shore," and a lone settlement "on Taylor's Creek, a small stream which enters the northwest corner of the lake, a few miles east of the mouth of the Kissimmee."[34] The only other people on the lake were hunters and fishermen and women who pursued their prey on either land or lake as the season and opportunity dictated.

With the exception of alligators, which were shot at any time of the year, hunting presented seasonal opportunities. Otter and raccoons were the most sought-after fur-bearing animals, and they were trapped in the winter, when their fur was thickest. Very plentiful, raccoon hides sold for only seventy-five cents in 1915, while the relative scarcity of otter skins insured that these pelts fetched at least eight dollars, and really fine ones sold for twelve to fifteen dollars.[35] Plume birds, especially egrets, were shot during the spring nesting season, when their valuable aigrettes—actually, the feathers that the birds used to signal their readiness for mating—could be taken, and this plumage sold for as much as thirty-two dollars per ounce, the price of gold in 1915.[36]

Although Lake Okeechobee initially produced an abundance of valuable animals, overhunting soon reduced their numbers, and the region could not for long sustain the likes of hunter Bill Brown, who killed 172 otters and 250 alligators in a single outing.[37] But plume hunting was even more devastating to the birds valued in the millinery trade. Hunters secreted themselves in large rookeries, then fired at the birds with small-bore rifles, using "the lightest kind of cartridge," whose "report is hardly greater than the snapping of a branch, and is scarcely noticed by the birds." In this way, one Florida hunter recounted that "he had been able to get over four hundred 'plume birds' in less than four days."[38] Because many of these birds were killed during the nesting season, when their plumage made them most valuable, the death of adult birds meant "the starving to death of a little brood." Indeed, one young Florida hunter was so distressed at the sound of young birds "calling so plaintively for frogs and fish" that he and his brother "went 'gator hunting, and worked a month to make a day's wages of plume hunting" because he "couldn't stand the little birds."[39]

Not all plume hunters were so squeamish. When the naturalist W. E. D. Scott toured Florida's lower west coast, from Tarpon Springs to Punta Rasa, during the spring of 1886, he secured "the name and addresses of some fifty dealers in various towns in Florida and the principal cities of the country." One of these dealers, J. H. Batty of New York City, employed at least sixty hunters, who sought birds "along the entire Gulf Coast from Cedar Keys to Key West." According to one hunter, Mr. Batty purchased "almost anything that wore feathers, but particularly the Herons, Spoonbills, and showy birds," at prices that, in 1887, ranged from as little as ten to fifteen cents for the back plumes of the Louisiana heron to as much as five dollars for the entire skin of a roseate spoonbill. Few hunters could resist the lure of these prices, especially when they knew that a good day could yield one hundred birds.[40]

London, Paris, and New York were the major destinations of the plumes, and the demand of the fashion industries in these cities was seemingly insatiable. Maximo Rookery, in Boca Ciega Bay, at the southern end of the Pinellas Peninsula (the peninsula that encloses Tampa Bay, modern-day Pinellas County), offers a dramatic example of the effect that fashion's demand for feathers had on Florida's birds. Scott reported that, when he visited the area in 1881, the birds nested on a group of small islands in the bay, about three miles from the mainland. These islands, "of at least two hundred acres in extent," were separated from one another only at high tide, and they provided a home for "a dense growth of several kinds of mangrove." The birds so crowded the island that "every tree and bush on this large area contained at least one nest," and Scott had "never seen so many thousands of large birds together at any single point."

Of course this large number of birds attracted the attention of plume hunters, and A. Lechevallier, "the Frenchman" in the argot of the plumers, maintained a camp there for "five breeding seasons." At the end of this time, Lechevallier and his men had, "by killing and frightening the birds away," completely destroyed the rookery. So completely had the birds been decimated that, when Scott returned in 1887, he saw "only a few Cormorants, possibly seventy five, and though I spent several hours looking over various parts of the island I found no large birds breeding."[41]

As the numbers of birds declined at Maximo and other easily accessible sites, hunters sought out more remote rookeries, until protective legislation and the changing tastes of fashion all but ended the plume trade in the 1920s. Although the number of birds that inhabited the peninsula is hotly debated, no one doubts that the 129,000 wading birds that nested in south Florida during the 1974–75 season represent but a small portion of the birds that inhabited the peninsula before fashion dictated their demise. Indeed, after hunters were restrained, habitat loss accounted for a second period of population decline that began during the 1930s.[42]

Declining numbers of otters, raccoons, alligators, and water birds meant that the hunters who lived on Okeechobee, too, soon needed other sources of income. A Louisiana Creole couple exemplified this breed. The pair lived on a houseboat, because that vessel offered the most reliable home in a region often subject to storms and floods. During violent weather in 1910 (probably a hurricane), the husband remembered, "me and the old woman clung to a sapling for 32 hours," and their peril was so extreme that, "I prayed for the first time in fawty years." To earn a living, the couple hunted, working more than one hundred otter traps, and the wife bragged that she killed forty-two bobcats in a single season. When fishing offered them the chance to earn a few dollars, they engaged in that activity too. Near their home, the pair maintained a fish pond where live catfish were stored until a commercial fishing boat arrived, at which time the Cajuns killed, cleaned, and sold their fish for the accustomed rate of three cents a pound.[43]

Commercial fishing began on Lake Okeechobee in 1883, soon after the opening of Hamilton Disston's canal between the lake and the Caloo-sahatchee River. At that time, Benjamin Franklin Hall sailed a boat to the lake and began buying all the fish that the district's sparse population could supply. In the early days, fishermen used trot lines and pound nets (actually, a fish trap), but they soon switched to seine nets, to increase their catches.[44]

Four- or five-man crews were required to deploy these nets properly, most of which were between five hundred and one thousand yards long. A seine crew secured one end of the net to a pole, either on the beach or out in the lake, and then the pullboat towed a small rowboat filled with net, usually referred to as the "seineboat," out into the lake until all of the net was deployed. The pullboat then made a great circle that ended back at the starting point, dragging the net behind. When the pullboat arrived, the rest of the fishing crew got into the shallow water and pulled in the net, folding it carefully back into the seineboat, until the fish were all confined to a small circle of net, the "pocket," in the parlance of the fishermen. The pocket was then towed to the holding pond, where the fish remained until the arrival of the runboat, the vessel that transported dressed fish to market, at which time the catfish were killed and cleaned. Each net deployment took, on average, about three hours, and the men usually completed two such operations per day.[45]

Few residents of the lake had the capital that such extensive operations required, and fish buyers soon hired their own crews, although they continued to buy the catches of independents, and even allowed some of these fishermen to live at the company camps. The fish companies paid their hired hands and these live-in independents in different ways. Hirelings received thirty-five to fifty dollars per month, plus board, while the men who lived at the company camp and fished for themselves were paid on a production basis, three cents per pound for cleaned catfish and one cent for scale fish, less the cost of their board.[46]

Blatchley wrote that a typical company-owned camp consisted of "a rough board shack" containing "one long front room with porch in front, and a smaller back room used as kitchen, dining room, and store house." The men slept on "folding cots each of which is overhung at night by mosquito netting," and a cook prepared the camp's food. A typical breakfast consisted of "cream-of-wheat, canned milk, rice, beef stew, hot biscuits and coffee or tea," served "in tin basins from which each helps himself generously," since the men did not receive lunch while working out on the lake.[47]

In addition to housing facilities, the fish camps required one or more skinning shacks located near the holding ponds. Blatchley describes a typical skinning shack as "a crude shelter with sheet iron roof, set on palmetto piling four feet above the water."[48] Here, the fishermen cleaned their fish in assembly-line fashion, and the organization of the work allowed a good hand to skin three hundred pounds of catfish per hour, after gutters cleaned and deheaded the fish.[49] Once the fish were cleaned and skinned, the men shoveled them "into the front hold or icebox of a large gasoline launch," the runboat, where "a third man with shoes on," a rarity among the fishermen, "was in the hold breaking up chunks of ice and jumping up and down on both ice and dressed fish to press them closely together."[50]

Once loaded on the runboats, the fish were transported to Fort Myers, via the Caloosahatchee Canal and River, or to Fort Lauderdale, after the North New River Canal was completed in 1913, where they sold the catfish for five cents a pound. In these cities, the fish catch was loaded onto freight trains and transported in carload lots to such destinations as Kansas City, St. Louis, and Indianapolis, where retailers charged twenty-five to thirty cents a pound for the dressed fish.[51] However, after January 1915, when the Florida East Coast Railway completed its track extension to Okeechobee City, these routes were largely abandoned—periods of low water made canals less than reliable shipping arteries—and the vast majority of the catfish went to the new terminal on the lake's northern shore for train shipment to the rest of the country.[52]

The arrival of this rail line, the first to reach Lake Okeechobee, offers a good illustration of how quickly the area grew once the isolation was broken. When the first train ran in January 1915, the rude pioneer community of Tantie had just been renamed Okeechobee City by the agents of the Model Land Company, the rail line's land sales company, and the community consisted of no more than a handful of log houses and a combination post office and school.[53] But when Isham Randolph visited Okeechobee City in November 1915, only ten months after the arrival of the first train, he found eleven hundred people residing in a town that featured "a bank, electric light and ice plants, and other modern conveniences and comforts."[54]

Similarly, agricultural development on the south shore of the lake could not begin in isolation, and farming did not start in earnest until Moore Haven was established[55] and the Atlantic Coast Line Railroad completed its rails to that city in 1918.[56] Transportation problems were not the only difficulties facing the pioneer farmers on the newly reclaimed muck lands. In spite of the claims of land promoters, disappointment and back-breaking labor more accurately characterized the early years of Everglades agriculture, and it must have seemed to many pioneers that the very land itself resisted human efforts to domesticate it. As one disillusioned pioneer farmer put it, the land companies advised prospective settlers to "take a tent, a bag of beans, and a hoe; clear a few rows in the sawgrass, plant the seed, and in 8 weeks you will have an income," but the reality was that such advice "may have provided income for the land offices, but the settlers found out differently."[57]

New arrivals soon discovered that clearing the land proved much more difficult than they had anticipated. James Bock, who settled near the lake in March 1920, realized that, instead of saw grass, "the growth on the best muck is elder or elder and custard apple," which grew "so dense that it is almost impossible to penetrate it except by cutting a path with a machete." In order to clear this tangle effectively, the pioneer had to "pull up bodily the smaller brush and to cut out the larger roots," a task so arduous that he should plan to clear only "about an acre a week." But clearing presented a more intractable problem than simply investing ten weeks' work in preparing a newly purchased ten-acre farm site—the average-size holding in the district—since, at the end of that time, "there would be a healthy new growth of elder on the first land cleared."[58]

The careful records of labor foreman George E. Tedder, who supervised the work crews during the building of the Florida Agricultural Experiment Station in 1921, provide the most comprehensive record of the efforts required to effectively clear Everglades elder land. In his words, the effort was "much slower work than I thought it would be, but the elders are thick." Indeed, on a typical day, eleven men grubbed the elder from three-quarters of an acre, and Tedder "was satisfied that they all did a good day's work." In order to avoid the regrowth of the stubborn elder, the crews found it necessary to go over grubbed land with a shallow plow—they tried disking, but found it to be ineffective—so that additional roots could be removed.[59]

Saw grass land, too, proved difficult to prepare for agriculture. In the early days, all clearing was done by hand because, as Everglades pioneer Thomas Will wrote, "there was no machinery available, not even a horse or a plow." The first step in the process called for felling the saw grass with a scythe and stacking the cuttings so that they would dry sufficiently to burn, usually in about two weeks. Then, Will continued, "the roots were belabored with a heavy hoe, to cut the long, tough runners, which were then pulled out with a potato hook." These were allowed to dry in place before they, too, were burned. Because the saw grass grew so thickly in the better land just below the elder land, this process "would require one man two months hard work to clear one acre of land."[60] Another pioneer farmer recalled, "One cultivator, devoting his entire time between March and the middle of July—three and one half months or more—prepared one and one third acres."[61]

Uprooting elders and saw grass represented only the first problem in the clearing process because the pioneer landowners had no other choice than to burn the refuse. In the Everglades this presented a severe problem. As James Bock admitted, "I had been told that the muck would catch fire, but I never had an idea that it would be such a job to keep it from burning." Some pioneers sought to avoid this problem by spreading the dried refuse in a thin layer over a wide area, so that the fires did not heat the dried muck enough to allow the ground to catch fire. Others burned their piles in stages, lighting them, then extinguishing the flames, then refiring the remains at a later date, so that the soil would not reach its kindling point. Others advised plowing before a burn, to bring moist soil to the surface, or after the fire, to insure that fires below the surface were extinguished. Still others did both. But, in spite of these precautions, the muck and peat often caught fire in the dry season and burned until the heavy rains covered them with water. In addition, cracks in the dried muck allowed surface fires to penetrate the soil to the shallow water table, where they spread to other districts as smoldering subterranean blazes (see fig. 5.2). Tragically, firing of refuse caused many hundreds of acres to be burned down to the underlying rock. Little wonder that Bock advised that burning was, "from our own experience, about the biggest thing a newcomer is up against."[62]

Nor did the pioneers' troubles end after the land was cleared. The nature of the newly reclaimed muck soils challenged the immigrants' powers of

Figure 5.2. Drying and cracking of Okeechobee peaty-muck in the willow and elder land near Canal Point. These cracks contributed to underground fires. Source: Charles B. Evans and R. V. Allison, "The Soils of the Everglades in Relation to Reclamation and Conservation Operations," *Soil Science Society of Florida Proceedings* 4-A (1942), p. 37.

improvisation. The earliest arrivals to the shore of Lake Okeechobee attempted to use draft animals to ease their intense labor, but the animals soon became mired in still-spongy muck soils unable to support their weight. To meet this problem, local residents fitted their animals with muck shoes—devices similar to oversized steel showshoes. Although these devices proved cumbersome to the draft animals, they did sufficiently distribute the animals' weight so that they did not bog down.[63]

When later residents imported tractors, they found that machines light enough to avoid getting stuck lacked the power needed to cultivate the heavy muck soils, while heavier, more powerful machines became hopelessly mired. After experimenting with numerous tractor designs, some of local construction, residents discovered that the caterpillar-treaded Elgin tractor proved satisfactory. Unfortunately for these farmers, however, the onset of World War I meant that the factory discontinued the manufacture of tractors, and worn-out Elgins could not be replaced until peace brought a resumption of normal production.[64]

Even successfully plowed fields proved troublesome. The drying muck soils caused a variety of inconvenient and sometimes disastrous problems. The pioneer Bock informed potential farm wives that "the 'dirtiness' of the muck" meant that they should expect "a hotel sized washing to be done every Monday or maybe every Monday and Thursday if you have a large family."[65] On a typical day, wrote Blatchley, "if one rides five miles over the roads he becomes so covered with the black dust of the dried muck that he looks like a Negro."[66] Almost incredibly, on exceptionally windy days the erstwhile wetlands experienced miniature dust storms. Labor foreman George Tedder remembered that on such days, with "dry Muck blowing bad," residents "could hardly get out of the house without wearing goggles." To make matters more uncomfortable, Tedder wrote, during these periods, "The dust blew in through closed windows and doors and caused burning when it came in contact with the skin." But windy conditions caused more than discomfort. Winds could damage crops when they blew "dry saw grass into the furrows so bad that the young plants were covered up," or by "blowing the muck from the roots" of some plants, while causing others to be "covered up with dry muck to where no plants could be seen."[67]

In addition to these problems, pioneer farmers discovered that their new land was far less fertile than they had expected. First-year plantings particularly demonstrated peculiar characteristics. If growers planted the standard truck crops—which, along the lake, usually meant beans, cabbage, lettuce, peppers, and corn—the plants emerged from the ground and grew vigorously for a few days, then, mysteriously they turned yellow and finally died.[68] Only new potatoes avoided this fate, although they hardly thrived; one observer described them as "not much larger than an average hen's egg."[69] Similarly, Bermuda grass, considered by many cowmen as the best dairy grass in the South, thrived after its introduction into the muck lands, causing Bock to gush that it "will sod in so thick and grows so fast that 50 cows could feed on a ten acre pasture." Disastrously, however, the cows that grazed on the grass, like truck crops, soon sickened and died.[70]

Although the new settlers did not know it, both crop failure and cattle diseases stemmed from the same source, a lack of trace elements, especially copper, in the apparently rich organic soils of the Everglades.[71] Pioneer growers referred to the mysterious malady as "reclaiming disease." As the name implied, the inability to raise truck crops disappeared after two or three years because, without the knowledge of the farmers involved, the powder they sprayed on potato plants to protect them from insects inadvertently added "blue stone" (copper sulfate) to the plots where they grew. Because potatoes enjoyed a conspicuous success, the acreage devoted to this crop expanded rapidly, and a few crops of potatoes prepared land for other crops. As for the cattle, they had failed to thrive because they, too, needed the trace elements that the district's grasses could not draw from the soil.[72]

Cold weather was another surprise to those who pioneered the reclaimed Everglades. As Blatchley noted, "the nights and early mornings in this extensive muck covered region are much cooler than in the higher sandy areas of southern Florida," and the experiences of the district's farmers corroborated the observation. John Newhouse remembered that when he arrived in the Everglades in 1914, "our party had been in the Glades less than three weeks, when the cold snap struck, and one morning the pump was frozen, and ice lay on a pail of water outside the house." During that winter "there was a frost about every two weeks" between November and the following April, and these cold spells damaged fragile truck crops.[73]

The story of F. E. Plank, who lost his "orange grove in a freeze in February 1917 at DeLand"[74] and sought a new start on Lake Okeechobee's Ritta Island in 1919, offers a good illustration of the effect these environmental difficulties could have on Everglades agricultural pioneers. Like so many others, Plank and his son cleared their land "with hoe and machete," then "piled and burned the custard apple." The islands along the lake attracted most of the earliest settlers, and Plank had been there long enough to clear "quite a good deal" of twenty acres in the manner described when he wrote to William A. McRae, Florida's Commissioner of Agriculture, in November 1919. Plank's land was located in an unsurveyed section—much of the Everglades was, and still is, in this condition—and the settler wanted to insure that he had the first opportunity to purchase the land upon which he lived once a survey was completed.[75] In response, Commissioner McRae told Plank that his land would sell for one hundred dollars per acre and assured him that he would, indeed, have the first opportunity to buy it.[76] By the next month Plank made arrangements with the state to divide the $1,984 purchase price of the 19.84-acre parcel into a down payment of $496 and three yearly payments of the same amount, plus 6 percent interest, and Plank assured the commissioner that he would make the first payment "in a very short time."[77] But Plank's "short time" continually receded.

Plank arranged to borrow against his tomato crop in order to make his down payment, but a frost on 6 March 1920, he reported, "killed every tomato in the neighborhood." Left without a crop or resources, Plank and his son "worked out"—that is, hired themselves out to others—so that they could pay for disking their land, in preparation for another planting. By June, however, Plank had to admit that "my tomato crop is a failure" because "we planted too late and the heat wave has ruined them," and he asked McRae for an additional year to make his down payment, a request which the commissioner granted.[78]

By August 1922, however, things had apparently not improved for Plank. He interested N. E. Drawdy in buying his improvements on the condition that Commissioner McRae would agree to sell the new investor the 19.84 acres for the original price of $100 per acre. But McRae replied that the value of Plank's land had "materially increased since you first applied for it," and the IIF trustees "will not now take less than $150.00 per acre for it." Clearly, the higher price not only ruined Plank's sale but also meant bankruptcy to the struggling pioneer, who, in spite of his back-breaking work and unfailing optimism, did not find a new beginning in this fickle new land.[79]

It was indeed difficult for men of limited means to establish themselves in the Everglades, and the high cost of land represented only one of many expenses. James Bock, the self-described amateur who, in 1920, wrote about pioneering in the Everglades, gave a detailed account of costs he incurred. Having land cleared, imperative if the new arrival wanted a return from the land as quickly as possible, "cost between $30 and $50 an acre." Seed to plant the land depended on the crop, but he estimated the per acre cost at "tomatoes $3, cabbage $5, potatoes from $30 to $50, corn $1, and peppers $5." If the farmer wanted to hire out the planting, Bock continued, "a man and a horse can be hired for $5 or $6 a day"; otherwise, "a good mule will cost about $150 and harness, wagon and implements will cost at least $150 more." Additionally, "every farm should have a good weather proof barn, set well off the ground to protect against dampness and rats," and such a structure "51x30" should cost "not over $700 if made of rough lumber," and "a fairly good crew will cost $100 to $150." In total, farmers were advised that "an expenditure of from $1,000 to $1,500 exclusive of the house, which would depend upon the owner's taste and means, is necessary to equip the farm."[80] All costs considered, then, the prospective Everglades pioneer could expect to spend at least $5,000 to establish a twenty-acre homesite on the newly reclaimed wetlands, a tidy sum in 1920—certainly for an untried venture.

But those who could not afford the total cost of homesteading in the Everglades had other options. During the early days the Everglades old-timer John Fritchey remembered, "most people moved from place to place farming except people who owned the land," and the nonlandowners merely "went out on the islands and ridges and cleared them and planted," because "no one ever knew who owned the land."[81] Others turned to sharecropping, and Herman Walker, another pioneer, remembered a farmer on the South New River Canal who, in 1912, "had a crew of white men working with him on shares."[82]

Knowledge of such conditions attracted a number of poor but ambitious immigrants to the lakeshore, among whom were African Americans. Some arrived aboard the mail boat that regularly traveled between Palm Beach and Clewiston. Blatchley saw one such boat, "its decks piled high with the cheap furniture of several families of Negroes who were aboard."[83] No doubt many of these families were sharecroppers from other areas of Florida and neighboring states, bound for a new start in the pioneer country. These people's agricultural experiences equipped them with just the array of skills that they would need in order to have at least the chance of success with the new land. If most lacked money, the region contained an abundance of work. "Clearing contractors (mostly Negroes)"[84] could earn up to thirty-five dollars per acre for clearing land, and, additionally, most had the skills required to build barns and perform other agricultural labors—all of which were commonly hired out by the farmers of the district. Although many of these black families no doubt suffered the same fate as F. E. Plank, surely others experienced varying degrees of success on the muck lands.

The formidable natural obstacles, numerous farming failures, and considerable economic costs associated with pioneering on the south shore of Lake Okeechobee prevented a population explosion below Lake Okeechobee, but the region did experience steady growth. Although many city dwellers bought Everglades land sight unseen, and some of these people even ventured to try homesteading, at least some of the immigrants had experience with muck soils.

During the mid 1910s, truck farmers had found the edge of the Everglades in the vicinity of Deerfield Beach ideal for their crops. At this location, natural drainage played into the growers' hands. Before the Hillsboro Canal—the last main canal dug by the state—was opened in 1917, "water flowed slowly from the middle of the Glades into the 'spruce ridge' and subirrigated it." (At this time many Floridians referred to sand pine as "spruce pine." The area that these farmers exploited was actually the border between the northern section of the Miami rocklands and the Everglades proper.) This situation created "an almost ideal condition, for the truckers 'followed the water down', planting in the same land as the water seeped." When the Hillsboro Canal "was cut to the ocean outlet," however, "it drained the adjacent land near the coast too much—so as to practically destroy the trucking industry in areas adjacent." The newly arid condition of their farms "tended to induce the truckers so affected to come to Lake Okeechobee for land that had enough moisture."[85] These experienced truck farmers doubtless enjoyed a greater degree of success than did their inexperienced or under-capitalized neighbors, and they helped establish a foothold in the new agricultural area below the lake.

6

Perfecting the Developmental System

During the First World War, the world demand for foodstuffs and other agricultural products fueled a second boom in the Everglades. In the words of Thomas Will, a pioneer settler and land developer, even "without advertising" people were "pouring in here,"[1] but the district's growers faced many difficulties. Truck crops, the staples of Everglades agriculture during these years, were in great demand, but harvesting presented problems for "plenteous" crops with "laborers few."[2] The war also generated a demand for exotic crops such as castor beans, which produced the castor oil that was, at the time, used as an aircraft lubricant, but by the end of hostilities, growers destroyed the trees because their yield had been disappointing.[3] In spite of mixed results, the end of hostilities did not dampen the enthusiasm for Everglades land, and, in the words of the pioneer farmer James E. Beardsley, "farmers flocked into the lake area after the war, seeking cheap, highly productive land, and began the foundation of the commercial vegetable industry."[4]

Howard Sharp, who served as managing editor of the *Palm Beach Post,* was fascinated with pioneer settlement around the lake and gave the area's activities prominent coverage in his newspaper. By 1924, Sharp could no longer abide being away from his interest, and he moved to Canal Point, where he established the *Everglades News.* On the pages of this weekly,

Sharp expressed his strong advocacy for development in the reclaimed Everglades, but he was, in the words of his obituary, "not a booster of the traditional type," which makes his accounts valuable.[5]

Sharp wrote that the war years and their immediate aftermath were favored with good weather: "the distribution of rainfall in the upper Glades in 1916, 1917, and 1918 was ideal." Rainfall during the winter growing season of January, February, and March for these years "was less than an inch and a half," "which is just about right, for a bean crop can be made in 45 to 50 days and tomatoes in 75 to 90." During these years, "rain fell in the summer, when no one wanted to farm; the ground was dry enough in November to put out seed beds, the moisture in the muck being sufficient to carry the crops through to maturity." But these favorable conditions began to change, Sharp recalled. During the postwar period the precipitation increased; "the rainfall totaled 53.90 inches in 1919 and 53.20 inches in 1920," but "the distribution throughout the year spread the water out so no great harm was done." The following year, 1921, "was a relatively dry year, the rainfall being 37.50," and the "lack of complete drainage facilities" continued "being no handicap."[6]

During 1922, the newspaper publisher recounted, the luck of the new Everglades agriculturalists changed dramatically, as "the abnormally heavy rainfall of the summer of that year was piled on the rain of 1921 which fell in the fall," and floods inundated the region around the south shore of Lake Okeechobee. More trouble followed. In 1923, only "a very small acreage of crops" was planted, and the country "was just drying off in 1924," when an October hurricane dropped "19 inches of rain in 3 days," and "flooded the whole country again." These changing conditions proved discouraging to the agricultural pioneers, and, although a few of the more hearty "continued to hang on," others "left by the thousands."[7]

In order to make the Everglades suitable to the needs of commercial agriculture, the region needed effective water control. This man-made system substituted the workings of canals, pumps, and dikes for nature's interactions among rock, water, and fire. Four broad plans directed this conversion. After J. O. Wright's report, which constituted the first of these plans, was discredited, the Randolph report provided the template for the state's revamped reclamation plan. But the devastating hurricanes of 1926 and 1928 forced a reassessment of this second strategy, and in 1928 the federal government stepped in with a new scheme, whose central feature was the construction of a massive levee, the Hoover Dike, around the southern shore of Lake Okeechobee.

Completed in March 1938,[8] this structure insured that the Everglades would never again experience disastrous flooding, but the subsequent drier conditions led to widespread muck fires in the interior and saltwater intrusion into coastal freshwater aquifers. By the 1940s the ills associated with an Everglades that had become too dry were readily apparent, and many experts recommended a more comprehensive system of water control as a solution to the district's ills. In 1948, the United States Army Corps of Engineers responded with the fourth Everglades reclamation plan—the *Comprehensive Report on Central and Southern Florida for Flood Control and Other Purposes.* This report incorporated the Kissimmee River basin into the Everglades reclamation project and provided the outline for the modern configuration of water control structures in peninsular Florida.[9]

Ever more complex, these strategies were also ever more expensive. In the end, the cost of effective water control within the Everglades Drainage District (EDD) was simply beyond the means of the district's residents to pay. After 1927, taxpayers who lived outside the EDD were required to help finance the Everglades developmental system. After the hurricane of 1926, the Corps of Engineers took virtual control of water-control projects in the Everglades, and the largesse of the federal government paid the cost of these works. By 1947, when drainage taxes were abandoned as the primary source of income for the EDD, any pretense that increased land values within the district could pay for the cost of reclamation became a memory.

Drainage in the Era of the Randolph Plan, 1913–1928

After its submission in 1913, the Randolph report provided the nominal master plan for the state's effort to reclaim the Everglades. In reality, however, lack of adequate funding severely hampered its execution. In practice, the reclamation effort during the 1910s and 1920s represented little more than an uncoordinated effort to meet problems on an ad hoc basis, and lack of money limited even these reactive responses. Indeed, by the end of the 1920s, the state-sponsored program was at a standstill.

The flooding during the early years of the 1920s established the need for more comprehensive water management in the Everglades, and commercial agriculturalists looked hopefully to the as yet incomplete St. Lucie

Canal for such control. The major innovation of the Randolph report, this canal, proponents believed, would control the overflow of Lake Okeechobee by providing an outlet to the Atlantic Ocean for the water that entered the lake from the north. Funding for the construction of the St. Lucie Canal proved elusive, however, because the state could not sell any of the $6 million in bonds authorized by the 1913 legislature. By 1915, the bonds were still unsold, but the IIF trustees nonetheless managed to reach an agreement with the Furst-Clarke Construction Company to begin dredging on the control canal. An exercise in creative finance, this agreement called for the contractor to accept "small monthly cash payments and notes of the Drainage Board, secured by drainage district bonds for the remainder."[10] To reduce costs, the revised plan decreased the size of the canal and eliminated construction of a power plant.[11] Opened in October 1926, the month following that year's devastating hurricane, the economized canal proved ineffective during the even more destructive hurricane of 1928.

Instead of constructing the ambitious system of additional main canals called for in the Randolph plan, state officials contented themselves with deepening the existing system, portions of which represented little more than ditches dug through the muck that rested on the limestone bedrock. To correct this situation, blast boats were required. Because deepening the canals meant excavating solid rock, blast boats preceded the dredges, bored holes in the rock, inserted sticks of dynamite, and broke up the limestone so that the steam shovels could remove the shattered substrata. Such an effort was slow going and consumed large sums of money that the state found increasingly hard to procure.

To compound the expense, engineers advocated construction of locks and dams in the main canals—namely, the Miami, North New River, South New River, Caloosahatchee, and Hillsboro canals. These control structures were required because, during periods of low water, the canals often reversed their flows, propelling water into Lake Okeechobee rather than into the Atlantic Ocean or Gulf of Mexico. Between 1913 and 1927, thirteen major control structures were completed at a cost of $1,835,648.62.[12]

In addition to this construction, in 1921 the EDD began erecting a dike from Moore Haven to Ritta, along the southern shore of Lake Okeechobee. Although drainage had lowered the lake from its normal level of about 20 feet to a level regulated at between 14 and 17 feet, subsidence of the organic soils along the southern shore had been 4.6 feet.[13] Reclamation had, in effect, not altered the relationship between the lowered lake level and the new surface of the adjacent land. This condition allowed the old blind rivers of the lake's southern shore to function in much the same way as they had in the predrainage system; that is, they continued to flow when the lake level rose to sufficient height. In the words of the pioneer John Newhouse, "There were many old rivers, sloughs and creeks through the lake shore ridge where water could flow through onto the land when the lake water was at a high stand."[14]

All these projects were expensive. To meet this need, the legislature authorized successive issues of new bonds, until, by 1927, the indebtedness of the EDD stood at more than $17 million.[15] Because these bonds were secured by the drainage taxes assessed on real estate within the district, the end of Florida's land boom in 1926 and the subsequent decline in property values spelled trouble for the entire financing scheme.

In addition to the debt of the EDD, there were additional bonds issued by the various subdrainage districts within the Everglades. Authorized by the drainage act of 1913, the first such district, the Palm Beach Drainage and Highway District, was founded in 1919. By 1926, the EDD had six additional subdrainage jurisdictions. By 1928, these subdrainage districts had spent a combined total of more than $2.5 million on water-control works, including a number of high-capacity pumps, mostly financed by bond issues.[16]

When the hurricane of 1926 passed over the lake, it devastated the area and rocked the already shaky enterprise of reclamation to its foundations. Because the St. Lucie control canal was not yet complete, the residents of the lakeshore were forced to rely on their dike and pumps to prevent flooding. The dike had previously failed during a storm in 1924. Since then, however, it had been enlarged and strengthened, and lakeshore residents now believed the new structure would hold. Irregular in height and constructed mostly of sand and muck, the enlarged levee proved no more reliable than had its predecessor, and water breached the structure in numerous places.[17]

Moore Haven suffered severe flooding after the dike burst. John S. Cottrell, the superintendent of the Disston Island drainage district, supervised the operation of the district's two pumping plants. Although these pumps could move 360,000 gallons of water per minute, they were unable to avert tragedy at Moore Haven. Two days before the storm, Cottrell toured the lake and observed that it stood at nineteen feet, only eighteen to twenty-four inches below the crest of the levee. The drainage superintendent told his assistant, "If we have a blow, even a gale, Moore Haven is going under water."[18]

The events of the next few days confirmed Cottrell's fears. When the winds began in earnest, the dike gave way, allowing a fourteen-foot wall of water to tear through the town of Moore Haven. As the dike began to cave in, at about 7 A.M. on 25 September, Cottrell left the lakefront for his home. By the time he arrived, the water was "about waist deep" in his yard, and he attempted to move his furniture and cars to the higher ground of a nearby road. As the water continued to rise, however, houses began to float by, and Cottrell's wife decided that it was time to flee to the relative safety of a nearby brick schoolhouse. Carrying two of his children through "water about breast deep," Cottrell managed to get them to the school, but, battling the current, he took two hours to return. When he arrived back at his home, he was forced to carry his wife to the road because the water "was over her head in the yard." Returning to the house, Cottrell gathered up his oldest daughter and youngest son and made yet another crossing of the flooded yard. Once on the road, Cottrell gave the girl to her mother and carried his son in his arms, "and we started back to the schoolhouse."[19]

The family traveled "about a block and from there on all the buildings on the storm side had been washed away." As soon as they left the protection of the remaining buildings, Cottrell related, "we were swept off the street" and "my wife was torn away from me." With his son, Cottrell "rolled over and over, part of the time above the water and part of the time under." When they finally came to rest against a displaced house, Cottrell dove under water so that he could enter through the submerged door frame, and he and his young son found refuge in the rafters of the partially submerged structure.

By two o'clock that afternoon, the eye of the storm passed, the wind direction changed, and the water level dropped. As soon as the water was shallow enough, Cottrell and his boy left the house and proceeded to the school, which they found empty; "then, of course," he realized "that my folks were gone." The next day, the bodies of his wife and daughter were found fifty feet from the road, and Cottrell took what solace he could from the thought that "they were probably drowned immediately."

Cottrell was not the only one who suffered personal losses. The sub-drainage superintendent recalled that survivors "buried 18 bodies" that first morning, and "from then on it was continuous." From his knowledge of the inhabitants of the area, Cottrell estimated that "at least 300 lives were lost," even though "lots of the bodies will never be found." In the aftermath of the tragedy, the state commissioned yet another reassessment of the troublesome reclamation project.[20]

In the politically supercharged climate of the postdisaster Everglades, however, the membership of this board generated heated controversy. Howard Sharp led the charge. On the pages of his paper, he accused the State of Florida of appointing a board that was sure to minimize the state's culpability in the making of the recent disaster. In Sharp's opinion, Fred Elliott, the state chief drainage engineer who had replaced Wright, had been allowed "to select the jury to try the case against him," and Sharp insisted that the board should have been selected without the engineer's knowledge. In spite of these objections, the board remained unchanged, and the state set about investigating the tragedy.[21]

The IIF trustees' charge to the 1927 Everglades Engineering Board of Review (EEBR) was threefold. First, the trustees wanted the EEBR to reassess the plans made by the Randolph Commission. Specifically, the Board of Review was to consider if the Randolph plan presented a proper course of action, and, if so, the trustees wanted to know if the reclamation activities since 1913 "have followed the Isham Randolph plan or not." Second, in response to widespread complaints about the performance of Chief Drainage Engineer Fred C. Elliott, the trustees wanted an evaluation of his competence. Finally, the EEBR was instructed to provide the trustees with "any and all information that you think would be needful and helpful in final drainage and reclamation of the Everglades."[22]

The EEBR's report found that the EDD, under the direction of Elliott, had indeed used the Randolph report as a general guide in Everglades drainage construction work, and the board gave the chief engineer a vote of confidence, despite the tragedy that had only recently taken so many lives.[23] As for future plans, the EEBR offered extensive changes in the state's master plan, based on "study of more accurate and extensive data, not available to the Randolph Commission, including the results of years of actual experience with the drainage works."[24]

The new plan, the third in fewer than twenty years, endorsed existing modifications to the Randolph plan and offered further suggestions for changes in the state's overall reclamation strategy that amounted to nothing less than a repudiation of the 1913 study. Specifically, the board's recommendations for further drainage-canal construction completely scrapped the Randolph report's canal system. In the place of long, diagonal canals running north and south, the EEBR advocated digging shorter canals that flowed west to east and emptied into the Atlantic Ocean[25] (see figs. 5.1 and 6.1).

More significantly, the board, for the first time, acknowledged the environmental difficulties that continued to dog the reclamation project, noting that "numerous observations have been made of subsidence of the Everglades." The rate of subsidence, they correctly maintained, depended on "the degree of drainage furnished the lands, the extent of occupancy and agriculture, the control of the ground water table, and the control of fires." As an example of expected subsidence, the report cited an area near Moore Haven, where, in a total of fifteen years, thirteen devoted to agriculture, subsidence amounted to "approximately 45 per cent of the original depth of the soil." Because such subsidence "may be expected to develop as a natural process under conditions of drainage and reclamation," the board suggested that, in the future, "advance provision in the design of all Everglades main drainage canals shall be made for subsidence of peat and muck soils to the extent of 3 feet below existing levels where the existing thickness is 6 feet or more."[26]

These bland admissions of fact contained a profound truth—the creation of the long-hoped-for agricultural cornucopia in the reclaimed Everglades meant the destruction of the very resource upon which the dream rested. Although "the data indicates that the rate of subsidence decreases through a period of years," the board did not hazard the opinion that such soil loss would ever stop completely. Indeed, every indication was that it would not. With little fanfare, soil loss became the salient factor in the minds of those who thought seriously about the long-term future of the region, and for the first time, an environmental consideration had found expression in a state plan.[27]

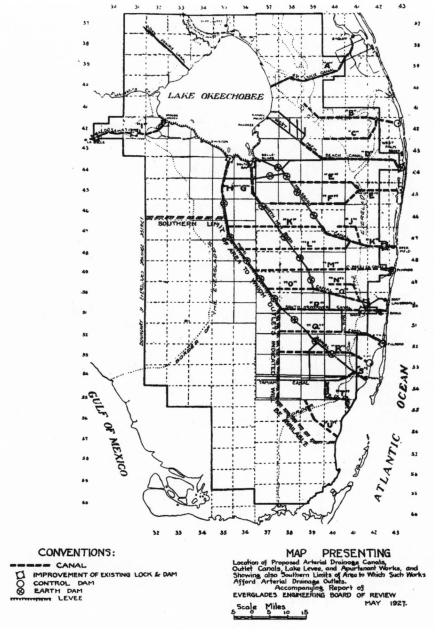

Figure 6.1. Canal system proposed by the Everglades Engineering Board of Review. Source: Anson Marston, S. H. McCrory, and George B. Hills, *Report of the Everglades Engineering Board of Review to the Commissioners of Everglades Drainage District* (Tallahassee: T. J. Appleyard, 1927), fig. 2.

The Corps of Engineers, 1926–1947

The EEBR's report was not the only study of the Everglades reclamation effort that grew from the damage engendered by the hurricane of 1926. The United States Army Corps of Engineers, too, studied the problem, and, after a reluctant beginning, the corps became the dominant player in Everglades reclamation. Like the state effort, federal attempts at water control in the Everglades suffered from parsimonious funding, but the greater wherewithal of the national government finally succeeded in creating a successful agricultural region in the erstwhile wetlands.

Americans have debated the proper role of the federal government in the funding of internal improvements since the earliest days of the republic. By the 1920s, the public attitude toward federally funded public works was in flux, but the thinking of those who advocated a more active role for the national government was coming to the fore. Still, tradition proved difficult to overcome, and conservatives occupied many positions of authority. Major General Edgar Jadwin, the head of the Corps of Engineers, held to the conservative line.

Even before the hurricane of 1926 Florida Congressman Herbert Drane tried to induce the federal government to get involved with south Florida's flood-control problems, but the Fort Myers Democrat had little success. In December 1924, Drane introduced a bill that called for a Corps-of-Engineers survey of the Caloosahatchee River to determine if deepening the river's channel could help alleviate seasonal flooding. Congress subsequently authorized one thousand dollars for such a project, but the corps maintained that the sum was not sufficient to accomplish the project. During the next congressional session, the authorization was increased to forty thousand dollars, but the corps claimed the appropriation had been misplaced, and it had not started the project when the hurricane of 1926 devastated much of the lake's southern shore.[28]

Although the extensive property damage and loss of life caused by the 1926 storm did prod the corps into action, its completed report recommended no federal action. Indeed, even after a round of public hearings in the Everglades, General Jadwin did not view a federal role as appropriate until after "the resources of the local interests and the State of Florida have been exhausted." And, even then, the corps chief advised Congress that the national government's role should be confined to works that played a "direct connection with navigation."[29]

By the time General Jadwin appeared before the Congress in 1929, however, almost five months had passed since the mammoth hurricane of 1928 churned through the Everglades. Even more destructive than the storm of two years earlier, this hurricane took more than two thousand lives and caused property damage over a more widespread area than had its predecessor. The physical devastation and human suffering prompted a change of opinion on Jadwin's part, and the general finally endorsed an active role for the federal government in the construction of flood-control works.

On 31 January 1929, Jadwin presented Congress with a three-part plan that discarded drainage in favor of flood control. First, he proposed increasing the depth of the Caloosahatchee River so that the stream could become a second control canal for Lake Okeechobee, and he also recommended expansion of the St. Lucie Canal, the existing control structure. Next, the general proposed dredging the channel of Taylor Creek and building a short section of dike around its mouth, so that the north-shore town of Okeechobee would not again experience flooding such as that which accompanied the 1928 hurricane. Finally, the plan called for building a much larger levee along the lake's southern shore.[30]

The planned works pleased the residents of the Everglades, but Jadwin's projection of costs gave them pause. The general, still a believer in local effort, projected a total cost of $10,740,000, and he projected that the state would pay $6,740,000, or 62.5 percent of the total.[31] In light of the financial situation in Florida, it seemed unlikely that the state would be able to raise its share.

In response to a torrent of criticism engendered by the Everglades disaster, Governor John W. Martin (1925–1929) had convinced the state legislature to pass yet another drainage law during its 1927 session. Among its proposals was the provision for the collection of an ad valorem tax on the district's real estate in the event that the drainage tax did not generate enough revenue to pay for new water-control works. But the hurricane of 1926 had marked the end of south Florida's land boom, and the district's taxpayers were in no mood to pay additional taxes. Accordingly, suits were filed in both federal and state courts, and a ruling by the federal district judge at Pensacola prohibited the sale of the new drainage law's bonds.[32]

The federal court ruling made the probability that the State of Florida could secure the more than $6 million called for in General Jadwin's plan seem extremely remote. Indeed, Everglades drainage operations had been suspended since June 1927, and the prospect of no further money from the sale of bonds caused the IIF trustees to institute further belt-tightening within the EDD. By July 1928, the financial crisis became so severe that even the EDD's clerical staff was cut to a minimum.[33]

The suspension of drainage operations in 1927 meant that, in a strictly business sense, Everglades reclamation had failed. Even the district's most ardent boosters admitted that growth within the EDD had failed to pay for the developmental system required to support agriculture. But the prestige of business logic suffered greatly in the years following the stock-market crash of 1929. Amid the economics of hard times, the federal government became more willing to spend money for public works, and this translated into an ever-diminishing state share of the new project's costs. In the end the State of Florida paid $500,000 in cash and supplied rights of way worth $800,000 for a project whose total cost was $19,145,000.[34]

Except for a short distance of levee built on the north shore, designed to protect Okeechobee City from flooding, all these works were designed to allow human control over the amount of water Lake Okeechobee could contribute to the Everglades. The improved output abilities for the Caloosahatchee and St. Lucie canals meant that the lake's level could be controlled during the normal yearly cycle of rainy and dry seasons, while the much larger levee prevented catastrophic overflows when the area was subjected to severe storms. After completion of the flood-control project, the main drainage canals had only precipitation and such irrigation water as farmers along Lake Okeechobee's shore sent south to drain. For the first time, total reclamation of the Everglades appeared to be a real possibility.

A Too-Dry Land, 1938–1948

Although early boosters, such as Napoleon Bonaparte Broward, viewed drainage as the solution to south Florida's problems, it soon became apparent that a desiccated Everglades created new concerns even as the old dilemmas disappeared. These new problems fell into three classifications: muck fires, soil subsidence, and saltwater intrusion. To the dismay of drainage advocates, the removal of the Everglades' surface water threatened the viability of the very land that drainage created, and the emergence of these new problems forced them to discard flood control for a much more complex program of water control.

Engineers lacked the requisite expertise to solve many of these new problems, and, for the first time, experts from other fields contributed to south Florida's reclamation project. Three organizations, in particular, contributed heavily to the emerging policy of water control: the Soil Science Society of Florida, the Soil Conservation Service of the United States Department of Agriculture (USDA), and the United States Geological Survey (USGS). Although the Corps of Engineers still constructed the required water-control works, its designs drew on the knowledge gathered by soil and water experts.

Advice from these sources was not always welcomed in the Everglades. During 1915, the USDA sent a team of three soil scientists into the Everglades to take soil samples along the route of the North New River Canal. The party's instructions directed the soil scientists to take core samples from both sides of the canal "on lines projected at right angles from the canals at each milepost, one at 300 to 1,000 feet from its bank, a second 1 mile out, a third 2 miles out, and in some cases a fourth 3 miles distance."[35] Based on these samples, the scientists classified 85.7 percent of the soils along the North New River Canal as "peat," either "brown fibrous" or "black nonfibrous," and they offered the opinion that "peat soils have everywhere been found difficult to utilize for agriculture," with the result that "the peat soils of the world have remained largely unutilized."[36] This judgment "was no water for the land agents' mill," John Newhouse remembered, and "a howl went up when this report became known," until "the report was hushed and soon disappeared from circulation."[37]

As drainage became more effective within the Everglades, however, the advice of such experts became more welcome. When the 1915 team of soil scientists surveyed in the vicinity of the North New River Canal, drainage was still incomplete. Indeed, they reported that in "68 per cent of the area" with peat soils, "the water table lay at the surface or the land was under water to a maximum depth of 38 inches."[38] As the Everglades became drier, however, problems with fire and, later, soil subsidence began to become obvious to even the most ardent booster, and the advice of soil experts became much desired.

Fire offered the most dramatic evidence of the adverse environmental

consequences of drainage. The organic soils of the Everglades were susceptible to burning when they became dry enough, and the occurrence of
muck fires were widespread throughout the region. The lowering of Lake
Okeechobee, John Kunkel Small wrote, exposed "several hundred yards of
new weed-clothed lake bottom," and the lack of water allowed fires to
transform "the once magnificent verdure" of shoreline hammocks into a
scene with "dead giant cypress trees, standing desolate, or prone in the
wholly or partially burned humus where once had thrived an almost impenetrable mass of ferns and other herbaceous plants." On the north shore
of the lake, the delta of the Kissimmee River presented a "doleful story"
because "the hammock and the humus there have been burning for years,
the heaviest rains having failed to extinguish it."[39]

Fires occurred in the Everglades Trough as well. John Kunkel Small again
related that he often encountered "small rocky reefs isolated in the Everglades," which "indicated the position of former hammocks" where only
"bare ragged rock" remained on sites that had once contained "shrubs and
trees growing in the accumulated humus."[40] As evidenced by an eyewitness
account, fires amid these hammocks often assumed peculiar forms. On
hearing that Paradise Key, the most storied of the Everglades Keys, was
again on fire, two interested naturalists hurried to the scene. When they
arrived, "very little flame could be seen," but the curious men discovered
that they "could not stand still, for the earth was so hot that our feet could
not stand the heat." The pair examined a downed royal palm and discovered that "to our surprise the trunk was not burned"; rather, "the soil and
roots had burned away, and only a smoldering hole was left." Later, the
naturalists witnessed "whole segments of the tree canopy," their roots
burned away, "sink down and finally rest on the ash-covered surface." By
the time the flames abated, "the fire actually consumed vegetation and
soil," leaving behind nothing but "a thin layer of ash, charcoal, and un-
burned trunks, limbs, and leaves."[41]

Small's observations also offered examples of areas where the soil had
burned away. In other fire-ravished areas, he wrote, "where the roots of the
big cypress trees were once buried in humus so spongy that one could walk
in it only with difficulty," repeated burnings had left the root systems exposed, "anchored only in sand, and one could crawl and even walk through
the network of once subterranean branched roots."[42]

During particularly dry years, fires often posed hazards to agricultural and residential areas. In February 1932, for instance, so much muck was aflame that the Board of County Commissioners in Dade County sent telegrams to Governor Doyle Carlton, in which they informed the governor that "Everglades fires are menacing this section," and that they were already destroying "the most fertile agricultural soils in the world." A Dade County private citizen gave the same warning, informing the governor that "dense smoke from glades fires has completely enveloped the entire western portion of the county for past four nights," causing "my family and hundreds of people I know to be suffering from its effects," and much "soil destruction" was occurring on "these valuable lands." During the same year, fire threatened agricultural land along the southern shore of Lake Okeechobee, and residents wired the governor, reporting burning "for the past several weeks," causing "an alarming amount of damage to the good lands around the lake," and prompting a United States Sugar Company executive to importune the governor for "any assistance that you can lend to this situation."[43]

The governor's answers to the entreaties of county officials, corporate officers, and private citizens were always the same. Although "the last session of the legislature passed a resolution authorizing the use of certain moneys to extinguish fires then existing," the governor explained, such an authorization did not pertain to "fires of later origin." The governor went on to acknowledge that although "an old statute" placed "at the disposal of the governor a sum of money for flood drainage," the law was mute "with reference to fires." This extremely narrow interpretation of governmental power insured that the state remained aloof from the crisis, and the fires were still burning in May, when residents of the Miami rocklands reported that "for several days past the people of this part of the state (Hollywood) have been unable to see the sun on account of the great amount of smoke that is in the air," and all this "without any apparent effort being made by anyone to stop or subdue these fires."[44]

As dramatic as these fires were, however, their damage represented but a small fraction of the soil loss that occurred throughout the drained wetlands. The organic soils of the Everglades formed under wet conditions in an oxygen-deficient environment. So long as water covered the ground, the bacteria that lived among the plant detritus could not get enough oxygen to

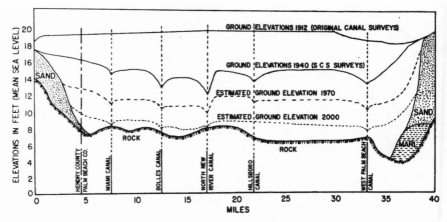

Figure 6.2. Cross-sectional view of the upper Everglades, showing sag valleys around canals. Source: John C. Stephens, "Subsidence of Organic Soils in the Florida Everglades—A Review and Update," in *Environments of South Florida Present and Past II*, Patrick J. Gleason, ed. (Miami: Miami Geological Society, 1984), fig. 2, p. 383. Reprinted with permission.

completely decompose the organic remains, and soil accumulated. Once the water was removed, however, there was no more barrier to oxygen, and bacteria were able to reverse the process of soil formation. The warm climate of the Everglades insured that these bacteria were extremely active, and biochemical oxidation of organic soils by microbes accounted for 55 to 78 percent of the soil loss within the Everglades region. At a 1950 experiment site, this soil loss amounted to 6.8 feet since 1912.[45]

The subsidence attributable to the biochemical action of bacteria is directly correlated with the level of the water table, whether or not the land is farmed. That is, regardless of the plant cover, the mere absence of water insures that the area's soils will deteriorate, and those losses have averaged about one inch per year since the inception of effective drainage. This correlation with the water table is clearly illustrated by the existence of sag valleys along the banks of canals, where these areas, the first sections of the Everglades to experience effective drainage, subsided more than the surrounding wetlands, which remained inundated for a longer period (see fig. 6.2).

Additionally, subsidence within the Everglades followed a pattern. In the years following the initiation of drainage, soil loss was quite rapid. But, since the loss of soil decreased the region's hydraulic gradient, after about five years the rate of subsidence became much slower because the lowered land surface provided only enough fall for sluggish water flow within the canals. Ironically, the land on the canal banks, which had attracted most of the early agricultural activity, now became reservoirs for runoff from surrounding lands that were now higher because they were not, at first, effectively drained. Faced with increased flooding and inefficient drainage, farmers created subdrainage districts, which installed pumps, and, again, the rate of subsidence increased, as drainage became more effective (see fig. 6.3). These patterns of subsidence did much to convince thoughtful experts that drainage was not an unmitigated boon and energized the search for a better long-term approach to reclamation.

Saltwater intrusion into coastal freshwater wells represented the third adverse effect that resulted from the dewatering of the Everglades Trough. Like problems associated with the district's organic soils, well contamination began soon after drainage became even partially successful. One of the city of Miami's early well fields was located along a creek that ran through the Spring Garden Golf Course, about three miles from Biscayne Bay. Before drainage, these shallow wells—which, at eighteen to thirty feet deep, were just deep enough to penetrate the water-bearing limestone—

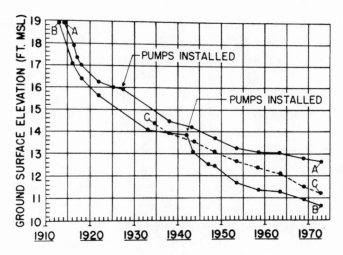

Figure 6.3. Sequence of subsidence in the Everglades. Source: John C. Stephens, "Subsidence of Organic Soils in the Florida Everglades—A Review and Update," in *Environments of South Florida Present and Past II*, Patrick J. Gleason, ed. (Miami: Miami Geological Society, 1984), fig. 2, p. 383. Reprinted with permission.

flowed without pumps. By 1919, however, these artesian wells had not only stopped flowing but also had experienced saltwater intrusion, as the loss of fresh surface water allowed water from the Atlantic to flow up the creeks at high tide and penetrate the porous limestone strata along its banks.[46]

The city responded to this early crisis by simply moving its well fields further inland, but, by 1938, more than one thousand of those wells too had become salty. Municipal officials then appealed to the USGS for help with the saltwater-intrusion problem, and the service dispatched a team of scientists, among whom was the geologist Garald Parker. By the next year Parker and the other scientists set about studying the substrata of south Florida. Parker found that wells at Coconut Grove and Coral Gables were being contaminated with salt water, and he soon became convinced that this water was entering the aquifer from underground. The removal of surface freshwater, coupled with pumping it from below ground, allowed heavier salt water to enter the porous limestone strata from below and intrude into the cones of depression created by the well field's pumps.[47]

In order to establish an encroachment pattern, Parker drilled rows of wells about a quarter of a mile apart, beginning on the coast and proceeding inland. What he discovered had serious implications for future water-use planning in south Florida. The shallow aquifer that supplies the Atlantic coastal cities' drinking water, named the Biscayne Aquifer by Parker, extended down only 90 to 180 feet "in an undulating depth, becoming shallower away from the shore." A 400–500-foot-thick layer of "heavy, thick, sticky, green clay," the Hawthorne Formation, marks the bottom of the aquifer. Referred to as an "aquiclude" by hydrologists, this impenetrable layer of clay separates the Biscayne Aquifer from a still deeper strata of water-bearing rock, the Floridan Aquifer. Parker found, however, that the water from this deeper strata was highly mineralized and was unsuitable for either domestic or irrigation use—in a word, nonpotable.[48]

This situation meant that the cities of south Florida's Atlantic coast had no other source of drinking water than the Biscayne Aquifer. Using the Ghyben-Hertzberg principle, which states that each foot of freshwater above sea level will displace forty feet of salt water in coastal strata, Parker determined that, in order to avoid saltwater intrusion into this source, the freshwater table had to be maintained at 2.5 feet above sea level.[49] He believed that this water table level could be established by building saltwater-control dams near the mouths of the canals that drained the vicinity of

Miami, and—with the cooperation of Miami, Miami Beach, Coral Gables, and Dade County—these works were constructed. Designed to maintain a 2.5-foot water table upstream of their locations, these dams insured that the well fields in the vicinity of Hialeah and Miami Springs could supply the metropolitan Miami area with as much as 90 million gallons of water per day.[50]

Comprehensive Water Control Begins in 1948

Construction of these dams marked the first time that scientifically determined realities dictated the construction of water-control works in the Everglades. It would not be the last. The loss of organic soils, both the dramatic and the mundane instances, concerned the residents of the reclaimed Everglades deeply. The agriculturalists who hoped to harvest wealth from the bounty of the district's organic soils found themselves faced with a conundrum: the Everglades could not be farmed unless drained, but that drainage led to the destruction of the very resource they sought to exploit. This irony led to another reassessment of the entire reclamation project, a reassessment that ultimately converted all of the Everglades into components of a developmental system.

A better understanding of the properties of the Everglades' water, soils, and bedrock had to be developed before answers could be found to the complex questions that confronted the district's residents. Garald Parker and his team developed the first real understanding about south Florida's groundwater, and they, and a host of other investigators, went on to supplement this knowledge with information about the region's surface water, soils, and bedrock.

The Soil Science Society of Florida played a crucial role in these enterprises by providing a forum where the new knowledge could be spread from the scientific community to the state's political leaders. Formed in 1939, the society noted the problems of the Everglades in the first issue of its *Proceedings*. In it, Dr. R. V. Allison, the president of the society and the head of the University of Florida's Everglades Agricultural Experiment Station, addressed what he viewed as the threefold problem of Everglades conservation.

Of the 2–3 million acres of organic soils in the Everglades, Allison estimated that only about 100,000 acres were actually in cultivation. These farmed acres represented the first problem of conservation. Allison urged that "we need to know more about the effect of cultivation" on soils being actively farmed so that the effect of "water control conditions involved in various systems of agriculture upon the permanence of the soil material" could be assessed. Secondly, Allison urged rewatering of undeveloped areas of organic soils so that "destruction of many of its most important natural features" could be avoided. Finally, Allison wanted to insure that "the recharge action by surface water" was restored "to the west of the metropolitan sections of the lower east coast" so that these areas would be assured adequate supplies of freshwater.[51]

When Allison addressed the Soil Science Society, the prospects for solutions to these problems appeared bleak. Not only was there a dearth of knowledge about the physical nature of the Everglades Trough, but also the bankrupt EDD lacked funds to implement changes in water-control structures. By the early 1940s, however, this situation changed, as scientific knowledge accumulated, and the EDD, at long last, settled on a refinancing plan that made it solvent.

Negotiations between EDD officials and representatives of the Reconstruction Finance Corporation (RFC) began in 1937, but disputes over the amount that bondholders would accept for their securities delayed a final settlement until 1941. In June of that year, the RFC agreed to refinance the EDD's debt of some $17,000,000 for $5,660,000, a settlement that assured old bondholders a return of fifty-six cents on the dollar. After 1941, the district was free to turn its attention to the concerns related to the over-drainage of the region.[52]

In the aftermath of the debt refinancing, the Soil Science Society provided an invaluable forum for the state's political and scientific leaders. During the 1940s, the society's annual meetings allowed scientists to apprise the state's political leaders of the newly acquired knowledge about south Florida's hydrology, geology, and soils, and Florida's political leaders exhibited a keen interest in the activities of the society. The most active of those political leaders, Florida's Secretary of Agriculture, Nathan Mayo, gave the keynote address at the 1942 session and actively participated in the 1943 meeting. Additionally, Mayo arranged a meeting between delegates from the society and Florida's governor and cabinet at Tallahassee in 1943, where the future plans for, and new knowledge about, the Everglades dominated the agenda.[53]

This exchange of emerging scientific knowledge led to the formation of a new consensus about the proper course for the restoration project's future. Abandoned was the notion that the entire Everglades Trough could become productive agricultural land. In the Everglades, the new consensus held, only soils that were five feet deep could be successfully developed, and these soils amounted to only approximately 435,000 acres in the district.[54]

In the words of John C. Stephens, a USDA drainage engineer from the Fort Lauderdale office, "the general rule is: good, deep agricultural peat—tight, relatively impermeable rock; shallow, nonagricultural peat—open permeable rock."[55] One such region of open permeable rock, containing only shallow, nonagricultural peat, lay in the southeast Everglades. Happily, this region bordered the Miami rocklands, where saltwater intrusion threatened the water supply of Florida's heavily populated lower east coast, and reflooding this district would help insure the 2.5-foot water table required to keep the ocean water out of the Biscayne Aquifer. To this end, the new consensus called for the construction of a system of levees that would create three interconnected reservoirs in Dade, Broward, and Palm Beach counties. Connected by gated spillways through the levees, these reservoirs (later usage, in deference to environmental sensibilities, termed them "conservation areas") allowed for containment of runoff from the area north of the West Palm Beach Canal, the Everglades agricultural area, and some flood discharge from Lake Okeechobee.[56]

Within the agricultural area, where soils were suitable for agriculture, a unit plan of development would be implemented. Water control would be accomplished by the construction of a canal network connected to eight pumping stations on the perimeter of the system.[57] The spoil from this canal-digging was used to create a system of dikes that would, in effect, divide the agricultural area into a system of zones, and the pumps would allow these zones to be either flooded or drained, as the need arose. In this way, the zones not actually in agricultural use—and only about 100,000 acres of the potentially productive 435,000 acres were being farmed in 1942[58]—could remain flooded, and their soils would not be destroyed needlessly.

As with any plan for such far-reaching change, the new consensus drew political opposition. The most effective of these opponents was Ernest Graham. Graham had come to Florida in 1921 to manage the operations of the Pennsylvania Sugar Company. Shallow soils and inadequate water control doomed the firm's efforts to grow sugar on the edge of the Everglades, just west of Miami, and, when the company failed in 1926, Graham gained control of their property. In the following decades, Graham built a thriving dairy business on the erstwhile sugar lands.

Graham's first concern was for his land. He claimed to see danger to his own land in the plan to control south Florida's water sources, and he was, in the words of an unnamed *Miami Herald* reporter, "spearheading an attack in Tallahassee against a bill whose purpose is to protect the state's fresh water supply."[59] As USGS hydrologist Garald Parker recalled, "In order for his dairy cows to keep their feet dry and prevent hoof rot, he had to have dry land," and the recommended 2.5-foot water table "did not allow his dairy to thrive."[60] In order to oppose the new water-control plan more effectively, Graham formed an alliance with two other large south Florida landholders, Sam Collier and John Lykes, and their faction nearly succeeded in abolishing the EDD at the 1947 session of the Florida legislature.[61]

Such powerful opposition could not, however, deny environmental facts, and the hurricane-driven floods that inundated south Florida in September and October of 1947 meant victory for those who advocated the new water-control strategy. Because the drainage canals allowed increased runoff from the northern Everglades, these floods affected the populous southeastern coast—Fort Lauderdale and suburban Miami were particularly hard hit—and the people involved demanded relief. Accordingly, the 1948 Corps of Engineers report, the *Comprehensive Report on Central and Southern Florida for Flood Control and Other Purposes,* incorporated urban flood control into preexisting plans for soil and water conservation, and the document heartily endorsed the new strategy of comprehensive water management (see fig. 6.4).

The *Comprehensive Report* linked the Kissimmee River to the Lake Okeechobee–Everglades Trough and, along with the Caloosahatchee River, considered all these waters as part of the same drainage area.[62] Beginning in the north, the plan called for the installation of control structures in, and channelizing of, the Kissimmee River. Because these works would accelerate discharge into the lake, the corps recommended expanding the lake levee so that it would completely encircle Okeechobee and enlarging the St. Lucie Canal and the Caloosahatchee River, so that, even with the greater discharges, these structures could maintain an acceptable lake level.[63]

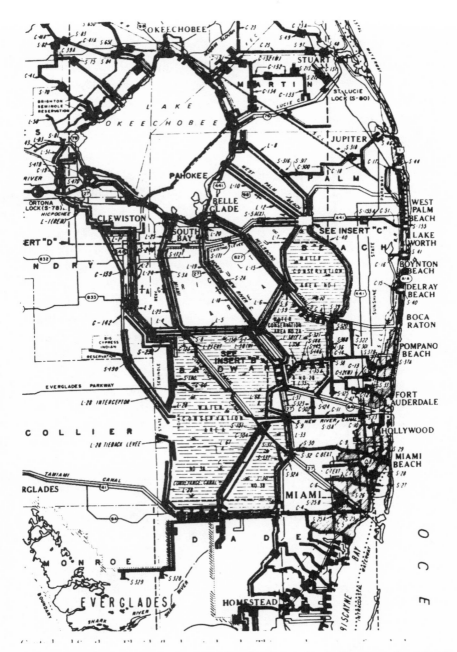

Figure 6.4. Water control system proposed in the *Comprehensive Report on Central and Southern Florida for Flood Control and Other Purposes. Summary of the Central and Southern Florida Flood Control Project Showing the General Plan of the Federal Project for the Control of Floods and Other Weather Conditions in the Basins of Streams and Lakes in Southeastern Florida,* Water Survey and Research paper no. 4, August 1950 (Tallahassee: State Board of Conservation Division of Water Survey and Research, 1950).

The corps also endorsed the division of the Everglades Trough into agricultural and water-storage areas. In the agricultural area, the *Comprehensive Report* maintained, "water control would be accomplished by the construction of a canal network connected by eight pumping stations on the perimeter of the system." In addition, three interconnected reservoir areas totaling about fifteen hundred square miles were to be constructed below the agricultural area. The lake, agricultural, and reservoir areas actually formed part of an integrated system, the corps maintained, because the agricultural area could "dispose of excess run-off" by "pumping from the canal network into the lake and/or the conservation area to the south."[64]

The conservation areas were, in reality, little more than sumps, and they were expected to provide relief from the two biggest concerns to south Florida's urban east coast: saltwater intrusion and flooding. According to the corps's report, the impoundment of water in these areas would "prevent their flowing eastward and flooding the developed areas along the coastal ridge" and would also "raise the ground water table and improve water supply for east-coast communities" by preventing "salt-water intrusion in the east-coast water supply well fields." Additionally, the system of levees that formed "the eastern boundary of the conservation area is the major feature for protection of the east coast" from future floods.[65]

The plan also proposed building a levee parallel to the Tamiami Trail, westward to the Collier County line, then northward to the western end of the agricultural area's rim canal. Gated spillways in the Tamiami Trail levee would allow for release of unusually large quantities of water to the south, and, hence, virtually eliminate the possibility of flooding in south Florida's agricultural or residential districts (see fig. 6.4). Taken as a whole, the corps's plan seemingly offered the possibility of real water management for south Florida, and contained features tailored to please every interest in the region.[66]

Even though the corps's plan overrode the wishes of Graham and his allies, these large landholders' desires still found expression in the funding plan for the vast project. Under the new plan, the State of Florida was responsible for 18 percent of the construction costs (some of these costs were rights of way rather than cash) as well as for the expense of maintaining the water-control works,[67] and rural interests did not want those costs allocated on the old benefit tax formula—that is, a graduated acreage tax. On 14 May 1949, at the Okeechobee County courthouse, delegates from the eighteen south Florida counties affected met to discuss financing. At this meeting, Ernest Graham and his coterie of large landholders proposed an ad valorem tax as a replacement for the traditional graduated acreage tax. After much discussion, delegates from fifteen counties accepted this proposal, and the state legislature subsequently enacted such a tax during its 1949 session.[68] This change meant that urban taxpayers would bear the burden of financing water control and was a tacit admission that the economic expectations of early drainage boosters were false—Everglades reclamation had failed as a self-sustaining project.

During the same session, the Florida legislature abolished the Everglades Drainage District, and replaced it with the Central and South Florida Flood Control District.[69] The new district's enlarged boundaries allowed it to exert the centralized authority over water policy so often called for by advocates of the new water-control program. The combination of centralized authority and a water-management plan based on a sound understanding of the physical realities of the Everglades finally opened the door to a prosperous commercial agricultural system in the restructured wetlands. Finally, the dreams of Buckingham Smith, Hamilton Disston, Napoleon Bonaparte Broward, and countless others could be realized.

7

The Fruits of Development

Despite early hopes that the reclaimed Everglades would prove ideal for small-scale farms, the Everglades Agricultural Area (EAA) became the home of large-scale commercial agriculture. Government policy played an active role in this outcome, and the success of Everglades agriculture was firmly grounded in indirect government subsidies. Effective water control, paid for in large part by city dwellers, represented the most important indirect government aid that the district's farmers received. Additionally, both the state and federal governments provided additional benefits to area growers when they underwrote the scientific research that was required before the fertility of the reclaimed muck soils could be utilized.

Considered together, however, these government benefits resulted in only a modest degree of success among the district's commercial growers. Indeed, it was not until after Fidel Castro came to power in Cuba that the EAA entered its current era of prosperity. After the United States imposed an embargo on all Cuban goods, sugar became involved in the dynamics of the Cold War, assuming the status of a strategic material, and the EAA became increasingly devoted to growing cane. Beginning during World War II, the federal government established a system that guaranteed sugar growers access to cheap offshore labor, and this arrangement assured them abundant profits from their newly expanded cane acreage. Such guarantees made sugar growing in the Everglades among the most profitable of agricultural enterprises and encouraged the creation of huge agricultural empires.

The engineering system that came to fruition after the flooding of 1947 insured the eventual success of commercial agriculture in the reclaimed Everglades. Yet the region's farmers still had three other major obstacles to overcome before their prosperity was assured. First in importance was the task of understanding the fertility of the muck soils. The district's pioneer farmers had long ago recognized that these soils, although undoubtedly rich in organic components, still lacked all of the elements required to turn the reclaimed lands into an agricultural cornucopia. Earlier generations of American agricultural settlers selected land based on its plant assemblage; that is, they knew that hardwoods, for instance, grew on soils that would support the crops they intended to grow. This strategy broke down in the Everglades, however, where the unfamiliar flora greatly reduced the value of traditional agricultural knowledge. In order to overcome the problems of inexperience, both the federal and state governments built agricultural research facilities in the Everglades, and the knowledge these facilities gathered greatly benefited the commercial growers.

The second obstacle arose from the promotional methods that had been used to sell land in the Everglades. A family could make a prosperous life for itself on ten acres of muck soil, the agents boasted, but their statements had little connection with the reality of Everglades agriculture. Of the thousands who bought these small tracts of land, only a relative handful attempted to farm their land. Among these wary pioneers a scattered few actually succeeded. But the land remained as it was sold, chopped up into thousands of small plots, much of it abandoned, and back taxes were owed on nearly all of it. The farmers who actually worked the muck lands knew that for their ventures to succeed, these holdings had to be consolidated.

The consolidation occurred in two episodes, one for sugar lands and another for truck farms. During the mid 1920s, Bror Dahlberg bought up small plots along the lake's western and southern shores. The first large-scale commercial agricultural operation in the Everglades, Dahlberg's Southern Sugar Corporation eventually gained control over more than 100,000 acres of reclaimed muck lands. The second spate of consolidation began in 1937, when the state legislature enacted the Murphy Act, and came to fruition after the 1941 session enacted legislation designed to bring reclaimed land back onto the tax roles. Taken together, these pieces of legislation allowed the district's vegetable growers, who were concentrated around the lake's southeast corner, to increase their holdings, although no single vegetable grower dominated this industry in anything like the way Dahlberg's firm controlled sugar.

Finally, the region's commercial growers required laborers, a commodity always in short supply around the lake. Both of the agricultural enterprises that prospered on the muck, raising vegetables and growing sugar, demanded large numbers of seasonal workers to insure their success. To attract sufficient workers, the district's farmers appealed to black sharecroppers from neighboring districts and states, and these appeals were largely effective, because Florida's growers needed labor during the winter months, when the sharecroppers were idle.

In spite of their similar needs, however, the labor procurement strategies of the vegetable and sugar growers soon assumed very different paths. For their part, the vegetable growers were able to rely on the vagaries of the free market to supply their labor needs. As vegetable fields came into widespread production in south Florida, they offered work to sharecroppers, many of whom were being displaced by the agricultural depression of the 1920s and by the Agricultural Adjustment Act's attempts to limit cotton production during the 1930s. Although south Florida's growers needed these workers only during the winter, the former sharecroppers soon discovered that they could patch together a living if they were willing to migrate north during the summer, picking various crops as they ripened, and return to the Everglades for the winter season.[1]

This east-coast stream of migrant labor, however, did not serve the sugar growers as well as they had hoped. The grueling nature of the work and the extreme regimentation large-scale sugar producers imposed on their workers made the cane fields a destination that knowledgeable field laborers carefully avoided. In order to attract sufficient numbers of cane cutters to south Florida, the sugar growers turned to the federal government, first to the United States Employment Service, and later to the Immigration and Naturalization Service. The Employment Service supplied workers from areas of the southeast where people were innocent of Everglades sugar-cropping practices. By 1942, however, the coercion that characterized workers' lives on the plantations led to United States Sugar's indictment for peonage. Although the charges were later dismissed, the threat to their labor supply deeply concerned U.S. Sugar's management, and, after the United States became involved in World War II, the company was able to convince the federal government to import workers from the Caribbean to replace the domestic workers who had, until then, cut the cane. This system proved so beneficial that, after the cessation of hostilities, the temporary labor importation program was reorganized and made permanent. This new program supplied the sugar growers with H-2 workers from the Caribbean until mechanical harvesters made the practice unnecessary in 1995.[2]

The solving of all three problems—soil productivity, land tenure, and labor supply—combined with the water-control works to allow commercial agriculture to prosper in the Everglades. That commercial system was, from the first, driven by the desire to earn a profit. Environmental considerations entered the thinking of Everglades farmers only when such concerns posed a serious threat to their pursuit of monetary gain. The system that emerged, the Everglades agricultural system, remains the single biggest impediment to any attempt to recreate at least a portion of the diverse environmental system that was the Everglades.

Soil Productivity

Pioneer farmers in the Everglades had found that the district's soils, whose treasure trove of organic matter seemed to offer so much promise, were difficult to master. Plants behaved strangely in the reclaimed muck soils. In some fields only recently brought into production, newly planted seeds sent forth young plants, whose apparent vigor pleased growers, but the leaves soon yellowed and the plants quickly died. In other plots, plants grew to amazing size, but they bore no fruit. Such puzzling behavior soon convinced the district's growers that they needed help if they were to overcome the intricacies of these new soils, and the farmers lobbied the state government for the creation of an agricultural experiment station in the Everglades.

In 1913, so beseeched, Governor Park Trammell proposed the creation of such a facility. The Florida legislature did not, however, respond for several years. In 1921, though, a law passed that instructed the trustees of the Internal Improvement Fund to set aside 160 acres as the site for the experiment station and ordered them to provide an annual appropriation of ten thousand dollars for the first two years and five thousand dollars during each of the following years to finance the venture. These appropriations were matched by similar allocations from the state treasury, and with this modest budget, the University of Florida's Everglades Agricultural Station became a reality.[3]

Beginning in 1924, with Director William Newell's experiments, the scientists at the station conducted tests to determine if the copper sulfate contained in Bordeaux mixture, the fungicide that was often sprayed on potatoes, was responsible for the stimulation of plant growth on raw sawgrass soil. During the next year, the scope of the experiment was expanded; the muck soil was treated with a number of common fertilizers, and then half of each sample was dusted with Bordeaux spray. At the end of two weeks, the scientists observed that, regardless of the fertilizer, the plants on the samples that had been sprayed with the fungicide prospered, while those on the plots without the spray died.[4]

These encouraging results led to further experiments in which other minerals commonly used by farmers were applied to a variety of crops, and the results of these applications were compared to similar plots treated with copper sulfate. Although the scientists noted some positive responses on the plots treated with sulfur and zinc, the areas that had received copper sulfate showed by far the best results. Over the next two years these experiments were refined and repeated until, by 1927, the experiment station's scientists concluded that the application of thirty to fifty pounds of copper sulfate per acre eliminated the reclaiming sickness that, until that time, had afflicted agricultural plants planted in raw peat soils.[5]

Announced in the initial report of the new Everglades Agricultural Experiment Station, calls for the application of copper sulfate served as the starting point for further experiments that ultimately resulted in a thorough understanding of the nutrients required to make the muck soils of the Everglades productive. R. V. Allison, one of the coauthors of the 1927 report, worked on refining his earlier experiments by treating plants with a combination of zinc sulfate and copper sulfate. The earlier tests revealed a delay in the response of some plants to application of copper sulfate, while zinc sulfate induced a rapid early growth in the same plants. At the end of six weeks, however, these results reversed themselves, and the plots treated with copper sulfate thrived, while those receiving zinc sulfate withered.[6]

Allison selected peanuts, a crop of commercial value to the region, for his experiments. The scientist reasoned that copper and zinc sulfates, used in tandem, should complement one another; that is, he hoped the zinc sulfate would encourage early growth, and the copper sulfate would facilitate growth after the effects of the zinc sulfate had subsided. Experimental results confirmed his insight. Applications of fifty pounds per acre of copper sulfate and sixteen pounds per acre of zinc sulfate produced peanuts that matured four to six weeks faster than plants receiving only copper sulfate.[7]

Allison's experiments with copper and zinc sulfate offered commercial growers a way to speed up the maturity of their crops, a prime consideration in a district where the climate permitted multiple plantings in a single year, but these tests suggested even greater advantage to growers if they introduced another mineral to their fields, manganese sulfate. Allison found that the application of fifty pounds of copper and manganese sulfate, combined with sixteen pounds of zinc sulfate, doubled the per-acre yield of peanuts when compared to fields where only copper and zinc sulfates were applied.[8]

Further experiments with manganese sulfate provided even better news for south Florida's commercial growers. Farmers who raised tomatoes on muck soils were accustomed to manuring the roots of their plants at planting, and they used, on average, about one ton of manure and three thousand pounds of commercial fertilizer per acre of tomatoes planted. Although farmers did not fully understand the interaction between manure and their tomato plants, they did know that without the manure the crops failed, and they stoically endured the considerable transportation and labor expenses its use entailed.

During the 1926–27 and 1927–28 growing seasons, scientists from the Agricultural Experiment Station began to experiment with manganese sulfate on tomatoes and other truck crops. Their tests showed that all attempts to raise tomatoes on muck soils using only commercial fertilizer failed. When fifty to one hundred pounds of manganese sulfate were added to the commercial fertilizer, however, the tomatoes produced a profitable harvest, without the addition of any manure. In addition, potatoes, beans, cabbages, cauliflower, carrots, beets, and corn profited from the application of the mineral. In summary, the experiments proved that Everglades peat soils lacked manganese and demonstrated that this deficiency could be corrected with the addition of either a ton of manure or fifty to one hundred pounds of manganese sulfate per acre. Given the relative costs, commercial growers were quick to abandon the manuring process and embrace the new method with its cost-cutting advantages.[9]

The addition of these three minerals—copper sulfate, zinc sulfate, and manganese sulfate—made commercial agriculture a profitable enterprise on the reclaimed muck soils of the Everglades, and further research did the same for cattle raising. Although the reclaimed Everglades supported luxuriant growths of forage crops, cattle did not thrive in the district; instead, they developed an ailment that locals referred to as "salt sick," a disease characterized by diarrhea, weight loss, growth retardation, and delayed sexual maturity.[10]

Cattle that suffered from this ailment refused normal feed, preferring to eat dry weeds that no healthy cow would touch, and some were even seen to eat such bizarre objects as clay, sand, and rags. In light of the earlier discoveries, scientists suspected that salt sick, too, was caused by mineral deficiencies, and they pursued this line of research from the beginning of their investigation. They soon discovered that the grasses that grew in the mineral-deficient soils of the Everglades were, themselves, lacking in certain minerals. Among the missing elements were iron and copper, both crucial to the development of healthy cattle. The investigators subsequently advised livestock owners that they could eliminate salt sick if they would feed their cattle a blend of twenty-five pounds of red oxide of iron, one pound of finely ground copper sulfate, and one hundred pounds of salt.[11]

Within a decade of its founding, the Everglades Experiment Station paid big dividends on the state's rather modest investment. Early studies provided the knowledge that vegetable growers needed to avoid the soil infertility traditionally associated with bringing new land into production, and later research provided the information these growers needed to improve yields on these acres. After the hard times associated with the nadir of the Great Depression in the early 1930s, south Florida's commercial agriculture flourished—thanks, in large part, to the contributions of the station's scientists.

Land Consolidation, 1920–1940

Sugar producers began consolidating land on the shores of Lake Okeechobee in the early 1920s. In 1920, a group of investors founded the Moore Haven Sugar Company and opened a small mill at Moore Haven. Although this firm was undercapitalized and quickly failed, the dream of growing sugar on the reclaimed muck persisted. In the summer of 1921, a better financed group bought four thousand acres and hired Anthony McLane to assess the potential for raising sugar on the newly acquired real estate. McLane, who had vast experience in both Louisiana and Cuban sugar, heartily endorsed the investors' ambition. By 1923, the new firm, the Florida Sugar and Food Products Company, opened a mill and began the commercial production of sugar.[12]

Ill-prepared to confront unfamiliar soils and inadequate water control, the Florida Sugar and Food Products Company, too, experienced financial reverses and was purchased by Frank W. Bryant with money he made from the development of the city of Lake Worth. Bryant renamed the firm the Southern Sugar Company, but he owned the enterprise only until 1925, when Bror Dahlberg assumed control. Dahlberg's primary interest was in Celotex, a wallboard made from bagasse, the waste product of sugar grinding, but when Dahlberg could not secure an adequate supply, he decided to raise sugar for himself and profit from both enterprises.

In the words of Everglades pioneer Lawrence Will, Dahlberg's arrival inaugurated the time when "the sugar company gobbled up the land so that there was no place left to farm."[13] Indeed, by 1929 the Southern Sugar Company controlled more than 100,000 acres along the western and southern shores of the lake, and even though this firm failed in 1931, its land holdings remained intact when the company's major stockholder, C. S. Mott, acquired all of Dahlberg's holdings.[14] Mott renamed the new firm United States Sugar, and by 1940 this company's extensive holdings produced an astonishing 86 percent of the sugar grown in the Everglades.[15]

Unlike sugar cultivation, where consolidation of land holdings occurred during the 1920s, Everglades vegetable production remained a very haphazard, small-farm industry well into the 1930s. From pioneer days, farmers had always known that tender vegetables grew best along the southeast corner of the lake, where that body's water ameliorated the effect of approaching cold fronts. As a result, truck farmers were concentrated in this district. Many growers, however, did not live there year-round; instead, they arrived in the fall, raised a crop or two, and departed as spring approached. These suitcase farmers, as they were called, usually rented their land, but some simply planted their crops on acres whose ownership was uncertain. Even among those who did reside in the region, few owned all of the fields they cultivated, because of the abundance of readily available land whose owners had either abandoned it or lived at such a distance that they remained ignorant of how their real estate was employed.

As the Hoover Dike made water control more reliable, however, the potential value of these lands increased. The farmers who grew truck crops on them became more concerned about clear titles, an issue that became more pronounced after 18 June 1936, when the Everglades Drainage District (EDD) began refinancing negotiations with the Reconstruction Finance Corporation (RFC). To secure a loan, the EDD had to convince the RFC that there was enough taxable real estate in the district to insure repayment, but with 95 percent of the land in arrears on those taxes for an average of eleven years, the EDD found it difficult to be persuasive.[16]

The state legislature hoped to bring these lands back onto the tax rolls by allowing current property owners and those interested in acquiring additional tax-delinquent lands an easy way to do so. Passed in 1937, the Murphy Act directed Florida's county clerks to advertise tax certificates on tax-delinquent lands for sale to the highest bidder. This law required only a three-week notice of such a sale, and it further directed that the purchasers of such certificates were free of all delinquent state and county tax levies.[17] Taking advantage of this opportunity, resident owners purchased tax certificates on their own land and cleared them of back taxes. In addition, these resident farmers purchased hundreds of ten- and twenty-acre tracts along Lake Okeechobee's southeast corner at very modest costs when absentee owners failed to place bids.

Laymond M. Hardy, an Everglades pioneer who was seventeen in 1937, recalled that his father asked him if he wanted some land. When he replied that he did, his father purchased ninety-two acres of the tax-delinquent land for his young son. Because neighbors made it a policy not to bid against each other, the purchase price was only forty-three dollars. This transaction was not exceptional, according to Hardy. The vast majority of the land acquired under the auspices of the Murphy Act went to Everglades residents, rather than to speculators, at prices similar to those paid by the elder Hardy. Overall, during the 1930s, the number of tenant farmers declined and the number of growers who owned their farms increased 241 percent.[18]

The Murphy Act relieved the district's property owners of state and county levies but not of drainage taxes. Assessed to pay for a series of bond issues authorized between 1917 and 1925, the highest rate of this tax was $1.50 per acre, and many landholders argued that the charge was unfair because it had been set during the boom conditions that existed only briefly. Indeed, amid the economic hard times of the Great Depression, most of the district's farmers owed more in back drainage taxes than their land was worth. Even those who could have paid, such as U.S. Sugar, refused to remit the drainage tax, arguing that the defunct EDD no longer maintained the water-control works within its jurisdiction.[19]

But the Everglades Drainage District Bond Holders Protective Association was determined to receive the bond revenue. The Everglades Drainage District had defaulted on its bonds on 1 January 1931, and, the next day, H. C. Rorick began organizing the association. Rorick ultimately succeeded in having 87 percent of the outstanding bonds deposited with his committee, and this organization kept state and EDD officials mired in litigation throughout the 1930s.

At this juncture, the newly elected governor, Spessard Holland (1941–1945), intervened. During March 1941, Holland arranged a meeting in Thomasville, Georgia, with representatives of the bondholders protective association, which he attended with his cabinet. Taking a hard line, Holland berated Rorick's ten-year practice of "negotiating with one hand and litigating with the other" and assured the bondholders' representatives that he had no intention of continuing this practice. In Holland's words, "I'm a fellow who wants to either negotiate or litigate, but I'm not going to do both at the same time. Let's get together. If you don't want to negotiate, we'll litigate till hell freezes over."[20]

Holland's approach brought a quick settlement. The RFC agreed to loan the bankrupt EDD $5,660,000, to be secured by refunding bonds, which were, in turn, supported by a revised drainage-tax structure. This refinancing scheme provided the bondholders with a settlement that amounted to 56 percent of the face value of their bonds, an amount they found acceptable, and the new drainage tax law that was passed by the 1941 session of the Florida legislature lowered the acreage tax on most land within the EDD. Additionally, this law provided that all delinquent drainage taxes could be settled by paying not more than two years' assessment at the new rate. New landowners—that is, those who purchased their property under the auspices of the Murphy Act—owed only one year of drainage tax. For Laymond Hardy, the young owner of ninety acres, this meant that he paid, at most, $181 for his real estate—quite a bargain.[21]

This generous settlement provided the second crucial ingredient for the success of commercial agriculture on the reclaimed muck soils. When coupled with the discoveries of the Agricultural Experiment Station's scientists, access to inexpensive farmland greatly enhanced the likelihood of financial success for farmers in the reclaimed Everglades. Only one problem remained for the hopeful commercial growers, that of ready access to inexpensive labor. Once again, government action provided crucial aid in overcoming difficulty.

Labor

The black southerners who entered the Lake Okeechobee region, so full of hope, soon had their expectations dashed. Many of these new arrivals were erstwhile sharecroppers from Florida and neighboring states. As such, they could ill afford to weather the environmental vagaries that plagued the district during the early years. Even when their dreams of land tenure were crushed, however, they, and their brothers and sisters, continued to come to the Everglades. They did this not because the new district's prospects were so good; rather, they came because the world of the cotton sharecropper was such a horror.

The growers on the muck needed labor only seasonally, but they paid cash—a commodity so scarce in the cotton belt that even the most meager wages attracted impoverished southerners. During the agriculturally depressed 1920s black southerners seized the opportunity, but during the Great Depression, whites replaced them, as economic hard times became more general. The agricultural dislocations of these decades forced many sharecroppers from their land and pickers became migrants, as field hands struggled to make ends meet by following the crops up the eastern seaboard. The migrants picked vegetables and citrus in Florida during the winter, then moved on through the Carolinas to Virginia and the truck farms of New Jersey, following the harvest season northward, until they ended their trek in upstate New York.[22]

In Florida, fruit and vegetable growers had little trouble attracting the harvest labor they needed, but such was not the case on the sugar-cane plantations. Zora Neale Hurston, who grew up in Eatonville, Florida, an all-black town located in what is now suburban Orlando, was among the many hopeful young blacks who made their way to south Florida in search of cash and adventure. Hurston depicted her experiences in a novel, *Their Eyes Were Watching God.* In Hurston's fictional account, a young couple, Tea Cake and Janie, decide to travel to the muck lands to work the harvest. Because Tea Cake was experienced with the region, he informed his lover, "You can always git jobs around heah in de season, but not wid de right folks." The couple took advantage of his knowledge and arrived at Lake Okeechobee's shore early enough to insure themselves jobs picking beans, avoiding the hated sugar cane.[23]

Much of the basis for Tea Cake's preference lay in the nature of the work itself. Although any field work is onerous, the demands of cane cutting require a combination of strength and endurance that few possess. Cutters must stoop low to cut the cane as close to the ground as possible, then rise so that they can chop the leaves from the tops of the plants and stack the clean stalks. Because this process is repeated thousands of times during the course of a workday, cutting cane exacts a great toll on backs and arms. Another significant hazard was the risk of cuts, or even blindness, from the cane's sharp leaves. Indeed, modern cutters prefer to wear two pairs of pants and layers of long-sleeved shirts, in spite of the south Florida heat, so that they will be protected from the leaves.[24]

In addition to the physical demands and dangers, the prospective cutters faced other problems. Large fields demanded that workers be organized into gangs, a mode of work much despised among black field hands since the end of slavery, and the huge acreage in cane required that the labor force remain in place for several months. In the vegetable fields, by contrast, pickers were paid a piece rate, based on individual effort, and the smaller scale of the operations insured that no harvest lasted more than a few weeks. As a result, migrant laborers could pick crops such as beans or tomatoes on as many small farms as they pleased, then return home whenever they wanted, without incurring the displeasure of their employers.

In the cane fields things were quite different. When sugar growers hired harvest hands, they forced them to pay certain expenses. Typically, cutters were charged $4.50 a week for board, $1.00 for a cane knife, and a $1.00 deposit for both a blanket and identification badge; all charges were paid in advance. Because most of the newly hired men were broke, the U.S. Sugar Company advanced each man $12.00 so that he could pay his charges and have some money left over for discretionary spending. Because many of the cutters were recruited from out of state, they also owed the sugar company for their transportation, which, in the case of one young man from Tennessee came to $15.44. Although travel charges were refunded if the cutter completed the harvest season, that debt as well as others was credited against future earnings.[25]

These charges were crucial to the sugar company's plan to maintain an adequate labor force for the entire season. State laws made legal the practice of withholding employees' earnings until such debts were paid. Two laws came into play here. The first made anyone guilty of a misdemeanor who, with intent to defraud, obtained an advance of money in exchange for an agreement to render services. The second made the mere failure to perform the services prima facie evidence of intent to commit fraud. In the cane fields, this meant that any cutter who quit his job before his debt was completely paid was guilty of a crime, and the pay practices of the sugar producers insured that the debt was not repaid quickly.[26]

Although the sugar company promised a wage of $3.00 per day, this rate took effect only after an undetermined length of time working for a daily training wage of $1.80. In the case of the cutter from Tennessee, this meant that he owed the wages for his first fifteen days of work—certainly not an unreasonable length of time for a training wage—to the company before he even entered the fields. But the cutter's problems did not end there because his board accumulated at the rate of $4.50 a week, and at the end of his first fifteen days, he still owed the company more than $13.50.

Still other practices helped to pull the harvest hands further into a quagmire of debt. In some camps the superintendents sanctioned illegal gambling and the sale of bootleg liquor, and they offered pay advances to workers who wanted to gamble or drink, adding to the cutters' debts.[27] Those who tried to leave the camps before their bills were paid had no other option than escape, because leaving while in debt was a crime. Often these escapees were taken into custody by the county sheriff—there was even a special black deputy empowered to police the movements of black citizens in Clewiston—and they were held until their employers paid their fines— creating an additional debt of $23 to $25.[28]

Such practices earned sugar growers a bad reputation among local blacks, and they were forced to search ever farther afield for their harvest hands. When U.S. Sugar advertised for one hundred cutters in Fort Lauderdale in 1932, the company received only two applicants, even though the offer came during the nadir of the Great Depression. According to a letter writer to Florida governor Doyle Carlton, this lack of interest stemmed from the common belief in the local black community that the sugar camps offered conditions "worse than the chain gang,"[29] and another wrote that payday brought only "an empty envelope or one with a few cents in it."[30] One former cutter remembered that his first payday consisted of $1.31, and added that "the next pay days I only drew small amounts."[31]

To aid them in their search for field hands, the sugar growers turned to the United States Employment Service, which recruited workers throughout the South. As workers began to experience the injustices and brutalities of the sugar camps, however, complaints about these conditions became more widespread. FBI offices in Birmingham, Memphis, Miami, Jackson (Mississippi), and Charlotte (North Carolina) received complaints from parents concerned about the welfare of their sons, and agents conducted investigations into their allegations.

As the complaints mounted, the press picked up on the story and gave wider publicity to the cutters' plight. When James Bates, Willie Bell, and James Butler staggered into Atlanta "ragged, unkempt, and exhausted," the Southern News Service put their story on the wire. The three young men had been recruited in Arkansas, along with three hundred other young black men, to cut cane in Florida, and they still carried a recruitment brochure that, reporter Charles W. Greenlea recounted, "carried pictures of carnivals, barbecues, and weekly entertainments for workers and gave the impression that a cane cutter's life was one of comfort and luxury." Once in Florida, however, the men complained that they worked from dawn to dusk under conditions of intimidation, and they asserted that their strenuous labor only left them "owing the boss for expenses." Discontented with their lot, the men fled the camp at Clewiston and hitchhiked to Atlanta, where the Travelers Aid Society helped them return to Arkansas.[32]

On 4 November 1942, the steady stream of complaints and rising tide of publicity finally resulted in U.S. Sugar's indictment for peonage at the federal district court in Tampa. The indictment's two counts charged that the firm's personnel manager, M. E. Von Mach, and three camp supervisors—Evan Ward McLeod, Oliver H. Sheppard, and Neal Williamson—combined to deprive the company's harvest laborers of rights guaranteed by the Thirteenth Amendment. The first count consisted of twenty instances of illegal beatings and intimidation, while the second, the peonage charge, maintained that Neal Williamson forcibly returned three cutters to the plantation at Miami Locks following a failed escape attempt.[33]

In April 1943, federal judge Fred Barker dismissed all the charges in the indictment, ruling that the grand jury had been improperly impaneled because its members all came from Hillsborough County, only one of the thirteen counties within the district.[34] Although Barker's ruling saved the sugar corporation embarrassment, its executives knew that the days of enforced labor were numbered. The United States Supreme Court had already struck down Alabama and Georgia laws that were similar to Florida's fraud statutes, and the case of Immanuel Pollock, a Florida farm laborer who alleged that he too had been held in a state of peonage, was working its way through the courts.[35]

Weeks before his ruling, however, Judge Barker's decision was rendered moot. On 16 March 1943 an intergovernment agreement was signed that authorized Bahamian workers to enter the United States for the purpose of agricultural employment, and a similar agreement was reached on 2 April that allowed the entry of Jamaicans. Because wartime conditions limited shipping and tourism, unemployment was high in the Caribbean, and men from the region eagerly accepted the jobs offered in the United States.[36]

The ready availability of imported agricultural laborers pleased Florida's growers for two reasons. First, they obtained the labor they needed during a time of maximum demand, and, second, the employment of offshore workers promised a continuation of labor control to which the state's farmers were accustomed. L. L. Chandler, the chairman of Dade County's United States Department of Agriculture War Board, offered the bluntest appraisal of this aspect of the new labor arrangement. While negotiations were under way, a number of options were explored, including moving domestic workers to Florida from other areas of the country and importing labor from Puerto Rico. Chandler opposed further attempts to harness domestic labor, because "there is no way of forcing such labor to work either effectively or regularly." As for Puerto Rican workers, Chandler believed that the same judgment applied, because, since they came from a U.S. possession, they could not "be deported and sent home, if it does not work."[37]

Between 1943 and 1947, the United States government played a direct role in negotiating employment contracts for offshore laborers and paid the cost of round-trip transportation for all workers between their homes and the United States. These contracts insured that all alien workers received adequate housing and medical care. Additionally, the imported workers were guaranteed at least thirty cents an hour, and they were given the added assurance that they would never be paid less than Americans who performed the same labor. To reassure American workers, the government promised that alien labor would neither displace any native employees, nor adversely affect the wage scale. Although not without flaws, the temporary labor program worked well enough, and its scope was eventually widened from the agricultural sector to include any industry benefiting the war effort.[38]

On 31 December 1947, the U.S. government withdrew as an active participant in contract negotiation. The years 1948–1951 were a period of transition between a wartime emergency program and the emergence of the system that lasted, at least in the cane fields, until 1995, when U.S. Sugar discharged its last twelve hundred Caribbean workers.[39] The Immigration and Nationality Act of 1952 provided the basis for the modern system, and the term "H-2 worker," often applied to Jamaican cane cutters, originated with the sections of the law that defined temporary nonimmigrant workers.[40]

The H-2 system lasted so long because it handsomely met the harvest requirements of the cane fields. In a typical year, Florida's sugar growers recruited a much larger number of workers than their needs demanded—only about one-third of the men who passed the rigorous selection process were hired—and the remainder provided a ready pool of prescreened applicants eager to replace any of the cutters found unacceptable during their stint in Florida.[41] The ready availability of replacements made the sugar growers intolerant of even the slightest breach in discipline. During a 1986 incident at the Okeelanta Corporation, for example, workers who were protesting their pay found themselves confronted by law-enforcement officers of the Florida Highway Patrol and the Belle Glade Police Department. Police dogs were set on the protestors after "it started getting real verbal and they would not let one of the supervisors out of his office near the barracks," and, the following day, three hundred of the protestors were deported. When the disturbance was over, all parties agreed that the protest would have no adverse affect on the sugar harvest, because, according to Florida Rural Legal Services attorney Rob Williams, Florida's sugar companies "have an unlimited number of workers no matter what they do."[42]

Although the ready pool of replacement workers made protests relatively harmless, two other policies made any expression of grievances unlikely. First, the cutters knew that any worker sent home for any alleged violation of contract would never again work in the cane fields, and most of these men wanted to be able to work for more than one season.[43] Their contractual pay agreement represented the second impediment to the free expression of discontent. Like their predecessors in the cane fields, H-2 workers' pay was subject to deduction for the cost of transportation, but this money was refunded if the cutter completed the harvest season. In addition to this deduction, however, money was withheld for a number of other reasons. Employers also withheld five dollars a day for meals, while 3 percent of wages went directly to the employees' home governments to defray the cost of administering the H-2 program, and 23 percent of each worker's pay was retained in the form of enforced savings. When any worker was judged in violation of his contract, therefore, he knew that his employer had ready access to the money in his savings account, and charges for transportation and other debts often consumed this hard-earned cash.[44]

In such circumstances, the sugar companies were guaranteed a more compliant work force than could be recruited from domestic labor. The strong arms and backs of these Caribbean cutters insured that the cane would be harvested in good time, at a predictable cost. Although not a direct subsidy, governmental guarantees of ready access to foreign contract labor played a crucial role in the profits enjoyed by Everglades sugar producers.

Everglades Agricultural Area, 1950 to the Present

The combination of effective water control, enhanced soil fertility, and abundant labor allowed commercial agriculture to flourish in the Everglades. By the 1950s the EAA provided a profitable home for growers of winter vegetables and sugar cane, as well as for stockmen who fattened their cattle on the luxuriant growth of grasses that thrived wherever the plows did not go. But this diversified system underwent a considerable simplification after 1961, when relations between the United States government and Fidel Castro soured, and, since that year, sugar cane has come to dominate the EAA, in terms of both acreage planted and profits earned.

In large measure, government subsidies account for the expansion of sugar-cane growing in the EAA. Every attempt by the residents of the Everglades to finance effective water control failed. Only after the federal government intervened and spread the cost of water-control works to taxpayers outside the district was Everglades agriculture able to prosper. Although this intervention did not favor sugar growers more than other farmers in the district, other federal programs did. The H-2 program, the offspring of wartime emergency, provided the sort of easily controlled labor pool that sugar growers wanted. Similarly, federal price supports for domestic sugar insured that the cane, once cut, would yield a guaranteed profit. Taken together, these federal programs created the sugar growers' land, provided them with reliable labor, and guaranteed their profits.

Cane growers continually assert that the nation's sugar policy does not cost the taxpayer any money, but this is only partially true. The direct subsidy that these growers receive from the government does, indeed, come in the form of a loan, and these loans are always repaid, with interest. But the money that the sugar growers use to settle their loans is derived from American citizens, if not in their role as taxpayers, then in their role as consumers of sugar.

The domestic sugar program is a complicated system. United States sugar producers, both those who grow beets and those who grow cane, are guaranteed eighteen cents a pound for sugar. Every year, the federal government loans these producers money based on this price, with the warehoused sugar as collateral. But sugar-program import quotas insure that growers will receive more than the base price for their sugar—twenty-two cents during the 1993–94 season, for example—and this higher price allows sugar growers to repay their nine-month government loans with money to spare.

This loan program does not cost the federal treasury any money. Indeed, the 4 percent interest that the sugar growers pay on their loans means that the program actually turns a profit, but the difference between the world market price of sugar and the domestic price comes from the pockets of every American with a sweet tooth. The 1993–94 world market price of sugar was eleven cents, but experts agree that this was artificially low and estimate the price would rise to seventeen cents a pound if the world sugar trade were freed of all restrictions. The difference, then, between the American domestic price of sugar and the price of sugar in a system of free trade is five cents, and this difference translates into huge profits for Everglades cane growers. The largest single beneficiary receives more than $64 million in excess payments because of this artificially high price of domestic sugar, and the benefits to Florida's sugar industry as a whole amount to more than $180 million annually.[45]

But sugar-growing in the EAA affects more than the purses of American consumers. The degree of water control that these growers require allows aerobic bacteria to oxidize the partially decayed organic remains that constitute the district's muck soil.[46] This biochemical oxidation destroys the organic components of muck soils, but these soils do not totally disappear, because the inorganic components remain. These inorganic remains contain high concentrations of nitrogen and phosphorus, and these minerals, in turn, are pumped south with the excess water that is routinely removed from the EAA.[47] Although these minerals are important to plant nutrition, in the southern Everglades and Florida Bay, they are pollutants, because the undisturbed ecosystem of the Everglades was a nutrient-deficient system.[48] In the engineered environment, however, these nutrients allow alien plants to replace indigenous inhabitants. Like the killer Macheath in "Mack the Knife," effective water control in the Everglades has left behind a victim oozing life, but that oozing represents a pollutant in a nutrient-deficient environment.

In spite of denials, the primary responsibility for the mineral enrichment that flows from the EAA rests with the sugar growers. Although sugar cane was always an important crop in the EAA, before the 1960s it was not dominant. During the 1953–54 growing season, more than 70,000 acres of muck land were planted in winter vegetables valued at $29,250,000, while only 48,200 acres were devoted to the $10,000,000 sugar crop, and some 50,000 head of cattle valued at $6,000,000 were being fattened in the EAA.[49] After Castro came to power in Cuba, however, the district's sugar producers converted the pastureland to cane and brought new land into production, until, by 1990, there were 440,040 acres within the EAA devoted to cane.[50] Because of the water-control demands associated with sugar production, the expansion of this crop into former pasture and fallow acres caused increased subsidence. That is, subsidence is directly proportional to the depth of the water table below the land's surface, and sugar cane requires a deeper water table than does either cattle-grazing or fallow land, which is usually allowed to remain flooded in the Everglades.[51]

EAA farmers routinely pump nutrient-rich water south, where it enters a man-made ecosystem that both benefits from and adds to the problem of nutrient enrichment. Many of the indigenous marsh plants, especially saw grass, have adapted to their native habitats by developing the ability to accumulate the nutrients that are generally lacking in these environments; that is, these plants store nutrients when they are available, for use at some future time when there is a shortage.[52] In the man-made ecosystem, however, the altered environment offers opportunities for other plants, which do not have the nutrient-fixing capabilities of plants that are adapted to Florida's marshes, to thrive. The predominance of these exotic plants, such as melaleuca, means, in essence, that the same amount of nutrient overload causes more adverse effects than would the surplus in an undisturbed environment. Drainage has created a complex feedback loop, in which exposed muck soils contribute the nutrients that encourage the growth of plants that do not have nutrient-fixing capabilities, and these plants, in turn, thrive on land made habitable because drainage has destroyed the dynamic storage and sheet flow of the pristine Everglades.

The muck soils of the Everglades are a finite resource, and their end is in sight. The Everglades pioneer Laymond Hardy, a well-known horticulturalist, has had reason to visit the Everglades Agricultural Experiment Station throughout his long career, and he is intimately familiar with the land it occupies. Hardy has probed the station's ground with an iron rod in many locations, and he is sure that the soil is no more than fourteen to eighteen inches deep within its confines—this on land where the muck was nine feet deep in 1924.[53]

It seems likely, however, that sugar production can continue in the Everglades even in the absence of soil. The farmers who grow fruits and vegetables on the rocklands between the urban sprawl of Miami and the entrance to the Everglades National Park do so on land that has virtually no soil. These growers are able to prosper because they rock plow; that is, they scarify and pulverize the limestone until they create a sort of artificial soil, and the sugar growers along Lake Okeechobee's southern shore could employ the same techniques on their land.

No one knows the total impact rock plowing will have in the northern Everglades, but the practice will convert the upper Everglades from a depleted environment to one that is completely destroyed. Because rock plowing destroys the limestone surface, the use of this technique will eradicate the thin layers of marine, brackish, and freshwater marls that lie between the bottom of the peat and the upper surface of the limestone bedrock throughout the EAA.[54] These marls are much less permeable than the underlying limestone, and this characteristic may well have been the precondition that allowed extensive saw grass growth and the subsequent accumulation of muck soils. Once these layers disappear, the physical characteristics that encouraged the growth of saw grass and the subsequent accumulation of peat will have disappeared.

It would be prudent to begin large-scale restoration of the Everglades before all of the organic soils disappear—that is, while some remnant of the original environment remains. But such a beginning seems unlikely, because the upper Everglades is no longer dominated by the interactions among rock, fire, and water. Today the upper Everglades is the EAA, and the relationships among land, labor, and profits determine the course of events. The businessmen-farmers who cultivate these acres conduct their affairs in a rarified commercial setting created by government subsidies, and they will never relinquish their prerogatives so long as these subsidies guarantee them a healthy profit.

Epilogue: Restoration

The fruition of the engineering plan that was formulated in the 1940s per-
fected the developmental system, but it effectively killed the Everglades. To
be sure, wetlands did not totally disappear from peninsular Florida, but
these remnants are decidedly *not* the Everglades, even though the name still
appears on maps. Of the three traits that characterized the predrainage
system in the Everglades—habitat heterogeneity, large spatial extent, and a
distinctive hydrologic regime—the new water-control works most directly
affected the last, but the destruction of the system's hydrologic regime led,
inevitably, to a reduction in the size and biotic diversity of the wetlands.

The goal of those who want to either re-create or rehabilitate, depending
on their perspective, the Everglades is the transformation of the developmental system into a sustainable one. This sustainable system must be able
to support wading birds, snail kites, alligators, otters, deer, panthers, and
people too. There are three elements that will be crucial to the attempt to
create this sustainable system, two very practical and the third conceptual.

The first of these practical elements is the re-creation, as nearly as possible, of the Everglades's predrainage hydrologic regime. The creation of a
sustainable system cannot begin until at least a portion of the district's sheet
flow and dynamic storage capacity, both dependent on the reestablishment

of the historic hydrologic regime, is again a reality. Stated simply, it takes water to re-create a wetlands system.

The form that the sustainable system will assume is the conceptual element of restoration. Currently, the metaphor "river of grass" and the image of the vast stands of saw grass that this metaphor suggests represent the historic Everglades in the minds of most Americans. This image must be replaced. The sustainable system must include the forests, tree islands, and mangrove swamps that characterized predrainage south Florida, and resurrection of the image of islands and seas, formulated before drainage altered the Everglades, would contribute greatly to the establishment of a sustainable system.

The final practical element is political. As with constructing the developmental system, the creation of a sustainable system in the Everglades will be a long-term project, deeply immersed in the political process. The temporal and political elements of this undertaking require that the goal of creating a sustainable system must be protected from the vagaries of transient political will. In this effort, the state of Florida would do well to emulate the state of New York. There, the state's Adirondacks park—which includes populated, developed, and wilderness areas—has, in large part, successfully maintained a sustainable wilderness system because the state's constitution mandates that the portions of the park designated as forest preserves must "be forever kept as wild forest land."[1] The Everglades, too, both its developed and undeveloped districts, must be fashioned into such a park.

A 1995 north-south trip through the Everglades nicely illustrates the degree to which the Everglades has been altered. In February of that year, two men—Robert McClure, a *Fort Lauderdale Sun-Sentinel* reporter, and Sean Dougherty, a photographer—set out to retrace the voyage made by the members of the *New Orleans Times-Democrat* in 1883. Because agricultural land now occupies all of Lake Okeechobee's southern shore, however, the modern explorers were forced to follow a route that, for much of its course, paralleled rather than followed the trail of the earlier expedition.[2]

McClure and Dougherty began their journey with a portage, the first of many, across the Hoover Dike, the giant levee that prohibits Lake Okeechobee from draining to the south. Once on the other side, the newspapermen encountered a world of immense change. Where the *Times-Democrat* expedition encountered blind rivers twisting through a labyrinth of pond apple, the modern explorers saw nothing but level farmland, and these fields also occupy the land where once stood the impenetrable stands of saw grass that so mightily vexed the earlier explorers.

The canals of the engineered Everglades provided easy transportation routes for the modern explorers, but the latticework of dikes, many with highways on top, that crisscrosses the entire district provided enough man-made barriers to make the trip toilsome. The newsmen spent their first night at one such man-made structure, the S-5A pumping station. One component in a fourteen-hundred-mile system of canals, dikes, pumps, and water-control gates, the S-5A was, until very recently, the largest pumping station in the world. Powered by six sixteen-hundred-horsepower engines, and capable of moving more than 3 billion gallons of water in a day, the S-5A is a key element in this system, providing a reversible path for water between the Everglades Agricultural Area and the water conservation areas to the south. Along with seventeen other pumps and some two hundred gates and spillways, the S5-A provides the degree of water control required to make commercial agriculture a viable proposition in the Everglades.

South of the pumping station, McClure and Dougherty encountered the demonstration project for the proposed Everglades Nutrient Removal Project. A man-made saw-grass wetland, this water filtration marsh is envisioned as the buffer between the agricultural area and the rest of south Florida. Designed to filter out the pollutants that leave the northern farmland, especially the phosphorus that artificially enriches the Everglades's water, this project will eventually cover 62 square miles, 39,680 acres, and cost at least $700 million to create. Although members of the *Times-Democrat* expedition would find this region familiar, nutrient enrichment will undoubtedly change the area into a cattail marsh, the unfailing indicator of this process within the Everglades. And many environmentalists fear that, over time, this cattail marsh will become nothing more than a toxic sump, as the pollution from agricultural runoff becomes more concentrated.

Below the filtration marsh, the modern travelers encountered the three water conservation areas that formed a key element in the report by the Corps of Engineers, the *Comprehensive Report on Central and Southern Florida for Flood Control and Other Purposes*. Little more than sumps themselves, these areas actually conserve very little water. In times of abundant rainfall, these conservation areas provide the retention ponds required to prevent flooding, but the water from such episodes is rapidly carried to the Atlantic Ocean. Similarly, when rainfall is inadequate, water from the conservation areas is pumped northward onto the fields of the EAA.

These practices mean that the misnamed water conservation areas have drastically altered the district's hydroperiod. In the words of Steve Coughlin, a biologist with the Florida Game and Fresh Water Fish Commission, "The number of drought years we have has increased dramatically," while, at the same time, "the number of high-water years has increased. We kind of just have highs and lows now. It's very rare when we're in the middle, where we belong."[3]

McClure and Dougherty saw evidence of these oscillations. The tree islands that were so abundant when the *Times-Democrat* party passed through the area have been almost totally obliterated by the artificial patterns of flood and drought, seriously depleting the number of nesting sites available for water fowl. The human-controlled water level poses yet another problem for these birds, because periods of low water, when the fish they eat become concentrated, no longer coincide with the natural rhythm of the birds' life cycle. But it was periods of high water that provided the newsmen with the most dramatic evidence for the harm caused by artificial water levels. On a bit of high ground known as Bergeron's Camp, the *Sun-Sentinel* reporters encountered numerous bones of the deer, raccoon, and possums that had starved to death during the most recent round of flooding within the conservation area.

After crossing the Tamiami Trail, the northern border of Everglades National Park, the modern explorers did encounter an extensive landscape that would have been familiar to Archie Williams and the other members of the *Times-Democrat* party, but the consciousness of the modern condition intruded into even this zone. The sight of snail kites, for instance, reminded McClure and Dougherty that fewer than one thousand of these animals still exist, because their only food source, the apple snail, has responded to the Everglades's new hydrological regime in a way that makes them unavailable to the kite—the snails now burrow into the mud because water control has made the pools of water that they prefer much more scarce. Similarly, as the newsmen approached Panther Mound, they reflected on the fate of its namesakes. After the death of a panther a few years ago—its liver full of mercury that no doubt entered its system via a route that began with fish and had an intermediate stop with raccoons—only one of these animals is known to roam the park.

Decompartmentalization has become the catchword among those who want to convert the Everglades that Robert McClure and Sean Dougherty saw in 1995 into the one more like what was seen by Archie Williams and the other members of the 1883 *Times-Democrat* expedition. Decompartmentalization entails the removal or modification of at least some of the fourteen-hundred-mile-long water-control devices that divide the Everglades into numerous zones. The removal or modification of these structures, properly done, would re-create the historic hydrologic regime of the Everglades, but only if the waters of Lake Okeechobee are allowed to flow south, as they did before construction of the Hoover Dike. That is, the sustainable system cannot be created as long as the southerly flow of water is controlled by the interests of the EAA's growers. The farmers of the EAA are the major impediment to the reestablishment of the historic hydrologic regime because the hydrologic regime of the developmental system provides for the maximization of their profits.

The creation of a state park that includes both the EAA and the land between that agricultural district and the Everglades National Park—most of the latter already belongs to the state—is the best way to insure that the historic hydrologic regime will be reestablished. Additionally, public land within this park should be constitutionally mandated as wild land, to be maintained in that state in perpetuity. The establishment of such a park will not be a cure-all; rather, it will insure that the debate over the creation of a sustainable system in the Everglades will remain at the center of public discourse until some sort of ecologically viable solution is found. As with the creation of the developmental system, the development of a sustainable system will ultimately be a political decision, and the necessary political foundation must be laid. The creation of a park with a constitutionally sanctioned mandate represents that political foundation.

The form that the ecologically viable solution takes must be modeled on south Florida's historic environmental realities, and it is here that the conceptual aspect of the sustainable system plays a crucial role. Marjory Stoneman Douglas's seminal book, *Everglades: River of Grass,* is the standard against which all other studies of the region are measured. From the first, this work sold well—its initial printing of 7,500 copies was released in

November 1947 and was sold out by Christmas—and this popular book's images powerfully affected the way Americans, and the world, think about south Florida.[4] But one image, that of the river of grass itself, so dominated all the others that it became the metaphor for the highly diverse environmental system that was, and to a much lesser extent still is, the Everglades. The dominance of this metaphor is unfortunate and hinders restoration of the complex wetlands system it so imperfectly describes.

Such an assertion will likely prove shocking to a generation whose consciousness of the Everglades has been so profoundly affected by *River of Grass,* but it is in no way intended as a criticism of Douglas or her book. Indeed, anyone who actually reads her work—and many who have opinions about the region seemingly have not done so—is aware of Douglas's appreciation for the complexity of the environmental system that she described. But the popularity of her work has indelibly imprinted the inaccurate metaphor "river of grass" on the American collective psyche, with the result that a literary expression has been assigned a physical reality that never truly existed.

The major flaw of the river-of-grass metaphor is the way the figure of speech distorts the truth about animal habitat in the Everglades. While traveling through the interior marsh, the members of the *Times-Democrat* expedition encountered a rich mosaic of dense saw grass stands, abundant flag marsh, and numerous tree islands, but very few animals. The most desolate areas of all were those where saw grass dominated. Indeed, Archie Williams, the reporter who documented the trip, contrasted the shores of Lake Okeechobee with its "10,000 alligators more or less" to the saw grass marshes, where "a deathlike oppressive stillness prevailed." Not only were the regions of saw grass "utterly devoid of game of any kind," but also "there were no fish in the water, no birds in the air." By contrast, Williams reported, the mangrove forest along the Shark River, like the forested shore of Lake Okeechobee, provided nesting sites for a vast rookery of "thousands of birds."[5]

Those who are interested in truly restoring the wetlands of south Florida would be better served if they discarded the river-of-grass metaphor for the more accurate portrayal offered by the naturalists John Kunkel Small and George V. Nash. Writing in 1902, before massive drainage altered the ecology of south Florida, these nature explorers appreciated the effect that the region's slight relief had on its plant and animal communities. Small and

Nash knew that south Florida's environmental health depended on the existence of the mangrove of Florida's coastal and riverine shorelines, the pine forest and tropical hardwood hammocks of the Miami rocklands, the pond apple and cypress forests of Lake Okeechobee's shoreline, as well as the saw grass and tree islands of the Everglads trough. Modern Floridians must be aware that the current myopic focus on saw grass will not lead to anything like an environmental restoration of south Florida; rather, the creation of vast stands of sawgrass will bequeath modern Florida the same sterile environment that Archie Williams encountered in 1883.

Taken together, the re-creation of the region's historic hydrologic regime, the formation of a constitutionally mandated state park, and the acceptance of an islands-and-seas image will provide the basis for a sustainable system in south Florida. The so-called water conservation areas of Broward, Palm Beach, and Dade Counties represent the fruition of the thinking that created the developmental system in the Everglades. Little more than sumps, these misnamed conservation areas neither conserve water nor support wildlife; rather, they play a key role in maximizing the profits of a sugar industry that owes the lion's share of its success to public largesse. There must be room for sugar growers in the sustainable system, but their interests cannot be allowed to block sustainability in south Florida. One need only contemplate the answer to the question "If not sustainability, what?" to understand the importance of converting the developmental Everglades to a sustainable system.

NOTES

Preface

1. Ritchie, "Both Sides Claim Victory on Sugar Tax," *Gainesville Sun*, 8 November 1996, 2B.

2. See Heilbroner, *Inquiry into the Human Prospect;* Schumacher, *Small Is Beautiful;* Ekins, ed., *The Living Economy,* for in-depth discussion about the relationship between economic thinking and human survival.

3. See Stephens, "Subsidence of Organic Soils in the Florida Everglades," in *Environments of South Florida*, ed. Gleason, 359, and Stephens and Johnson, "Subsidence of Organic Soils in the Upper Everglades," *Soil Science Society of Florida Proceedings*, 231.

4. Stewart, *Pyramids and Sphinx*, 28

5. See Stephens, "Subsidence of Organic Soils in the Florida Everglades," 359, and Stephens and Johnson, "Subsidence of Organic Soils in the Upper Everglades," 231.

6. Kirby, *Poquosin*, xi.

Chapter 1. A Changing Landscape

1. Gleason and Stone, "Age, Origin, and Landscape Evolution of the Everglades Peatland," in *Everglades: The Ecosystem and Its Restoration*, ed. Davis and Ogden, 153.

2. Webb, "Historical Biogeography," in *Ecosystems of Florida*, ed. Myers and Ewel, 71.

3. See Smith and Lord, "Tectonic Evolution and Geophysics of the Florida Basement," in *The Geology of Florida*, Randazzo and Jones, eds., 21–25; Sullivan, *Continents in Motion*, 259–74; and Dietz and Holden, "The Breakup of Pangaea," in *Readings from Scientific American*, 126–37.

4. Webb, "Historical Biogeography," 72.

5. Gould, *Wonderful Life*, 53–60.

6. Missimer, "The Geology of Florida," in *Environments of South Florida*, ed. Gleason, 385.

7. Ibid.

8. Healy, *Terraces and Shorelines of Florida.*

9. Widmer, *The Evolution of the Calusa,* 154–61.

10. Parker and Cooke, *Late Cenozoic Geology of Southern Florida,* plate 14.

11. Interview with Garald Parker.

12. See Widmer, *Evolution of the Calusa,* 154–65, and Gleason and Stone, "Age, Origin, and Landscape Evolution of the Everglades Peatland," 164.

13. See Brooks, "Lake Okeechobee"; Gleason, *Environments of South Florida, Present and Past II,* 38–68; and William A. White, *Geomorphology of the Florida Peninsula,* 68–85.

14. See Hoffmeister, *Land from the Sea,* 27–49, and Gleason, et al., "The Environmental Significance of Holocene Sediments," 327.

15. Gleason, et al., "Environmental Significance of Holocene Sediments," 299.

16. See Gleason, et al., "Environmental Significance of Holocene Sediments," 306–10, and Gleason and Stone, "Age, Origin, and Evolution of the Everglades Peatland," 169–70.

17. The soils in the Everglades have been arranged in a number of different classifications. The names used here have been selected because they provide the best context for a natural history. For the most modern scheme of classification, see Snyder, "Soils of the EAR," in *Everglades Agricultural Area,* ed. Botcher and Izuno. Also, in the Everglades, soils referred to as mucks contain a higher percentage of inorganic matter than do peats.

18. Gleason, et al., "Environmental Significance of Holocene Sediments," 301–4.

19. Gunderson and Snider, "Fire Patterns in the Southern Everglades," in *Everglades: The Ecosystem and Its Restoration,* ed. Davis and Ogden, 291–306.

20. Gleason, et al., "Environmental Significance of Holocene Sediments," 320–21.

21. Kushlan, "Freshwater Marshes," in *Ecosystems of Florida,* ed. Myers and Ewel, 335.

22. See Cohen, "Evidence of Fires in Ancient Everglades," and Hofstetter, "The Effects of Fire on the Pineland and Sawgrass Communities," in *Environments of South Florida, Present and Past II,* ed. Gleason, 459–76, for a discussion of the effects of fire on the saw grass environment.

23. Gleason, et al., "Environmental Significance of Holocene Sediments," 311.

24. Stephens and Johnson, "Subsidence of Organic Soils in the Upper Everglades," 2:220–21.

25. Kushlan, "Freshwater Marshes," 334.

26. Worster, "The Ecology of Order and Chaos," 13.

27. Tsu, *Tao Te Ching,* trans. Feng and English, 1.

28. Weaver and Brown, "Federal Objectives for the South Florida Restoration."

29. Kushlan, "Freshwater Marshes," 337.

30. Brooks, "Lake Okeechobee," 38–68.

31. Gleason and Stone, "Age, Origin, and Landscape Evolution of the Everglades Peatland," 182–86.

32. Davis, Jr., *Peat Deposits of Florida,* 41–46.

33. Burns and Taylor, "Nutrient-Uptake Model," 177–96.

34. Willoughby, *Everglades*, 119.

35. See Parker, *Water Resources of Southeastern Florida*, for an in-depth analysis of the role of solution in south Florida.

36. Dix and Maggonigle, "The Everglades of Florida," 521.

37. White, *The Geomorphology of the Florida Peninsula*, 9.

38. Williams, "North to South through the Everglades in 1883," ed. Wintringham, 71.

39. Ives, *Memoir to Accompany a Military Map*, 38.

40. Will, *Cracker History of Okeechobee*, inside fly leaf.

Chapter 2. Changing Peoples

1. McGoun, *Prehistoric Peoples of South Florida*, 7.

2. Ibid.

3. Meggers, *Prehistoric America: An Ecological Perspective*, 7.

4. Milanich and Fairbanks, *Florida Archeology*, 35. The authors date the earliest known finds at Little Salt Springs from 10,000–12,000 B.C. (hence the number in table 2.1), but they believe that the actual arrival of Paleo-Indians probably predates these finds by several thousand years.

5. Widmer, *The Evolution of the Calusa*, 155.

6. Ibid., 160–61.

7. Daniel, Jr., and Wisenbaker, *Harney Flats*, 168.

8. See Daniel and Wisenbaker, *Harney Flats*, 162–75, for a discussion of social and technological models of band societies.

9. Faeb, *Man's Rise to Civilization*, 206.

10. Daniel and Wisenbaker, *Harney Flats*, 145.

11. See McGoun, *Prehistoric Peoples of South Florida*, 60–62, and Milanich and Fairbanks, *Florida Archeology*, 48–60.

12. McGoun, *Prehistoric Peoples of South Florida*, 64.

13. Purdy, *Art and Archeology of Florida's Wetlands*, 95–96, 150–56, 174–77, and 188–92.

14. McGoun, *Prehistoric Peoples of South Florida*, 65.

15. Widmer, *Evolution of the Calusa*, 207–13.

16. Milanich, *Archeology of Precolumbian Florida*, 277–78.

17. See McGoun, *Prehistoric Peoples of South Florida*, 7. The author defines a cultural tradition as a "long-lasting manifestation of certain core cultural features."

18. Fontaneda, *Memoir of Do d'Escalente Fontaneda*, trans. Smith, 11–13, 17, and 20.

19. Goggin and Sturtevant, "The Calusa," in *Explorations in Cultural Anthropology*, ed. Goodenough, 189.

20. See de Meras, *Pedro Menendez de Aviles*, trans. Conner, 149. Solis de Meras was Menendez's brother-in-law and accompanied him to Florida as the official chronicler of the expedition—he wrote this account about 1567. See also Widmer, *Evolution of the Calusa*, 260.

21. See Fontaneda, *Memoir,* 13 and 16–17, and Goggin and Sturtevant, "The Calusa," 209.

22. Referred to as the cultural materialist interpretation, the model of a Calusa state based on the redistribution of locally scarce subsistence resources was first proposed by Widmer in *The Evolution of the Calusa.*

23. Cushing, "Exploration of Ancient Key-Dwellers' Remains," 347, 349, and 343.

24. Walker, "The Zooarchaeology of Charlotte Harbor's Prehistoric Maritime Adaption," in *Culture and Environment in the Domain of the Calusa,* ed. Marquardt and Payne, 265–68.

25. Ibid., 307 and 265.

26. Scarry and Newsom, "Archaeobotanical Research in the Calusa Heartland," in *Culture and Environment in the Domain of the Calusa,* ed. Marquardt and Payne, 375–402.

27. Fontaneda, *Memoir,* 13–14. This is according to Fontaneda, but the relationship between the Indians of Lake Okeechobee and coastal groups over time is not clear.

28. Laudonniere, *Three Voyages,* trans. Charles E. Bennett, 111.

29. Griffin, *The Archeology of Everglades National Park,* 298.

30. Gilliland, *The Material Culture of Key Marco,* 68–71.

31. Hahn, ed. and trans., *Missions to the Calusa,* 261–62.

32. Velasco, quoted in Swanton, *Early History of the Creek Indians,* 389.

33. "Father Rogel to Father del Portillo," 25 April 1568, in Hahn, *Missions to the Calusa,* 237–38.

34. Ibid., 241.

35. Ibid., 238. Rogel goes on to describe the other two gods: "the second one is greater than the third, that to him belongs the government of the kingdoms, empires, and republics. The third one, who is the least of all and the one who helps in the wars. And to the side to which he attaches himself, they say that one gains victory."

36. Laudonniere, *Three Voyages,* 110–11.

37. Cushing wrote a preliminary account of his discoveries, "Exploration of Ancient Key-Dwellers' Remains on the Gulf Coast of Florida," *Proceedings, American Philosophical Society* 35: 153 (1896; reprint, *Antiquities of the New World,* New York: AMS Press, 1973), and published an article, "Relics of an Unknown Race Discovered," *New York Journal,* 21 June 1896, 17–18, but he died before he could complete his analysis. Marion Gilliland's book *Material Culture of Key Marco* provides a good inventory and pictures of the artifacts Cushing recovered. Gilliland subsequently published another book, *Key Marco's Buried Treasure* (Gainesville: University of Florida Press, 1989), that provides an account of Cushing's expedition.

38. Gilliland, *Key Marco's Buried Treasure,* 2.

39. Sawyer, "Field Notebook," 84, 87, and 116.

40. Ibid., 127.

41. Cushing, "Exploration of Ancient Key-Dwellers' Remains," 363.

42. Fontaneda, *Memoir,* 14.

43. Sawyer, "Field Notebook," 126.

44. Gilliland, *Material Culture of Key Marco*, 152–56, 159–60, 184–87, and 245–46.

45. Ibid., 47–64 and 205–7.

46. Cushing, "Exploration of Ancient Key-Dwellers' Remains," 364, 366.

47. Sawyer, Letter, 12 March, Box 53, P. K. Yonge Library of Florida History, Gainesville, Florida.

48. Rogel, "Report on the Florida Missions," in Hahn, *Missions to the Calusa*, 287–88.

49. Gilliland, *Material Culture of Key Marco*, 75–84.

50. Sawyer, "Field Notebook," 122 and 125.

51. Cushing, "Exploration of Ancient Key-Dwellers' Remains," 374.

52. Gilliland, *Material Culture of Key Marco*, 72–75, 173–81, 207–9, and 221–23.

53. Sawyer, "Field Notebook."

54. Cushing, "Exploration of Ancient Key-Dwellers' Remains," 33.

55. See Gannon, *Florida: A Short History*, 4, and Tebeau, *History of Florida*, 19.

56. Menendez, "Pedro Menendez, Reports," in *Colonial Records of Spanish Florida*, ed. and trans. Conner, 35.

57. Indians poled canoes across the peninsula, following at least two routes. The first was from the mouth of the Miami River to Lake Okeechobee, and, from there, down the Caloosahatchee River to the Gulf. Another route was down the St. Johns River, then across its headwaters in the St. Johns Marsh to Lake Okeechobee, where the Caloosahatchee River was again the last leg to the Gulf. Probably neither of these routes was passable year-round (at least not every year), even by canoe, and neither was ever navigable by Spanish vessels.

58. See Herring, *History of Latin America*, 192–93; McAlister, *Spain and Portugal*, 370–71; and Perry and Sherlock, *History of the West Indies*, 36–38.

59. Lyon, "Enterprise of Florida," 418.

60. Tebeau, *History of Florida*, 34–35.

61. Hairing, *Spanish Empire*, 40, provides a good definition of the *encomienda* system: "the *encomienda* was a patronage conferred by royal favor over a portion of the natives concentrated in settlements near those of Spaniards; the obligation to instruct them in the Christian religion and the elements of civilized life, and to defend their persons and property; coupled with the right to demand tribute of labor in return for these privileges."

62. Lyon, "Enterprise of Florida," 418.

63. Fontaneda, *Memoir*, 13.

64. Lyon, "Enterprise of Florida," 418.

65. See Menendez to His Royal Majesty, in *Colonial Records of Florida*. In this letter Menendez discusses the dangers of the Bahama Channel at length, but he does not mention an alternate water route across Florida. Between 1567 and 1573, Menendez had presumably become convinced that no such route existed.

66. Romans, *Concise History of East and West Florida*, 291.

Chapter 3. The Derelict Land

1. Small and Nash, "Report of Small and Nash," 34–35.
2. Fritchey, *Everglades Journal*, 24.
3. Williams, "North to South through the Everglades, Part II," 63.
4. Letter of de Guemes to King of Spain, Hahn, *Missions to the Calusa*, 402.
5. Letter from Franciscans to King, in Hahn, *Missions to the Calusa*, 13.
6. Covington, "Trade Relations," 115.
7. Lopez, in Hahn, *Missions to the Calusa*, 165.
8. "Report on the Indians of Southern Florida," in Hahn, *Missions to the Calusa*, 419–31.
9. See Covington, *The Seminoles of Florida*, and Mahon, *History of the Second Seminole War*, for good accounts of the history of the Seminoles in Florida.
10. See Potter, *Hunting in Florida;* Hallock, *Camp Life in Florida;* and Scott, *Story of a Bird Lover* for a good sampling of the accounts written by these adventurers.
11. Fontaneda, *Memoir*, 13.
12. Will, *A Cracker History*, 34–37.
13. Harshberger, "Vegetation of South Florida," 153.
14. Dachnowski-Stokes, "Peat Profiles," 103.
15. Will, *A Cracker History*, 34–35.
16. Blatchley, *In Days Agone*, 101.
17. Denevan, "The Pristine Myth," 369–85.
18. "Notes on the Passage Across the Everglades," *St. Augustine News*, 8 January 1841, reprinted in *Tequesta*, 57–65.
19. Rodenbaugh, *From Everglades to Canon*, 30–31.
20. Williams, "North to South, Part II," reprinted in *Tequesta* 66, 71, and 73.
21. Willoughby, *Across the Everglades*, 110.
22. Williams, "North to South, Part II," *Tequesta* 85.
23. Ibid., 86–89.
24. Ibid., 78.
25. Ibid., 90.
26. Ibid., 91.
27. See Williams, "North to South through the Everglades," 47; Williams "North to South, Part II," 93; and Willoughby, *Across the Everglades*, 14.
28. "Florida Everglades Land Company," 8.
29. *Report of the Eighth International Geographic Congress*, 769.
30. Willoughby, *Across the Everglades*, 119.
31. Williams, "North to South, Part II," 62, 81, 92.
32. Small, *Flora of Miami*, iii.
33. Davis, Jr., *The Natural Features*, 165.
34. Moses, *The Journal of the Everglades Exploring Expedition*, reprinted in *Tequesta*, 29.
35. Harshberger, "Vegetation of South Florida," 96.

36. Harshberger, "Vegetation of South Florida," 105; Simpson, *In Lower Florida Wilds,* 196–97; and Small, "Report on Exploration in Tropical Florida," 51–52.

37. *Tropic Magazine.*

38. Harper, "Natural Resources of Southern Florida," 92.

39. See Harshberger, "Vegetation of South Florida," 89, and Davis, *Natural Features of Southern Florida,* 152.

40. Harper, "Natural Resources of Southern Florida," 90.

41. Small, "Exploration of Southern Florida," 54.

42. Collection 75, Model Land Company Records, University of Miami, Coral Gables, Florida.

43. See Davis, *Natural Features of Southern Florida,* 162–63, and "Suwannee River Pine," 57, 64.

44. Moore-Wilson, *Eight Royal Palm Hammocks,* 2.

45. Small, "Botanical Exploration in 1916," 101.

46. See Small, "Botanical Exploration in Florida in 1917," 279–80, and Simpson, *In Lower Florida Wilds,* 382–88.

47. George R. Bentley, "Colonel Thompson's 'Tour of Tropical Florida'," reprinted in *Tequesta* (1950): 3–12.

48. Small, "Exploration in the Everglades," 54.

49. MacGonigle, "Geography of the Southern Peninsula," 388.

50. Willoughby, *Across the Everglades,* 65.

51. Munroe and Gilpin, *Commodore's Story,* 118.

52. Davis, "Vegetation Map of Southern Florida," in *Everglades: The Ecosystem and Its Restoration,* insert.

53. Small, "Land Where Spring Meets Autumn," 86.

54. Small, "The Botanical Fountain of Youth," 150.

55. Small, "A Cruise to the Cape Sable Region," 191.

56. Small, "Botanical Fields," 204–5.

57. Small, "A Cruise to the Cape Sable Region," 199.

58. Heilprin, *Exploration on the West Coast of Florida,* 23.

59. Pierce, "Cruise of the *Bon Ton,*" reprinted in *Tequesta* (1952), 48.

60. MacGonigle, "Geography of the Southern Peninsula," 392.

61. See Doughty, *Feather Fashions,* 73, and Chapman, *Camps and Cruises,* 135.

62. Chapman, *Camps and Cruises,* 138–39.

63. Ibid., 135–41.

64. Ibid., 141, 145.

65. Willoughby, *Across the Everglades,* 111–12.

66. Bent, "Nesting Habits," 21–22.

Chapter 4. Drainage

1. Hahamovitch, *The Fruits of Their Labor,* 23.

2. U.S. Congress, Senate, *Everglades of Florida, Acts, Reports,* 34–35.

3. See Hays, *Conservation;* Nash, ed., *American Environment;* and Nash, *Wilderness.*

4. U.S. Congress, Senate, *Report of Buckingham Smith*, 17, 67.

5. *Comprehensive Report*, 2, 5.

6. *Report of Buckingham Smith*, 33–38.

7. De Bow, "Everglades of Florida," 297–304.

8. See "Act to Reclaim Swamp Lands," and "Patent to the Everglades, 1903," in *Everglades of Florida, Acts, Reports*, 67, 93–94.

9. *Minutes of the Trustees*, I, 401–2, 442, 449, 464, 466, 476.

10. Tebeau, *History of Florida*, 284.

11. See "Status of the Swamp Lands Patented August 6, 1904," in *Everglades of Florida, Acts, Reports*, 94.

12. Wallis, "History of Everglades Drainage and Its Present Status," in *Soil Science Society Proceedings* 4-A, 31–32; and *Everglades of Florida*, 10–14.

13. "Message of N. B. Broward to the Legislature," in *Everglades of Florida*, 99–109.

14. See *Jacksonville Florida Times-Union*, 7 April 1907, and *Journal of the House of Representatives of Florida* (1907), 658.

15. See *Minutes of the Trustees*, VI, 96–97, and Blake, *Land into Water*, 97–98.

16. Beard, "Excerpt of Address," *Pensacola News*, 17 May 1906.

17. See *Minutes of the Trustees*, VII, 144–45, 149–53, 462, 466; and IX, 610, 616.

18. *Minutes of the Trustees*, VI, 271, and VII, 553.

19. See *Everglades Hearings*, 143–44, and *Minutes of the Trustees*, VII, 502–13.

20. *Everglades Hearings*, 1039–40, 1328–29.

21. "Extract from a Report by J. O. Wright," 137.

22. *Minutes of Trustees*, IX, 248.

23. *Everglades Hearings*, 215–16.

24. Ibid., 1323.

25. Ibid., 1139.

26. Florida, *House Journal*, 1911, 61–62.

27. See Hanna and Hanna, *Lake Okeechobee*, 132, and *Minutes of the Trustees*, VIII, 428–45.

28. *Everglades Hearings*, 1323.

29. Packard, "Rush to Florida," 20–23.

30. *Florida Fruit Lands Review*.

31. *Everglades Hearings*, 1323.

32. *The Everglades, Richest Land in the World*, in Broward Papers, Box 9, P. K. Yonge Library of Florida History, University of Florida, Gainesville, Florida.

33. Weilding and Burghard, *Checkered Sunshine*, 38–40.

34. *Everglades Hearings*, 282, 882.

35. Ibid., 945–50.

36. *Minutes of the Trustees*, IX, 248.

37. *Everglades Hearings*, 879–83, and *Washington Post*, 5 March 1912, as quoted in *Congressional Record* 48, 2834.

38. *Everglades Hearings*, 3–7.

39. Ibid., 343–44, 352.

40. Ibid., 342–48.

41. Ibid., 337–95.

42. Ibid., 355.

43. Ibid., 10, 221, 841, 1041.

44. Ibid., 908.

45. U.S. Congress, House, *Majority Report*, 2–3.

46. Ibid., 4–5.

47. *Everglades Hearings*, 802–3.

48. *Majority Report*, 11.

49. *Everglades of Florida Acts, Reports*, 102.

50. "Report of a Preliminary Investigation," in *Everglades Hearings*, 569–70.

Chapter 5. Drainage Reconsidered and Pioneer Settlement, 1912–1924

1. See Cronon, *Nature's Metropolis;* Worster, *Dust Bowl;* and Reisner, *Cadillac Desert.*

2. U.S. Congress, House, *Everglades Hearings*, 643.

3. *Minutes of the Trustees*, X, 393–94.

4. See Hanna and Hanna, *Lake Okeechobee*, 160, and Weilding and Burghard, *Checkered Sunshine*, 43.

5. Blatchley, *In Days Agone*, 101.

6. *Minutes of the Trustees*, IX, 395.

7. Hanna and Hanna, *Lake Okeechobee*, 160–61.

8. See Blake, *Land into Water*, 119–20, and Dovell, "History of the Everglades," 321–23.

9. Will to Knott, 8 May 1912, Will Papers, Box 1.

10. *Minutes of the Trustees*, X, 138–42, 15.

11. Marquis, *Who's Who in America*, 1590, 1611, 1072.

12. Mead, Hazen, and Metcalf, *Report on the Drainage of the Everglades*, 7, 10–11.

13. Ibid., 8.

14. Ibid., 38.

15. Ibid., 33, 9.

16. Ibid., 9, 38, 34.

17. Tebeau, *History of Florida*, 338.

18. See Mead, Hazen, and Metcalf, *Report on the Drainage of the Everglades*, 38, and *Minutes of the Trustees*, X, 15.

19. *Laws of Florida*, 125–227.

20. *Report of the Everglades Engineering Commission*, 4.

21. Marquis, *Who's Who in America*, 1398, 1838.

22. Malone, ed., *Dictionary of American Biography*, 359–60.

23. *Report of the Everglades Engineering Commission*, 12.

24. Ibid., 5.

25. Ibid., 5, 12–14.

26. Ibid., 5.

27. Ibid., 6, 15.

28. *Minutes of the Trustees,* X, 1914.

29. See Mead, Hazen, and Metcalf, *Report on the Drainage of the Everglades,* 36, and *Report of the Everglades Engineering Commission,* 63.

30. Mead, Hazen, and Metcalf, *Report on the Drainage of the Everglades,* 33.

31. Randolph, "Reclaiming the Everglades," 49.

32. Ibid., 60.

33. *Everglades Hearings,* 337–38.

34. Blatchley, *In Days Agone,* 99–100.

35. "A Fine Otter Hide," *Fort Myers Press,* 8 February 1906.

36. Will, *Cracker History,* 94.

37. Ibid.

38. Scott, "Present Condition" (April 1887), 143.

39. "About the Aigrette," 232.

40. See Scott, "Present Condition" (April 1887), 143; "Present Condition" (July 1887), 217; and "Present Condition" (October 1887), 277, 283.

41. See Lindsey, *Bicentennial of Audubon,* 125–35, and Scott, "Present Condition" (October 1887), 281–82.

42. Lindsey, *Bicentennial of Audubon,* 131–32.

43. Blatchley, *In Days Agone,* 229–33.

44. Will, *Okeechobee Catfishing,* 11.

45. Ibid., 94.

46. Blatchley, *In Days Agone,* 239.

47. Ibid., 237–38.

48. Ibid., 239.

49. Will, *Okeechobee Catfishing,* 97–98.

50. Blatchley, *In Days Agone,* 239.

51. Ibid., 239–40.

52. Randolph, "Reclaiming the Everglades," 53.

53. Will, *Okeechobee Catfishing,* 40–42.

54. Randolph, "Reclaiming the Everglades," 53.

55. Sharp, "Farming the Muck Soil of the Everglades," 3.

56. Blake, *Land into Water,* 129.

57. Newhouse, "Pioneering in the Everglades," 3.

58. Bock, "What an Amateur Learned," 4.

59. Tedder, *Daily Reports,* 1924.

60. Newhouse, "Pioneering in the Everglades," 6.

61. Will, "Everglade Owners of Idle Lands Listen!" Will Papers, Box 37.

62. See Bock, "What an Amateur Learned," 236; Tedder, *Daily Reports,* February 22 and March 1.

63. Newhouse, "Pioneering in the Everglades," 14.

64. Ibid., 9–10, 15–16, 24–25.

65. Bock, "What an Amateur Learned," 6.

66. Blatchley, *In Days Agone,* 266.

67. Tedder, *Daily Reports,* March 3, March 12, May 12.

68. Ibid., May 8.

69. Blatchley, *In Days Agone,* 322.

70. Newhouse, "Pioneering in the Everglades," 63–66.

71. *Soils, Geology, and Water Control,* 61.

72. Newhouse, "Pioneering in the Everglades," 7.

73. Ibid.

74. Letter from Plank to McRae, 10 May 1920, file marked "Squatters, Lake Okeechobee Area." This collection is haphazard, neither organized nor indexed.

75. Plank to McRae, 10 November 1919.

76. McRae to Plank, 13 November 1919.

77. Letters from Plank to McRae, 17 December 1919; McRae to Plank, 23 December 1919; Plank to McRae, 9 February 1920.

78. Letters from McRae to Plank, 4 May 1920; Plank to McRae, 10 May 1920; McRae to Plank, 13 May 1920; Plank to McRae, 14 June 1920; McRae to Plank, 18 June 1920, Plank to McRae, 12 July 1920.

79. Letters from McRea to Plank, 3 August 1922, 11 August 1922.

80. Bock, "What an Amateur Learned," 5.

81. Fritchey, *Everglades Journal,* 16.

82. Walker to Will, 17 May 1912, Will Papers, Box 1.

83. Blatchley, *In Days Agone,* 324.

84. Ibid., 4.

85. Sharp, "Farming the Muck Soil of the Everglades," 4.

Chapter 6. Perfecting the Developmental System

1. Will to Fener, 1 February 1918, Will Papers, Box 9.

2. Will to Turner, 12 February 1918, Will Papers, Box 9.

3. Helm and Walker to Will, 20 November 1918, Will Papers, Box 9.

4. *National Defense Migration Hearings,* 12560.

5. "Biography Box," P. K. Yonge Library of Florida History, University of Florida, Gainesville, Florida.

6. Sharp, "Farming the Muck Soil," 3.

7. See Sharp, "Farming the Muck Soil," 3–4, and *National Defense Migration Hearings,* 12560.

8. Blake, *Land into Water,* 147.

9. See Wright, *Report on Drainage of the Everglades,* in *Everglades Acts, Reports,* 140–80; U.S. Congress, Senate, *Report of the Engineering Commission, 1913; Letter from the Chief of Engineers, 1928; Comprehensive Report for Flood Control, 1948.*

10. See *Journal of Florida Senate 1915,* 43, and Rose, "Swamp and Overflowed Lands," 135.

11. Marston, McCorory, and Hills, *Report of Everglades Engineering Board of Review,* 6, 34, 36.

12. See Marston, McCorory, and Hills, *Report of Engineering Board of Review,* 34–35, and *Biennial Report,* 19.

13. See *Report of Everglades Engineering Board of Review, 1927,* 48 and 74, and Brooks, "Lake Okeechobee," in *Environments of South Florida,* ed. Gleason, 257.

14. Newhouse, "Pioneering in the Everglades," 55.

15. See *Laws of Florida, 1923; Laws of Florida, 1925; National Defense Migration Hearings,* 12881.

16. See U.S. Congress, House, *Caloosahatchee River and Lake Okeechobee Drainage Areas,* 37–38, and Bestor, "Reclamation Problems of Sub-Drainage Districts," 161.

17. See Newhouse, "Pioneering in the Everglades," 55–56, and *Flood Control in Florida,* 87.

18. *Flood Control in Florida,* 87.

19. Ibid., 88–89.

20. Ibid., 87–90.

21. *Everglades News,* 26 January, 4 February, 25 March 1927, in Dovell, "History of the Everglades, 432.

22. *Report of EEBR, 1927,* 1–3.

23. Ibid., 34, 52.

24. Ibid., 34.

25. Ibid., 50–51, 88.

26. Ibid., 13, 74–75.

27. Ibid., 74.

28. U.S. Congress, House, *Hearings, Committee on Flood Control,* 247–48.

29. U.S. Congress, House, *Report from the Secretary of War, 1928,* 50.

30. U.S. Congress, Senate, *Letter from the Chief of Engineers, 1928,* 23, 6–7.

31. Ibid., 7.

32. See *Everglades News,* 2 September 1927, 23 December 1927, 17 February 1928, 15 June 1928, 20 July 1928, and Sharp, "The Dead Accuse," all cited in Dovell, "History of the Everglades," 456–58, 425–26; and Arthur, *The Taxpayers' Answer,* 22–23.

33. *Minutes of the Trustees,* XVII, 275–76.

34. See *Report of the Board of Commissioners of the Okeechobee Flood Control District, 1929–43,* 11 and 21, and Johnson, *Beyond the Fourth Generation,* 152–53.

35. Baldwin and Walker, *Soil Survey of Fort Lauderdale,* 18.

36. Ibid., 18, 35.

37. Newhouse, "Pioneering in the Everglades," 14.

38. Baldwin and Walker, *Soil Survey of Fort Lauderdale,* 39.

39. Small, "Old Trails and New Discoveries," 31–32, 39.

40. Small, "Coastwise Dunes and Lagoons," 195.

41. Alexander, "Paradise Key on Fire," 31–33.

42. Small, *From Eden to Sahara,* 83.

43. "Administrative Correspondence, Carlton," Box 44.

44. Ibid.

45. Stephens, "Subsidence of Organic Soils," in *Environments of South Florida,* ed. Gleason, 377–38.

46. Interview, Parker.

47. Ibid.

48. Ibid. However, north of Lake Okeechobee the Floridan Aquifer provides huge quantities of freshwater and serves as the reservoir for numerous municipalities.

49. Ibid.

50. Ibid. See also Parker and Cooke, *Late Cenozoic Geology;* Parker, "Notes on Geology;" Parker and Hoy, "Additional Notes."

51. Allison, "Soil and Water Conservation," 35–42.

52. See "Glades Refunding," *Palm Beach Post,* 7 June 1941, 1, and "Everglades Debts," *New York Times,* 11 June 1941, 31.

53. See *Soil Science Society Proceedings,* 5-A, 8; 4-A, 11–13.

54. See Ibid., 65; Gallatin and Henderson, "Progress Report on Soil Survey," 104.

55. Stephens, "Relationship of Sub-Surface Hydrology," 62.

56. Scott, "Central and Southern Florida Project," 125–27.

57. Ibid., 125.

58. Bestor, "Principal Elements," 93.

59. "Without Fresh Water," *Miami Herald,* 4 May 1945, 6-A.

60. Parker interview.

61. See Blake, *Land into Water,* 176, and Ernest Graham Papers, Franklin to Collier, 19 August 1947, Box 32.

62. *Comprehensive Report on Central and Southern Florida,* 1–5.

63. Ibid., 39–41.

64. Ibid., 42.

65. Ibid., 42–43.

66. Ibid., 43.

67. Ibid., 52, 55.

68. Heldt, "House Group OKs Flood Control," *Miami Herald,* 17 May 1949, 2-A.

69. Blake, *Land into Water,* 181.

Chapter 7. The Fruits of Development

1. See Jones, *The Dispossessed,* 167–204, and Hahamovitch, *Fruits of Their Labor,* 113–37.

2. Fowler, "Okeechobee: A Journey," 31.

3. *Laws of Florida, 1921,* 154–57.

4. Allison, Bryan, and Harper, "Stimulation of Plant Response," 40–41.

5. Ibid., 78.

6. Allison, *Agricultural Experiment Station Report 1928,* 113R.

7. Ibid., 114R.

8. Ibid.

9. Skinner and Ruprecht, "Fertilizer Experiments," 37–41, 64.

10. Becker, Neal, and Shealy, "Salt Sick," 6–7.

11. Ibid., 10–11.

12. See Blake, *Land into Water,* 131–33, and Sitterson, *Sugar Country,* 364.

13. Will, *Cracker History,* 215.

14. Sitterson, *Sugar Country,* 370–71.

15. "Pepper Explains Stand on Sugar Quota," *Tampa Morning Tribune,* 17 October 1940.

16. See Lewis, "The Economic Phase," and Beardsley, "Present Status of Plans for Refinancing," 101, 105.

17. See "Delinquent Tax Redemption Bill Signed into Law," *Clewiston News,* 18 June 1937, 1, and "Text of New Florida Law Relating to Taxation and Tax Certificate Purchases," *Clewiston News,* 16 July 1937, 1.

18. See Interview with Laymond M. Hardy, 3 November 1996, and Stephen, "Vegetable Production," 79–101.

19. Lewis, "Economic Phase," 100–101.

20. Ibid., 102.

21. See Lewis, "Economic Phase," 101–2, and Beardsley, "Status of Plans," 104–12.

22. Jones, *The Dispossessed,* 170–73.

23. Hurston, *Their Eyes Were Watching God,* 108.

24. Black, *H-2 Worker.*

25. "Report of the Federal Bureau of Investigation," compiled at Memphis, Tennessee, 11 March 1942. All FBI materials cited were obtained by Stephanie Black under the auspices of the Freedom of Information Act. She kindly shared copies of these documents with me, and I owe her a debt of thanks.

26. *Cases, Supreme Court of Florida 1943,* 338–43.

27. "FBI Report," Birmingham.

28. Letter from Coldman to Carlton, Florida State Archives, Series 278, Carton 54.

29. See Carlton, *Governors' Papers,* Series 204, Box 20, letter from Willie Johnson to Carlton, 7 April 1930; "FBI Report," Birmingham; and "FBI Report," Memphis. All of these documents provide extensive descriptions of the intimidation, beatings, and poor living conditions that characterized the cane cutters' lives in the Everglades sugar plantations.

30. Letter from Watts to Carlton, Florida State Archives, Series 204, Carton 91.

31. "FBI Report," Jackson.

32. Greenlea, "Peonage Story Told by Victims," article enclosed in a letter from Nellie Davis to President Franklin Roosevelt, 18 March 1942, included in the FBI file obtained through the Freedom of Information Act by Stephanie Black.

33. "U.S. Charges Sugar Corp. with Peonage," *Tampa Morning Tribune,* 5 November 1942.

34. See "Hearing to Be Held Today in U.S. Sugar Case," *Tampa Morning Tribune,* 26 April 1943; "Indictment against U.S. Sugar Thrown Out," *Tampa Morning Tribune,* 27 April 1943; and "Prosecuting a Producer," *Tampa Morning Tribune,* 29 April 1943.

35. See *Pollock v. Williams, Sheriff,* 322 U.S., 4–30. Pollock accepted a five-dollar

advance from J. V. O'Albora on 17 October 1942, and he was arrested for fraud on 5 January 1943. Convicted by a county judge the same day, Pollock was fined one hundred dollars or sixty days in the county jail. The state circuit court reversed the conviction, but Florida's Supreme Court reversed that decision on 27 July 1943. Pollock's case was heard by the U.S. Supreme Court during its October 1943 term, and the Florida fraud laws were declared unconstitutional on 10 April 1944.

36. U.S. Congress, Senate, *West Indies (BWI) Temporary Alien Labor Program: 1943–1947*, 3–6. See also Rasmussen, *History of the Emergency Farm Labor Supply Program 1943–47*, for a complete history of the temporary labor program.

37. Letter from Chandler, Florida State Archives, Series 406, Carton 66.

38. U.S. Congress, Senate, *West Indies (BWI) Temporary Alien Labor Program*, 3–6.

39. Fowler, "Okeechobee: A Journey," 31.

40. U.S. Congress, Senate, *West Indies (BWI) Temporary Alien Labor Program*, 8–9.

41. See Petrow, "Men Who Bring You Sugar," *St. Petersburg Times*, 7 December 1980; Brown and Lee, "Imported Muscle Fells Cane, Arouses Debate," *Tampa-Tribune News*, 4 December 1983; and Wilkinson, *Big Sugar*, 32.

42. See "Workers Returned to Caribbean after Melee over Pay," *St. Petersburg Times*, 27 November 1986, B2, and "Jamaican Official to Investigate Dispute," *St. Petersburg Times*, 27 November 86.

43. U.S. Congress, House, *Jobs of Domestic Workers*, 12.

44. U.S. Congress, Senate, *H-2 Program and Nonimmigrant*, 69–70. A cutter during the 1981 season was paid $4.69 per hour. From total wages of $450.24, the company withheld $70 for food—$5 per day—$11.41 for West Indies governmental administrative costs, $87.46 for savings, and $71.84 for transportation costs. From a gross salary of $450.24, this hypothetical worker received a check for $209.53, 47 percent of his gross wages.

45. See Vick, "Sweet Deal under Fire," *St. Petersburg Times*, 15 May 1994, 1A and "Sugar Subsidies Benefit the Few," *Gainesville Sun*, 16 May 1994, 1B.

46. Snyder, "Soils of the EAA," in *Everglades Agricultural Area*, ed. Botcher and Izuno, 38.

47. See P. Porter and Sanchez, "Nitrogen in the Organic Soils," and Sanchez and P. Porter, "Phosphorus in the Organic Soils," both in *Everglades Agricultural Area*, ed. Botcher and Izuno, 42–84. Although muck soils do not require the addition of nitrogen, EAA farmers routinely add fertilizers that contain phosphorous to their fields, and this phosphorous, too, contributes to enrichment.

48. See Kushlan, "Freshwater Marshes," in *Ecosystems of Florida*, ed. Myers and Ewel, 347–48, and Steward and Ornes, "Autecology of Sawgrass," 162–71.

49. See Ford, *Resource Use Analysis*, 57, 74–76, 85; and *Belle Glade Herald*, 1 July 1955.

50. See Coale, "Sugarcane Production in the EAA," in *Everglades Agricultural Area*, ed. Botcher and Izuno, 225. Also see Mase, "Sugar Industry Booms," 19 March 1961; "Millions Invest," 20 March 1961; and "Glades Land Boom," 21 March 1961, all in the *Tampa Tribune*.

51. Snyder, "Soils of the EAA," 38.

52. Kushlan, "Freshwater Marshes," 347–48.

53. See Stephens, "Subsidence of Organic Soils," in *Environments of South Florida,* ed. Gleason, 359, and Stephens and Johnson, "Subsidence of Organic Soils," 231. Hardy's observations confirm the predictions that Stephens and Johnson made in 1951. In that year, the soil scientists calculated that 88 percent of the organic soil in the Everglades would be gone, and fourteen inches represent 13 percent of nine feet.

54. Gleason, et al., "Environmental Significance of Holocene Sediments," in *Environments of South Florida Present,* ed. Gleason, 308.

Epilogue. Restoration

1. Terrie, *Contested Terrain,* 102.

2. McClure and Dougherty, "Journey on the River of Grass," *Fort Lauderdale Sun-Sentinel,* eight-part series, 30 April 1995–7 May 1995.

3. Ibid. "Day Four: Into the Wild."

4. Douglas, *Voice of the River,* 193.

5. Williams, "North to South, Part II," 62, 81, 92.

BIBLIOGRAPHY

"About the Aigrette." *Bird-Lore* XI (September–October 1909): 231–232.

Alexander, Taylor R. "Paradise Key on Fire." *Everglades Natural History* 2 (March 1954): 31–34.

Allison, R. V. "The Soil and Water Conservation Problem in the Everglades." *Soil Science Society of Florida Proceedings* 1 (1939): 35–58.

———. *University of Florida Agricultural Experiment Station Report for the Fiscal Year Ending June 30, 1928.*

Allison, R. V., O. C. Bryan, and J. H. Harper. "The Stimulation of Plant Response on the Raw Peat Soils of the Florida Everglades through the Use of Copper Sulfate and Other Chemicals." Bulletin 190. Gainesville: University of Florida Agricultural Experiment Station, 1927.

Arthur, P. H. "The Taxpayers' Answer to Governor Martin: An Analysis of the $20,009,000 Bond Issue." P. K. Yonge Library of Florida History, University of Florida, Gainesville.

Baldwin, Mark, and H. W. Walker. *Soil Survey of the Fort Lauderdale Area, Florida.* Washington, D.C.: Government Printing Office, 1915.

Beardsley, R. K. "Present Status of Plans for Refinancing the Everglades Drainage District." *Soil Science Society of Florida Proceedings* 4-A (1942): 104–12.

Becker, R. B., W. M. Neal, and A. A. Shealy. "I. Salt Sick: Its Causes and Prevention. II. Mineral Supplements for Cattle." Bulletin 231. Gainesville: University of Florida Agricultural Experiment Station, 1931.

Bent, A. C. "Nesting Habits of the Herodiones in Florida." *Auk* XXI (January 1904): 20–28.

Bentley, George R. "Colonel Thompson's Tour of Tropical Florida." *Tequesta* X (1950): 3–12.

Bestor, H. A. "Principal Elements of a Long Time Soil and Water Conservation Plan for the Everglades." *Soil Science Society of Florida Proceedings* 4-A (1942): n.p.

————. "Reclamation Problems of Sub-Drainage Districts Adjacent to Lake Okeechobee." *Soil Science Society of Florida Proceedings* 5-A (1943): 157–65.

Black, Stephanie. *H-2 Worker*. New York: Documentary film produced by First Run
Features.

Blake, Nelson M. *Land into Water—Water into Land: A History of Water Management in
Florida*. Tallahassee: University Presses of Florida, 1980.

Blatchley, W. S. *In Days Agone: Notes on the Flora of Subtropical Florida in the Days When
Most of the Area Was a Primeval Wilderness*. Indianapolis: Nature Publishing Company, 1932.

Bock, James. "What an Amateur Learned in Six Months Everglades Experience."
Florida Grower XXII (October 16, 1920): 4–5 and 18–19.

Botcher, A. A., and F. T. Izuno, eds. *Everglades Agricultural Area (EAA) Water, Soil, and
Environmental Management*. Gainesville: University Press of Florida, 1994.

Brooks, H. Kelly. "Lake Okeechobee." In *Environments of South Florida, Present and
Past II*, edited by Patrick J. Gleason. Coral Gables, Florida: Miami Geological Society, 1984.

Broward, Napoleon Bonaparte. Papers. P. K. Yonge Library of Florida History. University of Florida. Gainesville.

Brown, Loren G. *Totch: A Life in the Everglades*. Gainesville: University Press of Florida,
1993.

Brown, Robin C. *Florida's First People*. Sarasota: Pineapple Press, 1994.

Burns, L. A., and R. B. Taylor, III. "Nutrient-Uptake Model in Marsh Ecosystems."
Journal of the Technical Councils, ASCE 105: 177–96.

Carlton, Doyle Elam. Governors' Papers. Manuscript Division, Florida State Archives.
Tallahassee.

Chapman, Frank M. *Camps and Cruises of an Ornithologist*. New York: D. Appleton and
Company, 1908.

Congressional Record. 62nd Cong., 2nd sess., 5 March 1912. Vol. 48, part 3.

Conner, Jeanette Thurber, ed. and trans. *Colonial Records of Spanish Florida: Letters and
Reports of Governors and Secular Persons*. DeLand: Florida State Historical Society,
1925.

Cooke, C. Wayne, and Garald G. Parker. *Late Cenozoic Geology of Southern Florida,
with a Discussion of the Ground Water*. Geological Bulletin No. 27. Tallahassee:
Florida Geological Society, 1944.

Covington, James W. *The Seminoles of Florida*. Gainesville: University Press of Florida,
1993.

————. "Trade Relations between Southeastern Florida and Cuba, 1640–1840."
Florida Historical Quarterly XXXVIII (October 1959): 114–28.

Cronon, William. *Nature's Metropolis: Chicago and the Great West*. New York: W. W.
Norton and Company, 1991.

Cushing, Frank. "Exploration of Ancient Key-Dwellers' Remains on the Gulf Coast of
Florida." *Proceedings, American Philosophical Society* 35 (November 1896): 1–104.
Reprinted in *Antiquities of the New World: Early Explorations in Archaeology*, vol. 13

(New York: AMS Press, 1973), 329–448, for the Peabody Museum of Archaeology and Ethnology, Harvard University.

——. "Relics of an Unknown Race Discovered." *New York Journal,* 21 June 1896, 17–18.

Dachnowski-Stokes, Alfred P. "Peat Profiles of the Everglades in Florida: The Stratigraphic Features of the 'Upper' Everglades and Correlation with Environmental Change." *Journal of the Washington Academy of Sciences* 20 (19 March 1930): 89–107.

Daniel, I. Randolph, Jr., and Michael Wisenbaker. *Harney Flats: A Florida Paleo-Indian Site.* Farmingdale, New York: Baywood Publishing Company, 1987.

Davis, John H., Jr. *The Peat Deposits of Florida: Their Occurrence, Development, and Uses.* State of Florida Department of Conservation, Geology Bulletin No. 30.: Florida Geological Society, 1946.

——. *The Natural Features of Southern Florida, Especially the Vegetation, and the Everglades.* Tallahassee: Florida Geological Society, 1943.

Davis, S., and J. Ogden, eds. *Everglades: The Ecosystem and Its Restoration.* Delray Beach, Florida: St. Lucie Press, 1994.

De Bow, J. D. B. "The Everglades of Florida, and the Prospect of Reclaiming Them into Gardens for Every Variety of the Fruits of the Tropics." *Commercial Review of the South and West* VII (October 1849): 297–304.

de Meras, Gonzalo Solis. *Pedro Menendez de Aviles, Adelantado Governor and Captain-General of Florida.* Translated by Jeanette Thurber Conner. DeLand: Florida State Historical Society, 1923.

Denevan, William M. "The Pristine Myth: The Landscape of the Americas in 1492." *Annals of the Association of American Geographers* 82 (1992): 369–85.

Dietz, Robert S., and John C. Holden. "The Breakup of Pangaea." In *Readings from Scientific American: Continents Adrift and Continents Aground,* 126–37. San Francisco: W. H. Freeman and Company, 1976.

Dix, E. A., and J.M. Maggonigle. "The Everglades of Florida: A Region of Mystery." *Century Magazine* (February 1905): 512–26.

Doughty, Robin W. *Feather Fashions and Bird Preservation: A Study in Nature Protection.* Berkeley: University of California Press, 1975.

Douglas, Marjory Stoneman. *The Everglades: River of Grass.* 1947. Reprint, Sarasota: Pineapple Press, 1988.

——. *Voice of the River.* Englewood, Florida: Pineapple Press, 1987.

Dovell, Janius E. "A History of the Everglades of Florida." Ph.D. diss., University of North Carolina, 1947.

Ekins, Paul, ed. *The Living Economy: A New Economics in the Making.* London: Routledge & Kegan Paul, 1986.

Evans, Charles B., and R. V. Allison. "The Soils of the Everglades in Relation to Reclamation and Conservation Operations." *Soil Science Society of Florida Proceedings* 4-A (1942): 34–46.

"The Everglades of Florida, the Richest Land in the World." Chicago: Florida Everglades Land Company, n.d. P. K. Yonge Library of Florida History, University of Florida, Gainesville.

Faeb, Peter. *Man's Rise to Civilization as Shown by the Indians of North America from Primeval Times to the Coming of the Industrial State.* New York: E. P. Dutton, 1968.

Federal Bureau of Investigation. Reports, 1941–42. Stephanie Black, a documentary filmmaker, secured these documents under the auspices of the Freedom of Information Act and gave copies to the author.

Florida, State of. *Biennial Report, 1927–1928, to the Board of Commissioners of the Everglades Drainage District.*

———. *Cases Adjudicated in the Supreme Court of Florida During the January and June Terms,* A.D. *1943, from 7 May 1943 to 7 January 1944.*

———. *Journal of the House of Representatives of Florida.* 1907, 1911.

———. *Journal of the State Senate of Florida of the Session of 1915.*

———. *Laws of the State of Florida, Adopted by the Legislature of Florida at Its Regular Session, 1913, 1921, 1923, 1925 and 1929 under the Constitution of A.D. 1885.*

———. *Minutes of the Trustees of the Internal Improvement Fund.* I, 1902; VI, 1906; VII, 1909; VIII, 1910; IX, 1913; X, 1915; XVII, 1929.

———. *A Report of the Board of Commissioners of the Okeechobee Flood Control District on the Activities of the District and on Lake Okeechobee, 1929–1943.*

"The Florida Everglades Land Co." 1910(?). P. K. Yonge Library of Florida History, University of Florida, Gainesville.

"Florida Fruit Lands Review." Kansas City, Mo: Florida Fruit Lands Company, n.d. P. K. Yonge Library of Florida History, University of Florida, Gainesville.

Fontaneda, Hernando Descalante. *Memoir of Do d'Escalante Fontaneda Respecting Florida.* Translated by Buckingham Smith, 1854. Reprint, edited by David O. True. Miami: University of Miami Press, 1944.

Ford, Robert N. *A Resource Use Analysis and Evaluation of the Everglades Agricultural Area.* Chicago: University of Chicago Press, 1956.

Fowler, Connie May. "Okeechobee: A Journey." *Forum: The Magazine of the Florida Humanities Council,* Spring 1996, 4–44.

Fritchey, John. *Everglades Journal.* Edited by Beth R. Read. Miami: Florida Heritage Press, 1992.

Gallatin, M. H., and J. R. Henderson. "Progress Report on the Soil Survey of the Everglades." *Soil Science Society of Florida Proceedings* 5-A (1943): 95–104.

Gannon, Michael. *Florida: A Short History.* Gainesville: University Press of Florida, 1993.

Gilliland, Marion. *Key Marco's Buried Treasure.* Gainesville: University of Florida Press, 1989.

———. *The Material Culture of Key Marco, Florida.* Gainesville: University Presses of Florida, 1975.

Gleason, Patrick J., ed. *Environments of South Florida, Present and Past.* Coral Gables: Miami Geological Society, 1974.

———. *Environments of South Florida, Present and Past II.* Coral Gables: Miami Geological Society, 1984.

Gleason, Patrick J., and Peter Stone. "Age, Origin, and Landscape Evolution of the Everglades Peatland." In *Everglades: The Ecosystem and Its Restoration,* edited by S. Davis and J. Ogden. Delray Beach, Florida: St. Lucie Press, 1994.

Gleason, Patrick J., et al. "The Environmental Significance of Holocene Sediments." In *Environments of South Florida, Present and Past II,* edited by Patrick J. Gleason. Coral Gables: Miami Geological Society, 1984.

Goggin, John M., and William C. Sturtevant. "The Calusa: A Stratified, Nonagricultural Society (With Notes on Sibling Marriages)." In *Explorations in Cultural Anthropology: Essays in Honor of George Peter Murdock,* edited by Ward H. Goodenough. New York: McGraw-Hill, 1964.

Gould, Stephen J. *Wonderful Life: The Burgess Shale and the Nature of History.* New York: W. W. Norton & Company, 1989.

Graham, Ernest. Papers. Ernest Graham Collection. P. K. Yonge Library of Florida History, University of Florida, Gainesville.

Griffin, John W. *The Archeology of Everglades National Park.* Tallahassee: National Park Service Southeast Archeological Center, 1988.

Gunderson, L.H., and J.R. Snider. "Fire Patterns in the Southern Everglades." In *Everglades: The Ecosystem and Its Restoration,* edited by S. Davis and J. Ogden. Delray Beach, Fla.: St. Lucie Press, 1994.

Hahamovitch, Cindy. *Fruits of Their Labor: Atlantic Coast Farmworkers and the Making of Migrant Poverty, 1870–1945.* Chapel Hill: University of North Carolina Press, 1997.

Hahn, John H., ed. and trans. *Missions to the Calusa.* Gainesville: University of Florida Press, 1991.

Hairing, C. H. *The Spanish Empire in America.* New York: Oxford University Press, 1947.

Hallock, Charles. *Camp Life in Florida: A Handbook for Sportsmen and Settlers.* New York: Forest and Stream Publishing Company, 1876.

Hanna, Alfred Jackson, and Kathryn Abbey Hanna. *Lake Okeechobee, Wellspring of the Everglades.* Indianapolis: Bobbs-Merrill, 1948.

Hardy, Laymond M. Interview. 3 November 1996.

Harper, Roland M. "Natural Resources of Southern Florida." In *Florida State Geological Survey, Eighteenth Annual Report, 1925–1926.* Tallahassee: State Geological Survey, 1927.

Harshberger, John W. "The Vegetation of South Florida South of 27 Degrees 30 Minutes, Exclusive of the Florida Keys." *Transactions of the Wagner Free Institute of Science* 7 (October 1914): 51–189.

Hays, Samuel P. *Conservation and the Gospel of Efficiency.* New York: Atheneum, 1975.

Healy, Henry C. *Terraces and Shorelines of Florida.* Prepared by the United States Geological Survey in Cooperation with the Bureau of Water Resources Management, Florida Department of Environmental Regulation, and Bureau of Geology. Map Series 71. Tallahassee: Florida Department of Natural Resources, 1975.

Heilbroner, Robert L. *An Inquiry into the Human Prospect.* New York: W. W. Norton, 1974.

Heilprin, Angelo. *Exploration on the West Coast of Florida.* Philadelphia: Wagner Free Institute of Science, 1887. Reprint, Ithaca, N.Y.: Paleontological Institution, 1964.

Herring, Hubert. *A History of Latin America from the Beginnings to the Present.* New York: Alfred A. Knopf, 1968.

Hoffmeister, John Edward. *Land from the Sea: The Geological Story of South Florida.* Coral Gables: University of Miami Press, 1974.

Holland, Spessard. Governors' Papers. Manuscript Division, Florida State Archives, Tallahassee, Florida.

Hoover, Herbert. *The Memoirs of Herbert Hoover: The Cabinet and the Presidency, 1920–1933.* New York: Macmillan, 1952.

Hurston, Zora Neale. *Their Eyes Were Watching God.* New York: Lippincott Company, 1937.

Ives, J. C. *Memoir to Accompany a Military Map of the Peninsula of Florida South of Tampa Bay.* New York: M. B. Wynkoop, 1856.

Jennings, William Sherman. Papers. P. K. Yonge Library of Florida History, University of Florida, Gainesville.

Johnson, Lamar. *Beyond the Fourth Generation.* Gainesville: University Presses of Florida, 1974.

Jones, Jacqueline. *The Dispossessed: America's Underclass from the Civil War to the Present.* New York: Basic Books, 1992.

King, Lester C. *Wandering Continents and Spreading Sea Floors on an Expanding Earth.* New York: John Wiley, 1983.

Kirby, Jack Temple. *Poquosin: A Study of Rural Landscape and Society.* Chapel Hill: University of North Carolina Press, 1995.

Kushlan, James A. "Freshwater Marshes." In *Ecosystems of Florida,* edited by Ronald Myers and John Ewel. Orlando: University of Central Florida Press, 1990.

Lao Tsu. *Tao Te Ching.* Translated by Gia-Fu Feng and Jane English. New York: Vintage Books, 1972.

Laudonniere, Rene. *Three Voyages.* Translated by Charles E. Bennett. Gainesville: University Presses of Florida, 1975.

Lewis, R. K. "The Economic Phase Introduction." *Soil Science Society of Florida Proceedings* 4-A (1942): 100–103.

Lindsey, Alton. *The Bicentennial of John James Audubon.* Bloomington: Indiana University Press, 1985.

Lyon, Eugene. "The Enterprise of Florida." *Florida Historical Quarterly* 52 (April 1974): 411–22.

MacGonigle, John W. "The Geography of the Southern Peninsula of the United States." *National Geographic Magazine* 7 (December 1896): 381–94.

Marquardt, William H., and Claudine Payne, eds. *Culture and Environment in the Domain of the Calusa.* Gainesville: Institute of Archeology and Paleoenvironmental Studies, 1992.

Marston, Anson, S. H. McCrory, and George B. Hills. *Report of Everglades Engineering Board of Review to Commissioners of Everglades Drainage District.* Tallahassee: T. J. Appleyard, 1927.

Mahon, John K. *History of the Second Seminole War, 1835–1842, Revised Edition.* Gainesville: University of Florida Press, 1985.

Malone, Dumas, ed. *Dictionary of American Biography.* New York: Charles Scribner's Sons, 1935.

Marquis, Albert Nelson, ed. *Who's Who in America: A Biographical Dictionary of Notable Living Men and Women in the United States.* Chicago: A. N. Marquis, 1914.

McAlister, Lyle. *Spain and Portugal in the New World, 1492–1700.* Minneapolis: University of Minnesota Press, 1984.

McGoun, William E. *Prehistoric Peoples of South Florida.* Tuscaloosa: University of Alabama Press, 1993.

Mead, Daniel W., Allen Hazen, and Leonard Metcalf. *Report on the Drainage of the Everglades of Florida with Special Reference to the Lands of the Everglades Land Sales Company, Everglades Land Company, Everglades Sugar and Land Company in the Vicinity of Miami, Florida.* Chicago: Board of Consulting Engineers, 1912.

Meggers, Betty J. *Prehistoric America: An Ecological Perspective.* New York: Aldine Publishing Company, 1979.

Milanich, Jerald T. *Archeology of Precolumbian Florida.* Gainesville: University Presses of Florida, 1994.

Milanich, Jerald T., and Charles H. Fairbanks. *Florida Archeology.* New York: Academic Press, 1980.

Model Land Company. Papers. University of Miami, Coral Gables, Florida.

Moore-Wilson, Minnie. *Eight Royal Palm Hammocks in Florida: The Part the Seminoles Played in Their History.* Tampa: Tampa Tribune Publishing Company, n.d.

Moses, Wallace R. "The Journal of the Everglades Exploring Expedition, March 14–April 16, 1892." Edited by Watt P. Marchman. *Tequesta* 7 (1947): 3–43.

Munroe, Ralph Middleton, and Vincent Gilpin. *The Commodore's Story.* 1920. Reprint, Historical Association of Southern Florida, 1966.

Myers, Ronald L., and John J. Ewel, eds. *Ecosystems of Florida.* Orlando: University of Central Florida Press, 1990.

Nash, Roderick. *Wilderness and the American Mind.* New Haven: Yale University Press, 1967.

Newhouse, John. Papers. John Newhouse Collection. P. K. Yonge Library of Florida History, University of Florida, Gainesville.

"Notes on the Passage Across the Everglades." Reprinted in *Tequesta* 20 (1960): 57–65.

Packard, Winthrop. "The Rush to Florida." *Technical World* 16 (March 1910): 20–23.

Parker, Garald. Interview at his home in Tampa, Florida, 27 February 1992.

———. "Notes on the Geology and Ground Water of the Everglades of Southern Florida." *Soil Science Society of Florida Proceedings* 4-A (1942): 47–76.

———. *Water Resources of Southeastern Florida: With Special Reference to the Geology and Ground Water of Miami.* Geological Survey, Water Supply Paper No. 1255. Washington, D.C.: Government Printing Office, 1955.

Parker, Garald G., and C. Wythe Cooke. *Late Cenozoic Geology of Southern Florida, with a Discussion of the Ground Water.* Tallahassee: Florida Geological Survey, 1944.

Parker, Garald, and Nevin D. Hoy. "Additional Notes on the Geology and Ground Water of Southern Florida." *Soil Science Society of Florida Proceedings* 5-A (1943): 33–55.

Perry, J. H., and Philip Sherlock. *A Short History of the West Indies.* 3rd edition. New York: St. Martin's Press, 1956.

Pierce, Charles William. "Cruise of the *Bon Ton* in the Spring and Summer of 1885." *Tequesta* 22 (1952): 3–77.

Pollock v. Williams, Sheriff. 322 U.S.: 4–30.

Potter, John Whipple. *Hunting in Florida in 1874.* Providence, R.I.: self-published, 1884.

Purdy, Barbara A. *The Art and Archeology of Florida's Wetlands.* Boca Raton, Florida: CRC Press, 1991.

Randazzo, Anthony F., and Douglas S. Jones, eds. *The Geology of Florida.* Gainesville: University Press of Florida, 1997.

Randolph, Isham. "Reclaiming the Everglades of Florida." *Journal of the Franklin Institute* 184 (July 1917): 49–72.

Rasmussen, Wayne D. *A History of the Emergency Farm Labor Supply Program, 1943–47.* Agricultural Monograph No. 13. Washington, D.C.: Government Printing Office, 1951.

Reisner, Marc. *Cadillac Desert: The American West and Its Disappearing Water.* New York: Penguin Books, 1986.

Rodenbaugh, Theo. F. *From Everglades to Canon with the 2nd Dragoons (Second United States Cavalry): An Authentic Account of Service in Florida, Mexico, Virginia, and the Indian Country, 1836–1875.* New York: D. Van Nostrand, 1875.

Romans, Bernard. *A Concise History of East and West Florida.* 1775. Reprint, Gainesville: University of Florida Press, 1962.

Rose, Rufus E. "The Swamp and Overflowed Lands of Florida." P. K. Yonge Library of Florida History, University of Florida, Gainesville.

Sawyer, Wells. Papers. Wells Sawyer Collection. Box 54. P. K. Yonge Library of Florida History, University of Florida, Gainesville.

Schumacher, E. F. *Small Is Beautiful: Economics As If People Mattered.* New York: Harper and Row, 1973.

Scott, Earl Dodge. *The Story of a Bird Lover.* New York: Outland Company, 1903.

Scott, Harold A. "The Central and Southern Florida Project." *Soil Science Society of Florida Proceedings* 9 (1948): 121–31.

Scott, W. E. D. "The Present Condition of Some of the Bird Rookeries of the Gulf Coast of Florida." *Auk* 4 (April 1887): 135–44.

———. "The Present Condition of Some of the Bird Rookeries of the Gulf Coast of Florida." *Auk* 4 (July 1887): 213–22.

———. "The Present Condition of Some of the Bird Rookeries of the Gulf Coast of Florida." *Auk* 4 (October 1887): 273–84.

Sears, William H. *Fort Center: An Archeological Site in the Lake Okeechobee Basin.* Gainesville: University Press of Florida, 1982.

Sharp, Howard. "Farming the Muck Soil of the Everglades: Success of Big Reclamation Project Depends upon Perfection of Drainage Facilities." *Florida Grower* 32 (7 November 1925): 3–4, 22.

Simpson, Charles Torrey. *In Lower Florida Wilds: A Naturalist's Observations of the Life, Physical Geography, and Geology of the More Tropical Part of the State.* New York: G. P. Putnam's Sons, 1920.

Sitterson, Joseph Carlyle. *Sugar Country.* Lexington: University of Kentucky Press, 1953.

Skinner, J. J., and R. W. Ruprecht. "Fertilizer Experiments with Truck Crops." Bulletin 218. Gainesville: University of Florida Agricultural Experiment Station, 1930.

Small, John Kunkel. "Botanical Exploration in Florida in 1917." *Journal of the New York Botanical Garden* 19 (November 1918): 279–90.

———. "Botanical Fields, Historic and Prehistoric." *Journal of the New York Botanical Garden* 29 (August 1928): 185–209.

———. "The Botanical Fountain of Youth: A Record of Exploration in Florida in April, 1920." *Journal of the New York Botanical Garden* 23 (September 1922): 117–33.

———. "Coastwise Dunes and Lagoons: A Record of Botanical Exploration in Florida in the Spring of 1918." *Journal of the New York Botanical Garden* 20 (October 1919): 191–207.

———. "A Cruise to the Cape Sable Region of Florida." *Journal of the New York Botanical Garden* 17 (November 1916): 189–202.

———. "Exploration in the Everglades." *Journal of the New York Botanical Garden* 10 (March 1909): 48–55.

———. "Exploration of Southern Florida." *Journal of the New York Botanical Garden* 8 (February 1907): 23–28.

———. *Flora of Miami: Being a Description of the Seed-Plants Growing Naturally on the Everglades Keys and in the Adjacent Everglades, Southern Peninsular Florida.* New York: By the author, 1913.

———. *From Eden to Sahara: Florida's Tragedy.* Lancaster, Pennsylvania: Science Press Printing Company, 1929.

———. "The Land Where Spring Meets Autumn." *Journal of the New York Botanical Garden* 25 (March 1924): 53–94.

———. "Old Trails and New Discoveries: A Record of Exploration in Florida in the Spring of 1919." *Journal of the New York Botanical Garden* 22 (February 1921): 25–40.

———. "Report on Exploration in Tropical Florida." *Journal of the New York Botanical Garden* 5 (March 1904): 49–53.

Small, John K., and George V. Nash. "Report of Dr. J. K. Small and Mr. G. V. Nash upon a Trip to Florida." *Journal of the New York Botanical Garden* 3 (1902): 29–35.

Smith, Douglas L., and Kenneth M. Lord. "Tectonic Evolution and Geophysics of the Florida Basement." In *Geology of Florida,* edited by Anthony F. Randazzo and Douglas S. Jones. Gainesville: University Press of Florida, 1997.

Soils, Geology, and Water Control in the Everglades Region. Prepared under the direction of Lewis A. Jones, Chief, Division of Drainage and Water Control, Soil Conservation Service, United States Department of Agriculture. Bulletin 442. Gainesville: University of Florida Agricultural Experiment Station, 1948.

"Squatters, Lake Okeechobee Area." Papers. Florida Department of Natural Resources Vault. Marjory Stoneman Douglas Building, Tallahassee, Florida.

Stephen, L. L. "Vegetable Production in the Northern Everglades." *Economic Geography* 20 (April 1944): 79–101.

Stephens, John C. "The Relationship of Sub-Surface Hydrology to Water Control and Land Use in the Everglades." *Soil Science Society of Florida Proceedings* 5-A (1943): 56–76.

———. "Subsidence of Organic Soils in the Florida Everglades." In *Environments of South Florida, Present and Past,* edited by Patrick J. Gleason. Coral Gables: Miami Geological Society, 1974.

Stephens, John C., and Lamar Johnson. "Subsidence of Organic Soils in the Upper Everglades Region of Florida." *Soil Science Society of Florida Proceedings* 10 (1951): 191–237.

Steward, K. K., and W. H. Ornes. "The Autecology of Sawgrass in the Florida Everglades." *Ecology* 56 (1975): 162–71.

Stewart, Desmond. *The Pyramids and Sphinx.* New York: Newsweek Book Division, 1971.

"Suwannee River Pine and Cypress." Cross City, Fla.: Putnam Lumber Co., 1929.

Sullivan, Walter. *Continents in Motion: The New Earth Debate.* New York: McGraw-Hill, 1974.

Summary of the Central and Southern Florida Flood Control Project, Showing the General Plan of the Federal Project for the Control of Floods and Other Water Conditions in the Basins of Streams and Lakes in Southeastern Florida. Water Survey and Research Paper No. 4. Tallahassee: State Board of Conservation, Division of Water Survey and Research, 1950.

Swanton, John R. *Early History of the Creek Indians and Their Neighbors.* Washington, D.C.: Government Printing Office, 1922.

Tebeau, Charleton W. *A History of Florida.* Coral Gables: University of Miami Press, 1971.

Tedder, George E. *Daily Reports, Everglades Experiment Station.* Public Records Series 95, Institute of Food and Agricultural Sciences, Branch Stations, Field Laboratories, Research and Education Centers, Records and Correspondence, 1917–1971.

Terrie, Philip G. *Contested Terrain: A New History of Nature and People in the Adirondacks.* Syracuse, New York: Adirondack Museum/Syracuse University Press, 1997.

Tropic Magazine 1 (April 1917): no page numbers. P. K. Yonge Library of Florida History, University of Florida, Gainesville.

U.S. Congress. Senate. *Report of Buckingham Smith, Esq.* 30th Cong., 1st sess., 1848. Ref. Com. 242.

U.S. Congress. House. *Report of the Eighth International Geographic Congress Held in the United States, 1904.* 58th Cong., 3d sess., 1905. H. Doc. 460.

U.S. Congress. Senate. *Everglades of Florida Acts, Reports, and Other Papers, State and National, Relating to the Everglades of the State of Florida and Their Reclamation.* 62nd Cong., 1st sess., 1912. S. Doc. 89.

U.S. Congress. House. Committee on Expenditures in the Department of Agriculture. *Everglades of Florida Hearings.* 62nd Cong., 1st sess., 1912.

U.S. Congress. Senate. Committee on Expenditures in the Department of Agriculture. *Majority Report.* Report No. 1207. 62nd Cong., 2nd sess. 1912.

U.S. Congress. Senate. *Florida Everglades Report of the Everglades Engineering Commission to the Commissioners of the Everglades Drainage District and the Trustees of the Internal Improvement Fund, State of Florida, 1913.* 63rd Cong., 2nd sess., 1914. S. Doc. 379.

U.S. Congress. House. *Caloosahatchee River and Lake Okeechobee Drainage Areas, Florida, Letter from the Secretary of War, Transmitting Report from the Chief of Engineers on Survey of Caloosahatchee River and Lake Okeechobee Drainage Areas, Florida, with a View of Improvement for Navigation and the Control of Floods.* 70th Cong., 1st sess, 1928. H. Doc. 215.

U.S. Congress. House. *Letter from the Chief of Engineers, United States Army, Transmitting to the Chairman of the Committee on Commerce, United States Senate, in Response to a Letter Dated December 6, 1928, a Report on the Caloosahatchee River and Lake Okeechobee Drainage Areas, Florida, with a View to Improving for Navigation and the Control of Floods, April 9, 1928.* 70th Cong., 1st sess., 1928. H. Doc. 215.

U.S. Congress, House. Committee on Flood Control. *Flood Control in Florida and Elsewhere: Hearings before the Committee on Flood Control, House of Representatives.* 70th Cong., 2nd sess., 1929.

U.S. Congress. Senate. *Letter from the Chief of Engineers, United States Army, Transmitting to the Chairman of the Committee on Commerce, United States Senate, in Response to a Letter Dated December 6, 1928, a Report on the Caloosahatchee River and Lake Okeechobee Drainage Areas, Florida.* 70th Cong., 2nd sess., 1929. S. Doc. 213.

U.S. Congress. Senate. *Letter from the Chief of Engineers, United States Army, to the Chairman of the Committee on Commerce, United States Senate, Submitting a Review of the Report on the Caloosahatchee River and Lake Okeechobee Drainage Areas.* 71st Cong., 2nd sess., 1930. S. Doc. 115.

U.S. Congress. House. Select Committee Investigating National Defense Migration. *National Defense Migration Hearings.* 77th Cong., 2nd sess., 1942, Part 33.

U.S. Congress. House. *Comprehensive Report on Central and Southern Florida for Flood Control and Other Purposes.* 80th Cong., 2nd sess., 1948. H. Doc. 643.

U.S. Congress. Senate. Subcommittee on Immigration of the Committee on the Judiciary. *The West Indies (BWI) Temporary Alien Labor Program: 1943–1947.* By Joyce Vialet, Senate Committee Print, Study Paper. Washington, D.C.: Government Printing Office, 1978.

U.S. Congress. Senate. Subcommittee on Immigration and Refugee Policy of the Committee on the Judiciary. *The H-2 Program and Nonimmigration.* 97th Cong., 1st sess., 1981.

U.S. Congress. House. Subcommittee on Labor Standards of the Committee on Education and Labor. *Jobs of Domestic Workers: Florida Sugar Cane Industry.* 98th Cong. 1st sess. 1983.

Walker, Karen Jo. "The Zooarchaeology of Charlotte Harbor's Prehistoric Maritime Adaption." In *Culture and Environment in the Domain of the Calusa,* edited by William Marquardt and Claudine Payne. Gainesville, Florida: Institute of Archeology and Paleoenvironmental Studies, 1992.

Wallis, W. Turner. "The History of Everglades Drainage and Its Present Status." *Soil Science Society of Florida Proceedings* 4-A (1942): 29–33.

Weaver, James, and Bradford Brown. "Federal Objectives for the South Florida Restoration by the Science Sub-Group of the South Florida Management and Coordination Working Group." Privately published, 15 November 1993.

Webb, David. "Historical Biogeography." In *Ecosystems of Florida,* edited by Ronald L. Myers and John J. Ewel. Orlando: University of Central Florida Press, 1990.

Weilding, Philip J., and August Burghard. *Checkerd Sunshine: The Story of Ft. Lauderdale, 1793–1955.* Gainesville: University of Florida Press, 1966.

White, William A. *The Geomorphology of the Florida Peninsula.* State of Florida, Department of Natural Resources, Geological Bulletin No. 51. Tallahassee: Bureau of Geology, Division of Interior Resources, Florida Department of Natural Resources, 1970.

Widmer, Randolph J. *The Evolution of the Calusa: A Nonagricultural Chiefdom on the Southwest Florida Coast.* Tuscaloosa: University of Alabama Press, 1988.

Wilkinson, Alec. *Big Sugar.* New York: Alfred A. Knopf, 1989.

Will, Lawrence E. *A Cracker History of Okeechobee.* St. Petersburg, Florida: Great Outdoors, 1964.

————. *Okeechobee Catfishing.* St. Petersburg, Florida: Great Outdoors, 1965.

Will, Thomas Elmer. Papers. Thomas Elmer Will Collection. P. K. Yonge Library of Florida History, University of Florida, Gainesville.

Willey, Gordon R., and Philip Phillips. *Method and Theory in American Archeology.* Chicago: University of Chicago Press, 1958.

Williams, A. P. "North to South through the Everglades in 1883: The Account of the Second Expedition into the Everglades by the *New Orleans Times-Democrat.*" Edited by Mary K. Wintringham. *Tequesta* 23 (1963): 33–59.

————. North to South through the Everglades in 1883, Part II." Edited by Mary K. Wintringham. *Tequesta* 24 (1964): 59–93.

Williams, Lawrence Carroll. "A History of the Central and Southern Florida Flood Control District." Master's thesis, University of Denver, 1966.

Willoughby, Hugh L. *The Everglades: A Canoe Journey of Exploration.* Philadelphia: J. B. Lippincott Company, 1898.

Worster, Donald. "The Ecology of Order and Chaos." *Environmental History Review* 14 (Spring/Summer 1990): 1–23.

INDEX

developmental system, xvi, xviii, xix, 84, 106, 147, 175, 179

Disston, Hamilton: Atlantic and Gulf Coast Canal and Land Sales Company, 89; land purchase of, xviii, 61–62

Douglas, Marjory Stoneman, xvi, 179–80

drainage: drainage law of 1905, 92; of 1907, 92; of 1913, 110–11; of 1927, 139–40; goal of, xvi, xix; suspension of, 140

drainage engineers: Elliott, Charles G., 90–91, 101, 103; Elliott, Fred, 135; Kreamer, James M., 89, 103–4; Leighton, Marshall O., 111–12; Morgan, Arthur C., 101–2, 107, 116; Perkins, Edmund T., 111–112; Randolph, Isham, 111–12, 116

Elliott, Charles G., 90–91, 101, 103. *See also* drainage engineers

Elliot, Fred, 135. *See also* drainage engineers

encomienda system: defined, 187n 61; in Florida, 55

Everglades agricultural area, 154, 170–74, 177, 179

Everglades Agricultural Experiment Station, 122, 157–58, 173

Everglades Drainage District (EDD): abolishment of, 150, 153; creation of, 92; debt of, 133, 148, 162–164; dike project and, 132–33; failure of, 131; and Park Trammell, 110

Everglades Drainage District Bond Holders Protective Association, 163–64

Everglades Engineering Board of Review (1927), 135–37

Everglades Engineering Commission (1913) 111–14, 130–33, 135

Everglades National Park, 178

Everglades pioneers: Beardsley, James E., 129; Bock, James, 121–23, 125; Cottrell, John S., 133–35; Fritchey, John, 59, 127; Hall, Benjamin Franklin, 119; Hardee, W. R., 102; Hardy, Laymond M., 162–64, 173; Hutto, James T., 73; McCrimmon, D. Frank, 73; Newhouse, John, 125, 141; Plank, F. E., 125–26, 128; Sharp, Howard, 129–130, 135; Tedder, George C., 121–22, 124; Will, Lawrence, 64, 161; Will, Thomas, 122, 129

Everglades Trough: base flow and, 27–28; calcite mud in, 10, 23–24; decompartmentalization and, 179; dewatering of, 145–46; dynamic storage of, 27, 29, 175; floating islands in, 24; greater Everglades and, 59; habitat heterogene-ity in, 23, 175; hydrolic system of, 9, 26–27, 175; hydroperiod in, 8, 10, 14–15, 17–18, 20, 24, 178; islands in, 66–67; large spatial extent of, 23, 26, 175; mature system of, 21; new consensus about, 148–49; nutrient removal project and, 177; periphyton in, 15; sheet flow of, 27–29, 175

Felipe, Don, 46

fire: deep, 20–21; in muck or peat soils, 122–23, 140–43; subterranean 142, superficial, 18–20

Flagler, Henry M.: Florida East Coast Railroad, 90, 93, 101, 120; and land grant, 90

Fletcher, Sen. Duncan, 90, 96, 100, 114

Florida Bay, 79–80

Florida Sugar and Food Products Company, 161

Fontaneda, Hernando, 40, 45

Fritchey, John, 59, 127. *See also* Everglades pioneers

Furst-Clark Construction Company, 98, 102, 105, 132

geologic epochs: Cenozoic, 4; Holocene, 19, 32–33; Mesozoic, 5; Pleistocene, 5, 12, 33; Pliocene, 5; Triassic, 2

geologic formations: Fort Thompson, 8, 12, 14; Florida Platform, 2, 4–5; Atlantic coastal ridge, 12; Ocala arch, 4; dunes, 7

Gilchrist, Albert W., 93, 96, 107. *See also* governors, Florida

Gleason, William H., 75

governors, Florida: Bloxham, William D., 89; Carlton, Doyle E., 167; Gilchrist, Albert W., 93, 96, 107; Jennings, William, 90–91, 93; Martin, John W., 139; Trammell, Park, 110, 157

Graham, Ernest, 149–50, 152–53

groundwater, 9

Hall, Benjamin Franklin, 119. *See also* Everglades pioneers

hammocks: Royal Palm hammock, 74–75; 142; types, 71–73

Hardee, W. R., 102. *See also* Everglades pioneers

Hardy, Laymond M., 162–164, 173. *See also* Everglades pioneers

Harney, William, 65

Harper, Roland, 71. *See also* scientists

Harshberger, John, 64. *See also* scientists

Heilprin, Angelo, 78. *See also* scientists

Hoover dike, 162, 176, 179